Charles Seale-Hayne Library

University of Plymouth

(01752) 588 588

LibraryandITenquiries@plymouth.ac.uk

Resisting history

MANCHESTER
1824

Manchester University Press

ENCOUNTERS cultural histories

Series editors:
Roger Cooter
Harriet Ritvo
Carolyn Steedman
Bertrand Taithe

Over the past few decades cultural history has become the discipline of encounters. The issues raised by new 'turnings' – linguistic, pictorial and spatial – through theorists such as Bourdieu, Foucault, Derrida, Deleuze and Spivak have contributed to the emergence of cultural history as a forum for bold and creative exchange. This series places encounters – human, intellectual and disciplinary – at the heart of historical thinking. *Encounters* provides an arena for exploring new and reassembled historical subjects, for stimulating perceptions and reperceptions of the past, and for methodological challenges and innovations. It invites short, innovative and theoretically informed books from all fields of history.

Already published

Resisting history

Religious transcendence and the
invention of the unconscious

∾

Rhodri Hayward

Manchester University Press

Manchester and New York

Distributed exclusively in the USA by Palgrave

The right of Rhodri Hayward to be identified as the author of this work has been asserted by him in accordance with the Copyright, Designs and Patents Act 1988.

Published by Manchester University Press
Oxford Road, Manchester M13 9NR, UK
and Room 400, 175 Fifth Avenue, New York, NY 10010, USA
www.manchesteruniversitypress.co.uk

Distributed exclusively in the USA by
Palgrave, 175 Fifth Avenue, New York, NY 10010, USA

Distributed exclusively in Canada by
UBC Press, University of British Columbia, 2029 West Mall, Vancouver, BC,
Canada V6T 1Z2

British Library Cataloguing-in-Publication Data
A catalogue record for this book is available from the British Library

Library of Congress Cataloging-in-Publication Data applied for

ISBN 978 0 7190 7414 1 *hardback*

First published 2007

16 15 14 13 12 11 10 09 08 07   10 9 8 7 6 5 4 3 2 1

Typeset by Palimpsest Book Production Limited,
Grangemouth, Stirlingshire
Printed in Great Britain
by Bell and Bain, Glasgow

To Leonie – who makes all things possible.

Contents

Preface

Writing in the 1920s, Ezra Pound remembered, 'A day when historians left blanks in their writings . . . for things they didn't know'. I'm not sure that I can. The histories I studied at school and university from the 1980s onwards presented seamless stories of cause and effect. This book is about how that seamlessness was achieved and how troubling or baffling episodes of apparent magic or miracle have been incorporated into the historical record. Throughout its four short chapters, I argue that the ways that we imagine the past are inextricably connected to the ways that we imagine our selves. I show how our attempts to explain the lacunae in the historical record left by supernatural episodes have moved in tandem with the development of a psychological language – in particular, with the concept of the unconscious or subconscious self.

The changes wrought in our models of personality, memory, religion and history are intrinsically political and in my arguments I show how these intellectual transformations were part of a wider set of struggles over power and identity. The book describes how the concept of the subconscious self in the years before Freud was developed in episodes of supernatural contestation. Returning to those episodes helps to remind us about the assumptions we make and the tools we use in our own historical writing.

There are of course other ways of becoming aware of our own unspoken assumptions and I'd like to acknowledge my debt to many friends, colleagues and editors who've provided sound advice and questioned the many preconceptions that informed this work. I'm especially grateful to John Arnold, Peter Barham, Chris Bonell, Richard Deswarte, Henry French, Richard Gombrich, Piyel Haldar, Mathew Hilton, Mike Jay, Tony Melechi, Frances Neary, Michael Neve, Simon Nightingale, Carol Osborne, Paolo Palladino, Dorothea Pelham, Daniel Pick, Roy Porter, Eifion Powell, Stephen Pumfrey, Mathew Thomson, Damian Rafferty,

Preface

Graham Richards, Lyndal Roper, Justine Scott-McCarthy, Sonu Shamdasani, Carolyn Steedman and Bertrand Taithe. The staff at Lancaster
University Library, Cambridge University Library, the British Library,
the London Library, the Society for Psychical Research, the Wellcome
Library for the History and Understanding of Medicine and the National
Library of Wales have all been generous in their assistance. My parents
also provided constant help throughout this project. The original research
on which this work was based was funded by the ESRC and the leave to
write it granted by the Wellcome Trust. Roger Cooter has, as always,
given outstanding support. Roger Smith guided the project from its first
inception and without his intelligent engagement this book would never
have been written.

Notes

1 E. Pound, 'Canto XIII', *The Cantos of Ezra Pound* (London: Faber, 1975), p.
   60.

Abbreviations

ABA	*American Biographical Archive* (Munich: Saur, 1984)
Am. J. Psychology	*American Journal of Psychology*
AmericanDB	*American Dictionary of National Biography* (Washington: American Council of Learned Societies, 1926–37)
BBA	*British Biographical Archive* (Munich: Saur, 1984)
BMJ	*British Medical Journal*
DNB	*Oxford Dictionary of National Biography* (Oxford: Oxford University Press, 2004)
DWB	*Dictionary of Welsh Biography down to 1940* (London: Honourable Society of the Cymmrodorion, 1959)
ERE	James Hastings et al. (eds) *Encyclopaedia of Religion and Ethics* (Edinburgh: T. and T. Clark, 1908–26)
HWJ	*History Workshop Journal*
J.Hist.Behav.Sci.	*Journal of the History of the Behavioral Sciences*
JMS	*Journal of Mental Science*
J.Phil.	*Journal of Philosophy*
J.SPR	*Journal of the Society for Psychical Research*
NLW	National Library of Wales
Proc.SPR	*Proceedings of the Society for Psychical Research*
SE	Sigmund Freud, *The Complete Standard Edition of the Works of Sigmund Freud* ed. James Strachey et al. (London: Hogarth Press, 1953–)
SPR	The Society for Psychical Research

The invention of the self

When truth embodied in a tale (Tennyson, *In Memoriam*, 36)

There are moments when the pursuit of history can seem truly unnerving. Sometimes that past which was meant to ground our ideas and conceptions gives way and reveals something stranger, alien and uncanny. Although such episodes are rare events in most historians' lives, they form a recurring motif in fantastic literature, where they are widely associated with the breakdown of identity and personality. Stories of historians driven to madness and despair when their narratives are confounded recur repeatedly in novels, from Mary Ward's *Robert Elsmere* and the ghost stories of M. R. James to the works of modern authors such as Penelope Fitzgerald or Elizabeth Kostova.[1] They suggest that our failure to make sense of the past is reflected in a deeper failure to make sense of ourselves. Narrative incoherence invokes personal incoherence and the collapse of history in turn initiates a psychological collapse. At the point in our historical researches 'where we encounter an alien element which we cannot recognise as akin to ourselves ... the hope and purpose which inspired us dies, and the endeavour is thwarted'. As F. H. Bradley observed, this experience left 'in those to whom it has befallen, the bitterest pain of the most cruel estrangement'.[2]

This connection between history and sanity is perhaps unsurprising, since the past is now widely seen as the bedrock of our sense of self. We feel that our identities are somehow defined by memory and experience, and we look to our biographies when making sense of our own actions or those of our colleagues and our friends. Yet there is nothing straightforward about our ready equation of identity with history. Other societies and cultures maintain quite different conceptions of selfhood, seeing it as something defined through one's relationship with nature or one's position in the wider social order. And even in the West, many commentators believe that our historical or psychological understanding of the self is now giving way to new models based in neuroscience and biochemistry.[3] These cultural variations and transformations have, of course, been widely commented upon.[4] As anthropologists, philosophers and historians across the academy have all made clear, the self is not some kind of natural or pre-given entity with its own inherent form, but a contingent accomplishment which varies among cultures and between individuals.

All of us (I imagine) at some point become vaguely aware of these variations. We have moments when we identify so strongly with our work, our families or our friends that our personality seems to escape its basis in the body and instead extend out into the world. At other times we can feel so suspicious of the memories and desires which accompany our thoughts that the self seems to retreat into the mere moment of present consciousness.[5] The psychologist William James argued at the end of the nineteenth century that such variations turn the self into a kind of moral project. Those who embrace their histories and surroundings are rewarded with lives of vigour and joy. Those who retreat from the past and from contact with the wider world are condemned to suffer the agonies of the sick soul.[6]

This moral reading of the self has not been universally accepted. In the nineteenth and twentieth centuries many philosophers and theologians held history and identity under deep suspicion. Evangelical Protestants had long insisted that the self and its past were worldly distractions from the life of the spirit. European existentialists lamented the constraining effects of historical knowledge, seeing it as a fetter on self-awareness and future aspiration. The melancholy philosopher Søren Kierkegaard followed G. W. F. Hegel in seeing recollection as a form of unhappiness. He believed that our pursuit of a lost past was a mortifying process which absents us from the pleasures of life in the present.[7] Similarly Friedrich Nietzsche envied the bovine forgetfulness of the beasts in the field, believing that they had escaped the demands of memory and responsibility.[8] And of course this form of existentialist critique persists in the writings of post-structuralists today. Although their arguments are far from straightforward, Gilles Deleuze and Michel Foucault both argue that our modern idea of deep historical identity can be seen as an insidious form of political control.[9] In their works, historical knowledge achieves at best an ambiguous position. Although it can instil an awareness of contingency and hence the possibility of transformation, an uncritical knowledge of the past – be it political history or personal history – simply serves to fix the individual's place in a wider network of power.[10]

This book is about the conflict between these two opposed visions of the relationship between history and identity. It describes the triumph of the historicist perspective and the struggles that that victory has obscured. Returning to those struggles is important, for it helps to remind us of the contingency of our contemporary sense of self and of the political costs involved in its achievement. We live in an age in which understanding our personal past is held up as the key to an authentic life and individual fulfilment; an age in which the inability to maintain a coherent life narrative is regarded by medical professionals as a threat to physical health and survival.[11] It seems that other forms of selfhood have moved from being simply oppositional and instead are now seen as somehow unnatural or pathological. The failure of biography and the failure of narrative history are presented as threats to the natural order.

Yet despite the pathological associations of narrative failure, academics have managed to maintain a remarkable equanimity in the face of evidence and testimonies which apparently threaten the integrity of the historical record. Although the equation of narrative breakdown with personal breakdown might persist in contemporary fiction, one rarely sees historians succumbing to psychological collapse in the reading rooms of the Public Record Office or the British Library. Instead of being threatened or disturbed by reports of miraculous or supernatural events, academics seem drawn to them and the last decades of the twentieth century witnessed the emergence of a rich literature on the history of magic, hauntings, visions, spiritualism and witchcraft.[12] However, this turn to the occult, as we shall see, is based less in the recognition of the power of the supernatural to disrupt our conventional narratives or self images than in an assumption that such events can be used to launch new levels of historical explanation.

Instead of letting miraculous evidence mark the gaps in our historical knowledge, modern academics have used it as the starting point for virtuoso displays of intellectual analysis. The most common strategy renders the miraculous superficial in the most banal sense of the term, portraying it as the weird excrescence of a deeper historical process. Catholic visions of the Virgin or spiritualist encounters with the voluble dead are taken, variously, as psychoanalytic symptoms revealing scenes of maternal deprivation, sexual frustration or domestic oppression; alternatively, they are understood in functionalist terms, as attempts by those on the margins of society to achieve some sort of mystical empowerment or emotional release from the burdens of political control or economic disruption. The sheer brilliance of many of these accounts is undeniable and there is a satisfying sense of coherence achieved as strange and inexplicable events are mapped onto wider social, political or sexual agendas.[13]

The emotional satisfaction we experience in reading such histories reminds us of our psychological involvement in the historical project. As they render the strange familiar, such works turn the historical witness into a mirror of ourselves: beneath their miraculous claims, the witnesses of the past share the same economic motivations, political anxieties and sexual frustrations that animate our own twenty-first-century lives. History thus operates as a kind of psychological consolation, assuring us of the stability of our inner and outer natures, and revealing how the same mechanisms – be they physical or psychological – are shared across the expanse of time. As Raphael Samuel has argued, current methods serve to turn historical actors into our 'contemporaries, not so much by transporting us into the past, in the manner of the time traveller, not by piling up period detail, in the manner of the empiricist, but rather by investing the historical subject with a contemporary psyche or interpreting their actions in contemporary terms'.[14]

Samuel's insight is perceptive, yet it is difficult to see how the situation could be different. For in our interrogation of the historical evidence, we are forced into an ongoing assessment of the witness's veracity; an assessment which is guided by our psychological empathy and our common-sense knowledge of the natural order.[15] For these reasons Marc Bloch insisted that historical writing assumed that 'the universe and society possess sufficient uniformity to exclude the possibility of overly pronounced deviations', while his friend and colleague Henri Pirenne argued that, 'one cannot comprehend men's actions at all unless one assumes in the beginning that their physical and moral beings have been at all periods what they are today'.[16]

The writing of history, it can be argued, promotes a certain model of psychology. In our discriminations between what counts as reportage and what counts as mythical invention, we sketch out a map of the historical witness's character, values and motivations.[17] What we find alien in their reports does not threaten our worldview; instead it demonstrates their failure as witnesses. And this in itself operates as a consoling failure. It is a failure which reveals the power of human beliefs and desires while at the same time preserving our faith in the uniformity of the natural world.[18]

Of course the writing of history is rarely presented in this form. Historians no longer pursue the secularising agenda of nineteenth-century rationalists such as W. H. Lecky or Thomas Buckle, who used their histories of civilisation to expose and critique the mistaken apprehensions of the past.[19] Instead they maintain a very different sensibility, eschewing any judgement over the truth of various happenings and pursuing the more modest course of placing the events in a cultural or political context.[20] Yet even this procedure promotes a model of subjectivity – a subjectivity bound up in the body and society – which stands opposed to the pure, selfless experience claimed by many historical actors, from the religious mystic to the plain-speaking witness to the miraculous.

It seems that the historical approach is all encompassing, that once one adopts this interpretive method there is no escaping the power of its explanations.[21] Yet such power may be illusory. The Marxist critic Walter Benjamin famously likened the explanatory force of historical materialism to the operations of an impressive chess-playing automaton – an automaton whose apparent brilliance stems not from its mechanical organisation but from the efforts of a 'little hunchback' secreted in its innards. History, Benjamin maintained, is animated by its own obscure wizened dwarf: the venerable discipline of theology.[22] Although we might recognise the power of historical explanations, and readily perceive inevitable connections of cause and effect in the texts we read and the lives we live, these perceptions rest on older theological assumptions which guide our ways of seeing. Christianity, though widely ignored, infuses modern historical and psychological practice.

However we feel about dwarves and puppets, *Resisting History* shows that Benjamin's claim must be taken seriously, for our contemporary understanding of history and selfhood arises out of nineteenth-century religious debates over the boundaries of representation. These debates were generated by the Pauline Epistles, where a clear distinction is made between the spiritual and the human.[23] St Paul describes man as a being divided between a finite self created through the sin of Adam and an infinite spirit made possible through the example of Christ.[24] The boundary between these two aspects of the individual is death. It follows from this that whereas human experience is finite and amenable to narrative reconstruction, the spiritual or supernatural aspect of man necessarily lies beyond the possibility of historical description. This acknowledged boundary, as we shall see, was to become the crucial point of conflict between groups opposed to the concept of fixed personal identity and those whose claims to pastoral authority and expertise were predicated upon the idea of an individual's consistent psychological history. It was a conflict over different ways of imagining death, and would eventually lead to our modern conception of the unconscious.

Across nineteenth-century Europe and America, spiritualists, revivalists and Pentecostalists undermined the idea of a continuous narrative biography by claiming that the supernatural erupted into their everyday lives. Episodes of mediumship, inspiration and possession divided their actions from any easy identity with their bodies or the past. Divorced from the individual's historical biography, such supernatural events lay outside the forensic responsibility of the agent, undermining the conventional moral order. It was out of the elite's need to restore these events to history and narrative that the notion of the unconscious or 'subliminal self' was first developed.

Although Sigmund Freud depicted the discovery of the unconscious as a radical event that disrupted commonly held assumptions of personal identity and historical integrity, this was not the case.[25] In the chapters that follow I will demonstrate that the concept was first developed in an attempt to restore the contested life narratives of individual mystics. Against those histories which portray psychoanalysis as a revolutionary innovation that undermined bourgeois morality, this book demonstrates how the new rhetoric of the unconscious served a conservative purpose, being used to police the subversive mystical experiences of spiritualism and revivalism. The 'triumph of the therapeutic', to borrow Philip Rieff's evocative phrase, is the triumph of a particular version of the self and a particular conception of morality.[26]

Origin stories

In this chapter I argue that it was the appearance of new forms of religious narrative and theological argument in early nineteenth-century Europe which made possible the emergence of our modern understanding of history, authority, narrative and identity. Such an assertion is bound to be contested. Over the past three decades, historians, anthropologists, philosophers and literary theorists have all produced fine works making competing claims for the origin of this new form of deep subjectivity.[27] Changes in the Greek chorus, medieval inquisitorial practice, embryological discoveries, romantic literary style, clinical theories and consumer boycotts have all been held up as foundational moments in which a novel form of historically minded self-awareness first appeared.[28]

It is striking, however, that even the most secular of these origin stories remain indebted to Christian tropes and arguments. They imagine the birth of modern selfhood as a movement in which a dispersed, free-floating consciousness becomes bound up with a body (of flesh, knowledge or writing) which makes its articulation and representation possible. A clear example of this can be found in Michel Foucault's claim that our current conception of man emerged through specific innovations in the clinical and the human sciences of the eighteenth century. Foucault argued that the birth of the modern individual was made possible by the imagining of a space bounded by death. As he writes in *The Birth of the Clinic*: 'Western man could constitute himself in his own eyes as an object of science, he grasped himself within his language, and gave himself, in himself and by himself, a discursive existence, only in the opening created by his own elimination.'[29] Similarly, in *The Order of Things*, Foucault argues that the modern subject is born out of the intellectual discovery of mundane forces – biology, labour and language – that shape men's lives yet lie outside the ambit of individual cognition and control. These newly recognised forces 'traverse him as though he were merely an object of nature'. The sense of intellectual omnipotence that man had enjoyed as the 'sovereign subject of knowledge' is replaced by a new apprehension of personal finitude.[30]

The history of man that Foucault recounts is heavily indebted to the Christian story of the Incarnation. In his work, Foucault traces the entry of the transcendental bases of knowledge into the finite body of man, just as the Christian tradition of the Incarnation traces the entry of God, infinite and transcendent, into the human person of Christ. Both narratives map the passage of that which is beyond representation (God or, in Foucault's case, 'the sovereign subject of knowledge') into a human body which makes the act of representation possible. The apotheosis of both narratives is a divided figure: modern man who is at once empirical and transcendental; Christ who is at once both human and divine.

Although I think that Foucault's argument and those of many of his contemporaries are theological in their form and structure, I do not want to argue for the priority of Christianity's role in any explanation of the emergence of modern individuality. Many nineteenth-century authors believed that it was 'Christianity which raised to its true height the conception of the value of the single soul', but the transformation of this single soul into the finite historical individual we recognise today probably owes just as much to changes in the organisation of labour, literature and government.[31] My aim in returning to these theological writings is rather different. It is simply that the religious literature of the nineteenth century makes most readily apparent the deep connections between the new modes of historical writing, modern forms of subjectivity and the rise of hermeneutic expertise.

The historical and the mythological

It is widely acknowledged that the nineteenth century was characterised by a new interest in historical enquiry. Writing at the close of the Victorian era, the Anglican theologian Vernon Storr complained that '[t]he spirit of the age is pre-eminently historical and because it is that, it is also critical'.[32] Certainly there is a wide base of evidence to support Storr's claim. The rise of evolutionary theories in the sciences; romance and melodrama in literature, and historical criticism in theology demonstrates how the standards and aims of rational enquiry were transformed. As Storr noted, simply tracing the development or evolution of an idea, an individual or an institution now sufficed to explain them. This transformation created a situation in which the recovery of the past became the royal road to the achievement of truth and authority.[33]

In the case of theology the rise of the historicist approach has been attributed to a search for new forms of ecclesiastical authority. From the end of the eighteenth century, the established Church and its ministers were threatened by the growth of non-conformism and the widening powers of secular government.[34] These developments led sections of the Church of England to claim a new kind of historical authority in two areas. First, there was an assertion of the apostolic continuity of Anglican faith and doctrine.[35] In this claim, history was not imagined as a passive medium that preserved an unchanging faith: rather, the Christian religion was portrayed as a developing idea that is distorted and coloured by its times.[36]

Second, from the 1850s certain sections of the Church of England began to lay claim to a particular form of historical expertise in the interpretation of Christian texts. The new sense of the mutability of doctrine and the need for strict methods to recover its original meaning gave significance to this field. Its origins can be traced back to the new approaches to interpretation of the Bible that appeared in the eighteenth century, an attempt by philologists, notably Christian Gottlob Heyne and J. G. Eichorn, to distinguish between the elements of Jewish mythology in the New Testament and the true history of Christ.[37] It was in David Strauss's *Leben Jesu* published in 1835 that this approach received its clearest, albeit its most notorious, presentation.[38]

The publication of *Leben Jesu* is now widely celebrated as a foundational moment in the history of modern European thought.[39] It is a work infused by an absolute commitment to history and the sovereignty of natural law. Strauss shares with the eighteenth-century critics an uneasy suspicion of the Gospel narratives. With their frequent miracles and apparent contempt of the regular universe, the Gospels seemed to be little more than chronicles of episodic legerdemain. Yet unlike the earlier sceptics, Strauss is unwilling to dismiss the miracles as examples of straightforward imposture or religious fraud. Whereas rationalists such as H. E. G. Paulus or Tom Paine portrayed Christ as an impressive conjuror, Strauss portrays Him as a creation of His times: an invented Messiah whose every action was interpreted and redescribed in accordance with the prophecies and myths of the Jewish Messianic tradition.[40]

The recovery of the authentic story of Christ, Strauss believed, could only be achieved through a kind of policing operation. The mythical or unhistorical aspects of the Gospel narratives would have to be detected and excluded. He therefore set out clear criteria by which such acts of forensic discrimination might be achieved. In his introduction to the *Leben Jesu*, he argues that any narration which cannot be reconciled with known and universal laws must be rejected: 'When therefore we meet with an account of certain phenomena or events of which it is either expressly stated or implied that they were produced immediately by God himself (divine apparitions – voices from heaven and the like), or by human beings possessed of supernatural powers (miracles, prophecies), such an account is *in so far* to be considered not historical.'[41] This principle is extended to the assessment of human behaviour. Strauss argues that past actions must be judged against 'all those psychological laws which render it improbable that a human being should feel, think and act in a manner directly opposed to his own habitual mode and that of men in general'.[42] This method transformed the literary criteria of religious truth: events were no longer true simply because they were asserted within the Gospel record; they obtained their ontological validity from their place within a coherent historical and psychological sequence.[43]

Strauss's approach, as is well known, provoked a storm of controversy. In Zurich, his brief appointment to the chair of theology led to open fighting in the streets and the fall of the regional government in 1839.[44] In England, the appearance of rough translations of the *Leben Jesu* provoked calls in parliament for its suppression.[45] It was condemned by Anglican churchmen as an attack on the authority of the Gospels, although few of them had ever read the work.[46] It took a revision of the blasphemy laws before Marian Evans, writing as George Eliot, could publish the first complete English translation in 1846.

Yet it would be wrong to map the controversy surrounding the publication of the *Leben Jesu* onto the familiar conflict between secular rationality and ecclesiastical authority. The change the *Leben Jesu* wrought was subtler and more profound. It was, as Gerald Parsons argues, 'a conflict between different types of faith' and different ways of achieving a knowledge of the divine.[47] The doubts raised by the mythological theory introduced a new sense of distance to the reading of the Gospels: they were no longer the unmediated word of God; rather, as the *Westminster Review* insisted, they combined divine revelation with the 'psychological accidents' of a distant age.[48] The Bible's message – or *kerygma* – could only be recovered through disciplined enquiry; through the exercise and cultivation of the historical imagination. This discovery of historical distance in turn initiated a wider political and psychological transformation. It would change the way that the individual related to the sacred text and, more fundamentally, the way that individuals related to themselves.[49]

The story of the first of these transformations – the rise of a historical approach to the Bible – has been told many times.[50] Although the new or 'higher' criticism was initially resisted, by the end of the nineteenth century its method was firmly established in universities and theological colleges across the United Kingdom.[51] Indeed the new approach was inextricably linked with the development of these didactic institutions. For the admission that the Bible was bound up in history meant that the Scripture could no longer be taken on trust; rather, it could only be recovered through critical appraisal by an academic elite.[52] Just at the point when literacy and biblical literalism began to spread through the Victorian population, the truth of the Bible seemed to move further away from the grasp of its plebeian audience.[53] Although evangelical Protestants railed against the clerical mediation of the word of God, it now appeared that the word was mediated by history. And the recovery of religious truth, according to the champions of the higher criticism, only became possible through the dedicated work of the theologian and the historian.

The historical and the psychological

The rise of this historicist approach, I will argue, did not simply establish a new form of interpretive authority; it also made possible a new kind of psychological identity. Strauss's refusal of the miraculous and his insistence on the integrity of the historical record opened up new ways of thinking about the life of Christ. In the Gospels, Jesus is portrayed as a divided figure caught between the human and the divine. In His earthly life, He takes on the same opposed characteristics that Paul identifies in the individuality of every man – a finite self and an infinite soul – but for Christ the balance between these natures is very different. His Incarnation was understood by most early nineteenth-century Christians as the act of merely 'tabernacling in this very mortal flesh', his human form being a simple shell or husk housing the divine presence.[54] Thus the portrait of Jesus that emerges in the scattered parables and miraculous performances of the New Testament is to be understood as a fragmented, albeit deeply suggestive, sketch. The source and core of His identity lie outside the historical record. Strauss's arrangement of the Gospel material into a synthetic narrative transformed Christ into a historical character: Jesus emerged in the *Leben Jesu* as a kind of literary hero pursuing a Messianic *bildungsroman* from Bethlehem to Golgotha.[55] In Strauss's work, the supernatural aspect of Christ is consigned to the realm of the unhistorical. In his Incarnation, He remains, like all other men, a deathbound individuality, limited to a particular consciousness, living in a particular history. In his resurrection, He becomes a purely historical idea, a guiding force in the future evolution of humanity.[56]

Although the twentieth-century theologian Albert Schweitzer believed that 'the fertilising rain of the *Leben Jesu* brought up a crop of toadstools', it was a harvest which was to change forever the conception of spiritual identity.[57] Certainly the conservative reaction to the book was often doctrinaire and dogmatic. The critics, for the most part, rejected Strauss's sceptical attitude to the miraculous and his Hegelian understanding of the ascension of Christ. However, they remained enamoured of his literary approach and this concession was to change the shape of historical and theological argument in Britain.

From the 1840s onwards, narrative biographies of Christ began to appear across Western Europe. These had a tremendous impact on the British reading public.[58] The various English editions of the *Leben Jesu* were followed by translations of theologically conservative lives of Jesus prepared by Strauss's German critics.[59] In 1865, these stolid harmonies of the Gospel record were joined by the first English translation of Ernst Renan's *Vie de Jesus* (1863).[60] Renan's work, which combines his extensive biblical scholarship and personal experience of the Near East, presents a deeply romantic and evocative portrait of Christ that emphasises His personal humanity and psychological growth. That same year, it was joined by the anonymously published *Ecce Homo*, the first English life of Christ.[61] Written by the historian J. R. Seeley, the work lacks Renan's florid style and most of his candour. Yet this typically English compromise proved to be a publishing sensation. When Lord Shaftesbury condemned it as the 'most pestilential book ever vomited . . . from the jaws of hell' it quickly sold out, running through seven editions in as many months.[62]

The popularity of Seeley's dry book provided clear encouragement for others. Over the next four decades, more than 5,000 new 'lives of Christ' would appear. Among these many works the crowning success, in commercial terms at least, belonged to Dean Farrar's *Life of Christ*. Published in 1874, it became the best-selling biographical work of the Victorian age.[63]

These works were largely written in a spirit of orthodoxy, yet they maintain Strauss's most crucial innovation: the idea that the life of Christ can be adequately represented in the shape of a human narrative. In their commitment to a biographical representation they also assume a certain model of history and a certain conception of personality. This involves a commitment to what the critic Hayden White has called the 'middle style' in historical writing. As White explains, this approach restricts the possible contents of a narrative:

> the subordination of historical narrative to the deliberative mode of the middle style entails stylistic exclusions and this has implications for the kinds of events that can be represented in a narrative. Excluded are the kinds of events traditionally conceived to be the stuff of religious belief and ritual (miracles, magical events, godly events), on the one side and the kinds of 'grotesque' events that are the stuff of farce, satire, and calumny, on the other. Above all these two orders of exclusion consign to historical thinking the kinds of events that lend themselves to the understanding of whatever currently passes for educated common sense. They effect a disciplining of the imagination, in this case the historical imagination, and they set limits on what constitutes a specifically historical event.[64]

The explicit rules which Strauss brought into play to define what was 'real' and what was 'mythical' in history can be seen as exemplifying the middle style. They were rules which were reiterated with varying degrees of forthrightness and orthodoxy by the many contributors to the 'lives of Jesus' tradition.[65] Renan was perhaps the clearest in his belief that the consistency and integrity of the narrative should serve as the criteria of historical truth:

In histories such as this the great test that we have got the truth is to have succeeded in combining the texts in such a manner that they shall constitute a logically probable narrative, harmonious throughout . . . Each trait which departs from the rules of classic narration ought to warn us to be careful; for the feat which has to be related, has been living, natural and harmonious. If we do not succeed in rendering it such by the recital, it is surely because we have not succeeded in seeing it aright.[66]

Thus for Renan the supernatural or miraculous always becomes a sign of 'credulity or imposture' and the first duty of the historian is to explain it away.[67] Seeley is more defensive, arguing that: 'The accounts we have of the miracles may be exaggerated; it is possible that in some special cases stories have been related which have no foundation whatever.' However, he asserts, 'The Christ of the Gospels is not mythical . . . [since] the character those biographies portray is in all its large features strikingly consistent and at the same time so peculiar as to be altogether beyond the reach of invention both by individual genius and still more by what is called the "consciousness of the age".'[68]

Even in those 'lives of Jesus' which aimed to preserve the Gospel record from Strauss's historicist predations, narrative integrity and psychological consistency moved forward to become the new grounds of truth.[69] Evangelical critics who set out to undermine the portrait of Christ presented by Strauss and Renan found themselves deploying the same criteria as their enemies. The American divine Phillip Schaff argued that Renan's portrait of Christ was 'psychologically inconsistent' and should be rejected out of court.[70] The Scottish minister John Cairns derided Renan's aesthetic achievement, claiming that 'A more hopeless chaos than the character of Renan's imaginary Christ no artist ever mistook for a creation, and the eulogies heaped on this abortion are as offensive to literary taste as they are to moral feeling.'[71]

The narrativisation of the miraculous in the new 'lives of Jesus' thus led to a reconceptualisation of the self: against the old Christian model which had imagined individual actions as the outcome of combined human interests and inspired passions – passions which were shaped by external spiritual forces, whether demonic or divine – the new narrative model insisted that individuals were the sole authors of their actions. Their intentions were shaped only by their carnal desires and the memory of accumulated influences.[72] Reported miracles no longer indicated the failure of a human narrative and the entry of an ineffable divine force; rather they stood as demonstrations of the power of history and the psychological imagination.[73] Those who rejected the possibility of divine intervention were forced to posit new psychological mechan-isms of expectancy and anticipation to explain the persistence of troublesome interpretations in the religious records. As early as 1847, the *Westminster Review* could praise Strauss for having 'found a psycho-logical cause for early Christian fiction, and, in the cycle of Messianic notions, named a definite law of suggestion regulating its effects'.[74] By 1860, the Oxford mathematician Rev. Baden Powell, in his contribution to the controversial volume, *Essays and Reviews*, could argue that the perception of any apparent miracle (including those recorded in the Bible) was complicated by the 'enormous influence exerted by our prepos-sessions previous to the event and by the momentary impressions consequent upon it.'[75]

The critical histories developed in the 'lives of Jesus' tradition are thus inextricably linked with the appearance of psychological models of personhood in the nineteenth century. Psychological concepts of expec-tation and delusion were used to interrogate and repair the Gospel record; psychological criteria for the consistency of character were used to judge the portraits developed in the new biographies of Christ; but perhaps the most important and wide-reaching innovation was the new theo-logical model of personhood that developed from these accounts. As many commentators noted, the rise of historical criticism drew atten-tion to the 'self-consciousness of Jesus' and raised questions about the inner life of Christ.[76]

By the end of the nineteenth century, the psychological question of Christ's character was seen as one of the main problems raised by Strauss's achievement. As the Episcopalian theologian William Douglas Mackenzie noted in the *Encyclopaedia of Religion and Ethics*: 'Strauss's method of attack compelled men to think more seriously even than he did himself of that which lay behind all the separate utterances of Jesus, namely that consciousness of Himself from which His whole attitude, action, purpose and speech arose.'[77] The problem required a new theological model of His incarnate existence: a model which would reconcile His divine nature with the possibility of His literary representation. As Renan claimed in his *Life of Jesus*: 'His glory does not consist in being relegated out of history; we render him a truer worship in showing that all history is incomprehensible without him.'[78] For Christ to become truly incar-nate, the critics argued, His nature had to be transformed. In the new theology of the nineteenth century, Christ's personality was no longer portrayed as an ineffable force. It was instead understood as a limited entity – an entity which could be completely represented through narra-

tive and recovered through historical investigation. This reconceptualisation was made possible, in theological terms, by a return to the
controversial doctrine of the *kenosis*.

Kenosis and the morality of historical representation

The concept of the *kenosis* or the 'self-emptying' of Christ first appeared
in Paul's epistle to the Philippians, although passages in the Gospels of
Mark and Luke are also often cited to illustrate the idea.[79] The term
refers to a specific mechanism of incarnation, in which Christ became
Man through the complete surrender of His divine power. This act is
prefigured in Isaiah's prophecy of a Messiah who 'hath poured out His
soul unto death' and through this taken on the Adamic limitations of
mortal man.[80] It was an act of humility. As Bishop Lightfoot wrote in
1879, Christ 'did not cling with avidity to the prerogatives of His Divine
majesty, He did not ambitiously display His equality with God; but
divested Himself of the glories of heaven, and took upon Him the nature
of a servant assuming the likeness of man'.[81]

The idea of the living Christ as a deathbound individual had been a
point of controversy in the early Church: heretical groups – the Docetae,
the Apollinarians and the Arians – denied the existence of a human intelligence in Christ while the Ebionites originally denied the incarnation
of the divine presence. These doctrinal disputes were resolved in the
Church Councils at Nicaea, Ephesus and Chalcedon in the fourth and
fifth centuries, and the doctrine of *kenosis* remained largely ignored until
it was resurrected in the wake of the arguments over the *Leben Jesu*.[82]

The German theologians who pioneered a return to the kenotic
theology, Gottfried Thomasius and Wolfgang Gess, did not interpret the
Incarnation as a simple surrender of Christ's power.[83] Rather, they believed
that the humiliation of Christ also involved the renunciation of his
divine consciousness. It was a psychological process in which the absolute
omniscience of God was relinquished for the unconscious grace of a
child. This sacrifice was not seen as undermining the power of Christ,
for it was an act of voluntary surrender.[84] It involved the inhibition of
the external or physical attributes of God (omnipotence, omniscience
and omnipresence) by His internal or ethical attributes of love and sacrifice. By the end of the nineteenth century, this conception of Christ's
personality had been widely accepted by theologians across the British
Isles.[85] Given the developments described earlier in this chapter, its adop-
tion is unsurprising. The idea of Christ's self-limitation, His ethical

embrace of a finite self, made possible the projects of historical criticism and psychological representation. The fundamentalist argument that Christ had endorsed the stories of the Flood or Jonah and the whale and so placed them outside critical interrogation was rendered untenable, as Jesus himself was now seen as having taken on the limited intellectual outlook of first-century Palestine.[86] As a writer in the *Church Quarterly Review* quipped, 'The readiness to accept certain theories of kenoticism . . . in certain quarters seems to proceed not so much from the supposed satisfactory nature of the theories themselves, as from the fact they afford an easy mode of getting rid of certain sayings of our Lord about Noah and Moses and David and Jonah.'[87]

The ethical reading of the *kenosis* transformed a literary problem concerned with the organisation of historical narratives into a kind of moral injunction. The self-limitation of Christ and His achievement of a new finitude moved from being a point of doctrinal interest to a model for human existence. The example of Christ had of course always provided a template for Christian behaviour – but the new narrative 'lives of Jesus' extended that process, celebrating the *kenosis* as a model for the perfect inner life.[88] As A. J. Mason stated in his 1896 lecture series on *The Conditions of Our Lord's Life on Earth*: 'All the phenomena of Christ's inward experience during His life on earth which are recorded for us, combined to suggest that his moral growth . . . was of the same kind as ours only immeasurably better . . . Christ is not only our pattern but our example; and his methods of attaining to moral perfection are our methods.'[89]

The narrative structure of the 'lives of Jesus' became an archetype for the reader's internal experience. Engagement with these texts encouraged a moral transformation. As many clerics made clear, the Gospel stories created new networks of feeling, perception and connection within the reader. Dean Farrar wrote in the introduction to his *Life of Christ*: 'If the following pages in any measure fulfil the objects with which such a Life should be written, they should fill the minds of those who read them with solemn and not ignoble thoughts; they should add "sunlight to daylight by making the happy happier"; they should encourage the toiler; they should console the sorrowful; they should point the weak to the one true source of moral strength.'[90] This was, as Ieuan Ellis has remarked, a Pre-Raphaelite version of Christ, emphasising His humanity over the sacrifice of His atonement.[91]

From the perspective of modern criticism such narratives may be regarded as libidinal apparatuses: they provide a framework that structures the desires and perspectives of the reader.[92] Again, this idea was anticipated in the discourse of Victorian theology. The Oxford theologian William Sanday drew upon St Paul's Epistle to the Galatians to demonstrate the structuring influence of the life of Jesus. He believed that this example possessed 'a formative power which so fashions men in the likeness of Christ, that they become in turn a standing witness to those that have not come under the same influence'. Christ is formed within converts, Sanday wrote, as an embryo is formed in the womb.[93]

The complicity is now apparent between psychological examples held up in the 'lives of Jesus' tradition and the models of selfhood concurrently developed in Victorian Christology. To reiterate, the doctrine of *kenosis* suggests that normal human life involves a surrender to limitation; a voluntary engagement with our finite personalities and history. The example of Christ gives such limitation a moral imperative. This lesson is brought home by the late nineteenth-century glosses on the story of the Temptation.

The Temptation is usually portrayed as a kind of moral drama, in which Christ is pitted against the strength and cunning of the Devil. In the kenoticists' interpretation, His struggle is not so much with Satan as with the control of His own transcendent Person. Christ was tempted by the Devil three times: on the first occasion he was hungry, and the Devil urged him to turn stones to bread; on the second occasion he felt forsaken, and the Devil encouraged him to test His Father's wardship by throwing Himself from the pinnacle; in the third temptation, Satan offered to make Christ king of this world.[94] In the interpretation of the British kenoticists, Christ's success in this trial lay in His refusal to employ His transcendent or miraculous power.[95] As Andrew Martin Fairbairn wrote, 'to have yielded and used the power would have lifted the Person out of the category of humanity; placed Him above rather than under nature . . . Jesus was victorious because He refused to emancipate Himself from law, or to live otherwise than under the conditions common to man.'[96]

Christ's obedience lies in his adherence to the human limitations he has assumed. It is an example of His continuing sacrifice within the Incarnation.[97] Had he submitted, Renan claimed, 'the laws of history and popular psychology would have suffered so great a derogation'.[98] Christ's humanity rested upon His perpetuation within the finite boundaries of personality and earthly history. It was a message brought home very clearly to lay audiences: to be a person was an ongoing act of sacrifice; to be a person was to be 'embodied in a tale'. It involved the joyful acceptance of the carnal limitations of the deathbound self, a commitment to the interior life and history.

History and transcendence

We can now begin to see how new forms of historical enquiry opened up new ways of imagining the self – and these in turn made possible new kinds of hermeneutic authority and new kinds of individual action. The rise of historical criticism, as many nineteenth-century commentators noted, moved in tandem with a new theological understanding of the nature of Christ and man. The injunctions against the miraculous in historical narrative and the injunction against transcendence in the new theology could never be completely effective, however. Christ's whole life held out the promise of eventual transcendence. His crucifixion and atonement had made manifest the possibility of overcoming of the finite self and it was this idea of atonement which remained at the heart of Christian teaching until the rise of the kenotic theology.[99] Yet even the concept of transcendence would eventually succumb to the historical approach. When late nineteenth-century Anglican theologians imagined the life beyond death, it was no longer apprehended as a divine or ineffable state. Rather, it was imagined as another kind of history: a deeper history where the life of the individual joined that of other men.

This new view of transcendence as a movement from an individual to a universal history was first developed in Hegel's writings – and indeed in many ways it had been embraced in Strauss's speculative portrait of the ascension of Christ.[100] The British pioneers of this new view of transcendence, however, were neither as heterodox nor as marginalised as Strauss. As we shall see, they included the core of the Anglican establishment whose academic mentor, the Balliol philosopher T. H. Green, was widely acclaimed as the leader of the new school of British Idealism.[101]

Green propounded a version of Hegelian idealism (inspired by the work of Hermann Lotze) that takes personality as both the fundamental base and the absolute goal of human development.[102] Against those Hegelians who believed that man's personality was a contingent creation awaiting a general subsumption in the Absolute, Green insisted upon the perfect integrity of its existence. In the conclusion to his posthumously published work, *A Prolegomena to Ethics* (1883), Green argues that the idea of human development would be emptied of 'any real meaning, if we suppose the end of development to be one in the attainment of which persons – agents who are ends to themselves – are extinguished.'[103] Green's vision is some way from the idea of self-annihilation that had inspired centuries of Christian mysticism.

Green proposes that transcendence be imagined as a form of social engagement, in which the individual overcomes his or her personal history by joining in the history of others. This model was widely adopted by the Anglican hierarchy, receiving its most famous articulation in *Lux Mundi* – a collection of programmatic essays published in 1889 under the editorship of the Keble College theologian Charles Gore.[104] The contributors to *Lux Mundi* were drawn from the common rooms of Oxford, and they followed Green in identifying social fellowship with personal transcendence.[105] In his own essay, Gore argues that the Holy Spirit, 'treats man as a "social being" who cannot realize himself in isolation . . . the true, the redeemed humanity is presented to us as a society or Church.'[106] Likewise, his colleague William Campion states that a 'Christian anthropology', 'recognises man's inherently social nature. It is not good for man to be alone. The family, state and Church on earth are training places for a perfected common life in the City of God.'[107]

This identification of the transcendent aspect of man and achievement of social fellowship was to become the central tenet of the Anglo-Catholic contributors to *Lux Mundi*. John Richardson Illingworth, whom many regarded as the most intellectually able of *Lux Mundi* writers, defines man as, 'an individual but also a social being "he lives in and for others" . . . he can only realise himself through his essential dependence upon other men . . . And when we probe this dependence to its utmost depth, we are carried in the last resort, to the infinite Personality of God.'[108] The vision of the soul articulated by the *Lux Mundi* authors was rooted in Green's philosophy and a distinctive programme of social action.[109] Yet their identification of transcendence with the experience of fellowship and communion was widely shared by the end of the nineteenth century. The language of influence and sympathy, developed in Victorian literature, sustained this vision. Tennyson claimed at the end of his life that his long meditation on friendship, *In Memoriam*, expressed his belief that 'We are parts of the infinite whole'. Indeed, the poem's description of a child's consciousness presents its growth as a kind of *kenosis* – a movement from an extended universal self into a sense of separate individuality:

> The baby new to earth and sky,
> What time his tender palm is prest
> Against the circle of the breast,
> Has never thought that 'this is I'.

But as he grows he gathers much,
And learns the use of 'I' and 'me',
And finds 'I am not what I see,
And other than the things I touch.'

So rounds he to a separate mind
From whence clear memory may begin,
As thro' the frame that binds him in
His isolation grows defined.[110]

This same sense of connection and loss informs Matthew Arnold's poem, 'To Marguerite', which was widely quoted in the late nineteenth-century literature on the philosophy of personality. Arnold describes the same sense of separation that Tennyson apprehended in the maturing child, but sees it as bereavement suffered by the population as a whole:

Yes! In the sea of life enisled,
With echoing straits between us thrown,
Dotting the shoreless watery wild,
We mortal millions live *alone*.
The islands feel the enclasping flow,
And then their endless bounds they know.

O then a longing like despair
Is to their farthest caverns sent;
For surely once, they feel, we were
Parts of a single continent!
Now round us spreads the watery plain –
Oh might our marges meet again!

Who order'd that their longing's fire
Should be, as soon as kindled, cool'd?
Who renders vain their deep desire? –
A God – a God their severance ruled?
And bade betwixt their shores to be
The unplumb'd, salt, estranging sea.[111]

This cataclysm, which transforms the human species from a united continent to an archipelago of individuals, obscures man's true foundation in the experience of human fellowship. The myth also serves a deeper purpose. In its identification of man's true nature with his social being, the fable promotes a general reconciliation between the individual and the goals of a wider society. The recovery of man's essential substance could only be achieved, as Green and his followers had argued, through his coordination with the collective demands of others. Thus incarnate man emerged around a double imperative: to realise his finite individuality, and yet transcend it through subordination to society.

In the new model of man developed in nineteenth-century Christology and British idealism, the domain of individual history expanded outwards. It overflowed the limiting deaths of the *kenosis*, forming a 'single continent' with the social world. Yet this egress of personality did not betoken the end of narrative and psychological representation; instead, it encouraged the extension of personality and history into new domains. Within the work of Anglican theologians, the extended personality achieved only the loosest of formulations in its romantic yet political identification with the social world. Its most detailed articulation was delegated to another project, where the overflowing personality was defined and contained within the many new deaths discovered in the practices of spiritualism and psychical research.

Notes:

1 Alongside Mary Ward, *Robert Elsmere* [1888] (Oxford: Oxford University Press, 1987); M. R. James, *Ghost Stories of an Antiquary* [1904] (London: Dover, 1971); A. S. Byatt, *Possession* (London: Vintage, 1991) and Elizabeth Kostova, *The Historian* (New York: Little Brown, 2005) other examples might include John Cowper: Powys, *Wolf Solent* [1929] (Harmondsworth: Penguin Books, 1964); Michael Stewart, *Belladonna* (London: Harper Collins, 1992); Robert Girardi, *Madeline's Ghost* (London: Sphere, 1995); M. P. Dare, *Unholy Relics and Other Uncanny Tales* (London: Edward Arnold, 1947) esp. the title tale, 'Bring out your dead', and 'The haunted drawers'; Richard Malden, *Nine Ghosts* (London: Edward Arnold, 1943); Frances Cowles, *The Horror of Abbot's Grange* (London: Frederick Muller, 1936) and *The Night Wind Howls* (London: Frederick Muller, 1938).

2 F. H. Bradley, *The Presuppositions of Critical History* [1874], ed. Lionel Rubinoff (Chicago: Quadrangle Books, 1968), p. 39.

3 W. Barrett, *Death of the Soul: From Descartes to the Computer* (Oxford: Oxford University Press, 1987).

4 P. Heelas and A. Lock (eds), *Indigenous Psychologies: An Anthropology of the Self* (London: Academic Press, 1981); M. Carrithers, S. Collins and S. Lukes (eds), *The Category of Person* (Cambridge: Cambridge University Press, 1985).

5 William James, *The Principles of Psychology* [1890] (London: Dover, 1950), ch. 9.

6 William James, *The Varieties of Religious Experience: A Study in Human Nature* (London: Fontana, 1960), pp. 92–171; James, *Talks to Teachers* [1899] (London: Longmans, 1917), pp. 248–54; Cushing Strout, 'William James and the twice-born sick soul', Daedalus 97 (1968), 1062–82. James's ethic will be discussed in more detail in chapter 3.

7 See for example, 'The unhappiest one', in *Either/Or* [1843], ed. and trans. H. V. Hong and E. H. Hong (Princeton NJ: Princeton University Press, 1987), pp. 219–30; G. W. F. Hegel, *The Phenomenology of Mind* [1807], trans. J. Baillie (New York: Harper Torchbooks, 1966), pp. 251–67.

8 Friedrich Nietzsche, 'The use and abuse of history', in *Thoughts Out of Season*, ed. Oscar Levy (Edinburgh: T. N. Foulis, 1909). This image of bovine happiness rooted in a lack of historical awareness forms a recurring motif in continental philosophy. See the fourth thesis of Immanuel Kant, 'Idea for a universal history from a cosmopolitan point of view', in *Kant's Political Writings* (Cambridge: Cambridge University Press, 1991).

9 Among their many examples, see: M. Foucault, *Discipline and Punish* (London: Penguin, 1979); Gilles Deleuze and Felix Guattari, *Anti-Oedipus: Capitalism and Schizophrenia*, trans. Robert Hurley, Mark Seem and Helen Lane (London: Athlone, 1982).

10 On the different possibilities of history, see: M. Foucault, 'Nietzsche, genealogy and history', in James Faubion (ed.), *Michel Foucault: Aesthetics, Method and Epistemology* (London: Allen Lane, 1998); Foucault, 'The subject and power', in H. Dreyfus and P. Rabinow, *Michel Foucault: Beyond Structuralism and Hermeneutics* (Hemel Hempstead: Harvester, 1987).

11 J. W. Pennebaker, J. K. Kiecolt-Glaser and R. Glaser, 'Disclosure of traumas and immune function: health implications for psychotherapy', *Journal of Consulting and Clinical Psychology* 56 (1988), 239–45; J. W. Pennebaker, 'Telling stories: the health benefits of narrative', *Literature and Medicine* 19 (2000), 3–18; M. A. Stewart, 'Effective physician–patient communication and health outcomes: a review of the literature', *Canadian Medical Association Journal* 152 (1995), 1423–33.

12 Among the most important examples are: David Blackbourn, *Marpingen: Apparitions of the Virgin Mary in Nineteenth-Century Germany* (New York: Knopf, 1994); Ruth Harris, *Lourdes: Body and Spirit in the Secular Age* (London: Allen Lane, 1999); Alex Owen, *The Darkened Room: Women, Power and Spiritualism in Nineteenth-Century England* (London: Virago, 1989); Owen, *The Place of Enchantment: British Occultism and the Culture of the Modern* (Chicago: University of Chicago Press, 2004).

13 Psycho-historical narratives of supernatural phenomena, include: Lyndal Roper, *Oedipus and the Devil: Witchcraft, Sexuality and Religion in Early Modern Europe* (London: Routledge, 1994); Dianne Purkiss, *The Witch in*

History (London: Routledge, 1989); Owen, *Darkened Room*; Michael Caroll, *The Cult of the Virgin Mary: Psychological Origins* (Princeton NJ: Princeton University Press, 1986).

14 R. Samuel, 'Reading the signs: II. fact-grubbers and mind-readers', *HWJ* 33 (1992), 244.

15 Bradley, *Presuppositions*, pp. 114–15, 118, 121; R. G. Collingwood, *The Idea of History* (rev. edn), ed. Jan van der Dussen (Oxford: Oxford University Press, 1994), pp. 137–8.

16 Marc Bloch, *The Historian's Craft* (Manchester: Manchester University Press, 1959), p. 115. Henri Pirenne quoted in V. A. Harvey, *The Historian and the Believer* (London: SCM Press, 1971), p. 71. See also, Hans Frei, *The Eclipse of the Biblical Narrative: A Study in Eighteenth and Nineteenth Century Hermeneutics* (New Haven: Yale University Press, 1974), p. 240.

17 Bloch, *Historian's Craft*, pp. 100–1, 112.

18 *Ibid.*, pp. 135–6; Harvey, *Historian and the Believer*, p. 97.

19 W. H. Lecky, *History of the Rise of the Spirit of Rationalism in Europe* (London: Macmillan, 1865); H. T. Buckle, *History of Civilization in England* 1 (London: Longman, Green and Co., 1871), pp. 18–35; J. B. Crozier, *Civilization and Progress* (London: Longman, Green and Co., 1892), pp. 36–42, 226–28.

20 This even applies to some of the most careful and sensitive accounts, see for example, Kathryn A. Edwards, 'Female sociability, physicality and authority in an early modern haunting', *Journal of Social History* 33 (2000), 601–21; Susan Juster, 'Mystical pregnancy and holy bleeding: visionary experience in early modern Britain and America', *William and Mary Quarterly* 57 (2000), 249–88.

21 This is the position established by Ernst Troeltsch. See his entry on 'Historiography', in *ERE* VI (1914), pp. 716–23. For background: A. O. Dyson, 'Ernst Troeltsch and the possibility of a systematic theology', in John Clayton (ed.), *Ernst Troeltsch and the Future of Theology* (Cambridge: Cambridge University Press, 1976), pp. 85–93; Harvey, *Historian and the Believer*, ch. 1.

22 W. Benjamin, 'Theses on the philosophy of history no. 1', in *Illuminations* [1955] (London: Fontana Press, 1992), p. 245.

23 Romans 5.12–14, 7.7ff.

24 1 Corinthians 15.21–3, 45–9. For other nineteenth-century commentaries on this the Pauline conception of man, see: David Somerville, *St Paul's Conception of Christ* (Edinburgh: T. and T. Clark, 1897); R. L. Ottley, *The Doctrine of the Incarnation* [1896] (London: Methuen, 1902), pp. 113–17; William Sanday and Arthur C. Headlam, *The Epistle to the Romans* [1895] (Edinburgh: T. and T. Clark, 1911), pp. 131–47; George Baker Stevens, *The Theology of the New Testament* [1901] (Edinburgh: T. and T. Clark, 1911), pp. 349–62; H. R. Mackintosh, *The Doctrine of the Person of Christ* [1912] (Edinburgh: T. and T. Clark, 1914), ch. 3.

25 Sigmund Freud, 'Introductory lectures on psychoanalysis' [1917], in *SE* XVI, pp. 284–5; Freud 'A difficulty in the path of psychoanalysis' [1917], in *SE* XVII, pp. 139–43; Freud, 'The resistances to psychoanalysis' [1925], in *SE* XIX, p. 221.

26 Philip Rieff, *The Triumph of the Therapeutic* (Harmondsworth: Penguin University Books, 1973).

27 For overviews, see: Roy Porter (ed.), *Rewriting the Self: Histories from the Renaissance to the Present* (London: Routledge, 1997); John Shotter and Kenneth J. Gergen (eds), *Texts of Identity* (London: Sage, 1989); T. C. Heller and D. Welberry (eds), *Reconstructing Individualism: Individuality and Self in Western Thought* (Stanford CA: Stanford University Press, 1986).

28 Julian Jaynes, *The Origin of Consciousness in the Breakdown of the Bicameral Mind* (London: Penguin Books, 1990); Eve Keller, 'Embryonic individuals: the rhetoric of the seventeenth-century embryology and the rhetoric of early modern identity', *Eighteenth-Century Studies* 33 (2000), 321–48; N. Izenberg, *Impossible Individuality: Romanticism, Revolution, and the Origins of Modern Selfhood, 1787–1802* (Princeton: Princeton University Press, 1992); Ian Watt, *The Rise of the Novel* (London: Hogarth Press, 1987); Michel Foucault, *The Birth of the Clinic* (London: Routledge, 1997); Charles Taylor, *Sources of the Self* (Cambridge: Cambridge University Press, 1989).

29 Foucault, *Birth of the Clinic*, p. 197.

30 Foucault, *The Order of Things* [1970] (London: Routledge, 1988), p. 313.

31 Henry Powell, *The Principle of the Incarnation* (London: Longmans and Co., 1896), p. 145. The most famous statement of this idea was given in J. R. Illingworth, *Personality: Human and Divine, Being the Bampton Lectures for the Year 1894* (London: Macmillan and Co., 1894).

32 V. F. Storr, *Doctrine and Development* (London: Methuen, 1906), p. 212.

33 Useful overviews can be found in: J. H. Buckley, *The Triumph of Time: A Study of Victorian Concepts of Time, History, Progress and Development* (Cambridge MA: Harvard University Press, 1967); J. W. Burrow, *A Liberal Descent: Victorian Historians and the English Past* (Cambridge: Cambridge University Press, 1981); Dwight Culler, *The Victorian Mirror of History* (New Haven: Yale University Press, 1985); Alan Davidson, *History: Sacred and Profane* (London: SCM Press, 1964); Peter Hinchliff, *'God and History': Aspects of English Theology, 1875–1914* (Oxford: Clarendon Press, 1992); David Newsome, *The Victorian World Picture* (London: John Murray, 1997), ch. 3; Roger Smith, *The Fontana History of the Human Sciences* (London: Fontana Press, 1997), pp. 337–92.

34 A. J. Engel, *From Clergyman to Don* (Oxford: Clarendon Press, 1983).

35 On the Oxford Movement, see: Geoffrey Rowell, *The Vision Glorious: Themes and Personalities of the Catholic Revival in Anglicanism* (Oxford: Oxford University Press, 1983).

36 This was the position famously advanced by J. H. Newman in his *Essay on*

the Development of Christian Doctrine [1845], ed. J. Cameron (Harmondsworth: Penguin, 1974).

37 Horton Harris, *D. F. Strauss and his Theology* (Cambridge: Cambridge University Press, 1973), ch. 23.

38 D. F. Strauss, *The Life of Jesus Critically Examined* [1835], trans. George Eliot, ed. Peter C. Hodgson (London: SCM, 1973).

39 A. M. Fairbairn, 'David Friedrich Strauss: a chapter in the history of modern religious thought', *Contemporary Review* 27 (1876), 961–6; V. A. Harvey, 'D. F. Strauss' *Life of Jesus* revisited', *Church History* 30 (1961), 192–211; Basil Willey, *Nineteenth-Century Studies: Coleridge to Matthew Arnold* (Harmondsworth: Penguin Books, 1964), p. 230; Karl Barth, *Protestant Theology in the Nineteenth Century: Its Background and History* (London: SCM Press, 1972), pp. 542–3.

40 On Strauss's departure from Reimarus and Paulus, see: W. L. Craig, 'The problem of miracles: a historical and philosophical perspective', in *Gospel Perspectives* VI, eds D. Wenham and C. Blomberg (Sheffield: JSOT Press, 1986), pp. 9–40; Barth, *Protestant Theology*, pp. 542–3; Hans Frei, 'David Friedrich Strauss', in *Nineteenth-Century Religious Thought in the West* 1, eds Ninian Smart, John Clayton, Patrick Sherry and Steven T. Katz (Cambridge: Cambridge University Press, 1988), esp. pp. 222–3.

41 Strauss, *Life of Jesus*, p. 88.

42 *Ibid.*

43 Strauss derived his category of the 'unhistorical' from Hegel's *Philosophy of History*. For useful commentaries, see, G. D. O'Brien, 'Does Hegel have a philosophy of history?', *History and Theory* 10 (1971), 295–317; Burleigh Taylor Wilkins, *Hegel's Philosophy of History* (Ithaca: Cornell University Press, 1974); and Hans Kellner, *Language and Historical Representation* (Madison: University of Wisconsin Press, 1989), pp. 26–54.

44 Harris, *Strauss*, ch. 12.

45 T. Larsen, *Contested Christianity: The Political and Social Contexts of Victorian Theology* (Waco: Baylor University Press, 2004), pp. 43–58, 113–30; O. Chadwick, *The Victorian Church* 1 (London: Adam and Charles Black, 1966), pp. 487, 532.

46 M. A. Crowther, *Religious Controversy in Mid-Victorian England* (London: David and Charles, 1970), pp. 46–60.

47 Gerald Parsons, 'Biblical criticism in Victorian Britain: from conflict to acceptance?' in Parsons (ed.), *Religion in Victorian Britain II: Controversies* (Milton Keynes: Open University, 1988), p. 250.

48 [Anon.], 'Strauss and Parker', *Westminster and Foreign Quarterly Review* 47 (1847), 136.

49 On the creation of this sense of historical distance, M. de Certeau, 'The historiographical operation', in *The Writing of History* (New York: Columbia University Press, 1988), pp. 56–115. For its psychological implications,

Mark Salber Phillips, 'Distance and historical representation', *HWJ* 57 (2004), 123–41.

50 On the growth of historical criticism, see: Frei, *Eclipse of Biblical Narrative*; Bernard Reardon, *From Coleridge to Gore* (Harlow: Longmans, 1971), ch. 10; J. W. Rogerson, 'Philosophy and the rise of biblical criticism', in S. W. Sykes (ed.), *England and Germany: Studies in Theological Diplomacy* (Frankfurt: Springer, 1982), pp. 63–79; L. E. Elliot-Binns, *English Thought 1860–1900: The Theological Aspect* (London: Longmans, Green and Co., 1956), pp. 116–90.

51 The most notorious point of controversy was the publication of *Essays and Reviews* in 1860, see: Peter Hinchliff, *Benjamin Jowett and the Christian Religion* (Oxford: Clarendon Press, 1987), ch. 5; Ieuan Ellis, *Seven Against Christ* (Leiden: Brill, 1980); J. L. Altholz, *Anatomy of a Controversy: The Debate over Essays and Reviews, 1860–64* (Aldershot: Scolar Press, 1994); Reardon, *Coleridge to Gore*, pp. 321–43.

52 On the rise of this form of hermeneutic authority, see: Frank Kermode, 'Institutional control of interpretation', *Salmagundi* 43 (1979), 72–86. For an extreme example of this new hermeneutic, see: Bernard Bosanquet, 'How to read the New Testament', in *Essays and Addresses* (London: Swann Sonnenschein, 1889), pp. 131–61.

53 J. Vincent, *Literacy and Popular Culture: England, 1750–1914* (Cambridge: Cambridge University Press, 1989), pp. 1–49, 171–9; J. Rose, *The Intellectual Life of the British Working Classes* (New Haven: Yale University Press, 2002), pp. 93–106.

54 L. J. Ellicott, *Historical Lectures on the Life of our Lord* [Hulsean Lectures 1859] (London: Longman, Green, Longman, Roberts and Green, 1865), p. 42.

55 Franco Moretti, *The Way of the World: The Bildungsroman in European Culture* (London: Verso, 1987).

56 Strauss, *Life of Jesus*, pp. 777–81.

57 A. Schweitzer, *The Quest of the Historical Jesus* [1906] (London: Adam and Charles Black, 1948), p. 96.

58 Daniel L. Pals, *The Victorian Lives of Jesus* (San Antonio: Trinity University Press, 1982), pp. 28–50; Chadwick, *Victorian Church* II, pp. 60–8.

59 Johann Neander, *Leben Jesu* (Hamburg, 1837), trans. J McClintock and C. E. Blumenthal, *The Life of Jesus in its Historical Connexion and Historical Development* (London: Bohn's Standard Library, 1851); Carl Ullman, *Die Sundlosigkeit Jesu* (Hamburg, 1842) trans. R. C. L. Brown, *The Sinlessness of Christ* (Edinburgh: T. and T. Clark, 1858).

60 Ernst Renan, *The Life of Jesus* (London: Trübner [Cheap Edition], 1865).

61 [Sir John R. Seeley], *Ecce Homo* [1865] (London: George Routledge, n.d.).

62 Chadwick, *Victorian Church* II, p. 65.

63 F. W. Farrar, *The Life of Christ* [1875] (London: Cassell and Co., 1903). For Farrar's sales figures, see, Pals, *Lives*, pp. 79–80.

64 H. White, *The Content of the Form* (Baltimore: Johns Hopkins University Press, 1987), p. 66.

65 Barth, *Protestant Theology*, pp. 554–5.

66 Renan, *Life of Jesus*, p. 32.

67 *Ibid.*, p. 30.

68 [Seeley], *Ecce Homo*, p. 41.

69 Troeltsch, 'Historiography', pp. 716–23; Schweitzer, *Quest*, p. 111.

70 Phillip Schaff, *The Person of Christ: The Miracle of History* (Boston: American Tract Society, 1865), p. 185.

71 J. Cairns, *False Christs and the True* (Edinburgh: Edmonton and Douglas, 1864), p. 22. On Cairns, see A. Alexander, *John Cairns: His Life Story* (Stirling: Drummond's Tract Depot, 1898).

72 Thomas Dixon, *From Passions to Emotions: The Creation of a Secular Psychological Category* (Cambridge: Cambridge University Press, 2003).

73 Lorraine Daston and Katherine Park, *Wonders and the Order of Nature, 1150–1750* (New York: Zone Books, 2001), pp. 339–43; L. Daston, 'Preternatural philosophy', in *Biographies of Scientific Objects* (Chicago: Chicago University Press, 2000), pp. 14–41.

74 [Anon.], 'Strauss and Parker', 152–3.

75 Baden Powell, 'On the study of the evidences of Christianity', *Essays and Reviews* (London: J. W. Parker, 1860), p. 106; see fn. 51.

76 James Stalker, 'Our present knowledge of the life of Christ', *Contemporary Review* 77 (January 1900), 125.

77 W. D. Mackenzie, 'Jesus Christ', in *ERE* VII (1914), p. 506.

78 Renan, *Life of Jesus*, pp. 34–5. See Owen Chadwick, *The Secularisation of the European Mind in the Nineteenth Century* (Canto edn) (Cambridge: Cambridge University Press, 1990), pp. 219–20.

79 Philippians 2.5–8. Other passages cited in justification, included: Mark 13.32, 2 Corinthians 7.9 and Luke 2.52.

80 Isaiah 53.12.

81 J. B. Lightfoot, *St Paul's Epistle to the Philippians* (London: Macmillan and Co., 1879), p. 110. On John Barber Lightfoot (1828–89), Bishop of Durham: G. R. Eden and F. C. Macdonald (eds), *Lightfoot of Durham: Memories and Appreciations* (Cambridge: Cambridge University Press, 1932).

82 Illingworth, Personality, lecture 1; R. L. Ottley, *The Doctrine of the Incarnation* [1896] (London: Methuen, 1902), pp. 165–82.

83 Thomasius's position was popularised among anglophone audiences through translations of Franz Delitzsch, *A System of Biblical Psychology* [1855], trans. R. E. Wallis (Edinburgh: Clark's Foreign Theology Library, 1867) and Frederic Godet, *Biblical Studies*, trans. W. H. Lyttleton (London: Hodder and Stoughton, 1876). For general summaries of continental Christology cf. A. B. Bruce, *The Humiliation of Christ* [1876], 5th edn (Edinburgh: T. and T. Clark, 1914), app. notes A and B to lecture IV (pp. 386–410); J. B. Orr,

The Christian View of God and the World (Edinburgh: Andrew Elliot, 1902), app. to lecture VI (pp. 248–57).

84 Bruce, *Humiliation*, pp. 16–35; Ottley, *Doctrine* II, pp. 286, 605–18; A. M. Fairbairn, *The place of Christ in Modern Theology* [1893] (London: Hodder and Stoughton, 1894), pp. 476–7. R. C. Moberly, *Atonement and Personality* [1901] (London: John Murray, 1909), p. 97; Thomas Charles Edwards, *The God-Man* [The Davies Lectures for 1895] (London: Hodder and Stoughton, 1895); Lewis Edwards, *Person Crist* (Bala: Davies ac Evans, 1897).

85 Outlines of the development of kenotic Christology in England are given in Frances J. Hall, *The Kenotic Theory* (London: Longmans, Green and Co., 1898); Mackenzie, 'Jesus Christ', pp. 545–6; Elliot-Binns, *English Thought*, ch. 11; R. Morgan, 'Historical Criticism and Christology: England and Germany', in S. W. Sykes (ed.), *England and Germany: Studies in Theological Diplomacy* (Frankfurt: Springer, 1982), esp. pp. 85–96. For the controversy surrounding the *kenosis* in Wales, see: R. Tudur Jones, *Ffydd ac Argyfwng Cenedl* II (Swansea: John Penry, 1982), ch. 2.

86 Matthew 24.37–9; 12.40. The most famous statement of this argument occurred in Charles Gore's essay, 'The Holy Spirit and inspiration', in [Charles Gore] (ed.), *Lux Mundi: A Series of Studies in the Religion of the Incarnation*, 2nd edn (London: John Murray, 1890), pp. 359–61.

87 [Anon.], *Church Quarterly Review* 52 (1898), 268.

88 For background, see: M. H. Abrams, *Natural Supernaturalism: Tradition and Revolution in Romantic Literature* (London: Oxford University Press, 1971), ch. 1; Joseph W. Reynolds, *The Mystery of Miracles* (London: C. Kegan Paul, 1881), p. 75.

89 Arthur James Mason, *The Conditions of Our Lord's Life on Earth* [The Bishop Paddock Lectures, 1896] (London: Longmans Green and Co., 1896), pp. 12, 210; Robert Ottley, 'The Incarnation', in James Hastings (ed.), *A Dictionary of the Bible* (Edinburgh: T. and T. Clark, 1899), p. 459. On Mason (1851–1928), Lady Margaret Hall Professor at Cambridge, see Peter Davie *DNB*, pp. 564–5.

90 Farrar, *Life of Christ*, p. xxxv.

91 I. Ellis, 'Dean Farrar and the quest for the historical Jesus', *Theology* 89 (1986), 108–15.

92 For the idea of the libidinal apparatus or framework, see: Deleuze and Guattari, *Anti-Oedipus*, bk 4; Fredric Jameson, *The Political Unconscious: Narrative as a Socially Symbolic Act* (London: Routledge, 1989), p. 17; Jameson, *Fables of Aggression* (Berkeley: University of California Press), pp. 8–11.

93 Galatians 4.19; William Sanday, 'Jesus Christ', p. 651, repr. *Outlines of the Life of Christ* (Edinburgh: T. and T. Clark, 1906), p. 228. There was a considerable literature which argued for the formation of character through the imitation of Christ, Charles Barrows, *The Personality of Jesus* (London: James Clarke, 1906), p. 210; W. S. Bruce, *The Formation of Christian Character*

(Edinburgh: T. and T. Clark, 1902), pp. 87–93, ch. 5; R. W. Church, *The Discipline of Christian Character* (London: Macmillan and Co., 1885), pp. 102–13, 128–30; J. R. Illingworth, *Christian Character* (London: Macmillan, 1904), pp. 33 8; J. R. Miller, *The Building of Character* (London: Sunday School Union, n.d.), ch. 3.

94 Matthew 4.1–11; Luke 4.1–13; Mark 1.12–13.

95 Mason, *Conditions*, pp. 58–67; Ottley, *Doctrine*, pp. 613–16; [Seeley], *Ecce Homo*, ch. 2, esp. pp. 36–41; F. Montgomery Hitchcock, *Christ and His Critics* (London: Robert Scott, 1910), pp. 112–19; H. J. C. Knight, *The Temptation of Our Lord* [Hulsean Lectures, 1905–6] (London: Longmans, 1907), pp. 91–5, 146–7; Henry Latham, *Pastor Pastorum* [1890] (Cambridge: Deighton Bell and Co., 1907), pp. 112–46.

96 Fairbairn, *Place of Christ in Modern Theology*, pp. 350–1. On Fairbairn, Principal of Mansfield College, see: W. B. Selbie, *The Life of Andrew Martin Fairbairn* (London: Hodder and Stoughton, 1914).

97 Most of the authors cited above believed that the Temptation extended beyond the simple episode given in this parable and instead accompanied Jesus throughout his Incarnation. Some went even further. Alfred Garvie argued the whole history of the natural universe represented the kenotic surrender of God to natural law: *Studies in the Inner Life of Jesus* [1902] (London: Hodder and Stoughton, 1908), p. 524.

98 Renan, *Life of Jesus*, p. 196.

99 For evangelical versions of the atonement, see: Edward Garbett (ed.), *Evangelical Principles* (London: William Hunt and Co., 1875); R. W. Dale, *The Atonement* (London: Congregational Union of England and Wales, 1875). On the shift, see: Boyd Hilton, *The Age of Atonement: The Influence of Evangelicalism on Social and Economic Thought* (Oxford: Clarendon Press, 1988), ch. 8.

100 M. C. Massey, 'The literature of Young Germany and David Friedrich Strauss's *Leben Jesu*', *Journal of Religion* 59 (1979), 298–323; Barth, *Protestant Theology*, p. 161.

101 On British Idealism, see: H. D. Lewis, 'The British Idealists', in John Clayton et al. (eds), *Nineteenth Century Religious Thought in the West* II (Cambridge: Cambridge University Press, 1989), ch. 8; P. P. Nicholson, *The Political Philosophy of the British Idealists* (Cambridge: Cambridge University Press, 1990); Peter Robbins, *The British Hegelians, 1875–1925* (New York: Garland Publishing, 1982); John Passmore, *One Hundred Years of British Philosophy* (Harmondsworth: Penguin, 1968), ch. 5. For its background, see: K. E. Willis, 'The introduction and critical reception of Hegelian thought in Britain, 1830–1900', *Victorian Studies* 32 (1988), 85–111. On Green (1836–82), fellow of Balliol College, and later Whyte's Professor of Moral Philosophy at the University of Oxford: M. Richter, *The Politics of Conscience: T. H. Green and his Age* (London: Weidenfeld and Nicolson, 1964).

102 Despite Lotze's massive influence on Victorian philosophy and theology, he has attracted little attention from modern scholars. For a nineteenth-century exposition of his work, see: Sir Henry Jones, *A Critical Account of the Philosophy of Lotze* (Glasgow: Robert MacLehose, 1895).

103 T. H. Green, *Works* III, ed. R. L. Nettleship (London: Longmans Green and Co., 1889), p. 111. For a similar argument, see: James Iverarch, *Theism in the Light of Present Science and Psychology* (London: Hodder and Stoughton, 1907), pp. 219–20.

104 On Gore (1853–1932), Principal of Pusey House and Bishop of Oxford, see G. L. Prestige, *Charles Gore: A Great Englishman* (London: William Heinemann, 1935). For the significance of *Lux Mundi*, see, Robert Morgan (ed.), *The Religion of the Incarnation: Anglican Essays in Commemoration of Lux Mundi* (Bristol: Classical Press, 1989); Hinchliff, *God and History*, ch. 5; Reardon, *Coleridge to Gore*, pp. 430–46.

105 For the influence of Green on the *Lux Mundi* group: B. M. G. Reardon 'T. H. Green as a theologian', in A. Vincent (ed.), *Political Philosophy of T. H. Green* (Aldershot: Gower, 1986); S. Paget, *Henry Scott Holland: Memoir and Letters* (London: John Murray, 1926), pp. 24–69; Richter, *Politics of Conscience*, ch. 5.

106 [Gore] (ed.), *Lux Mundi*, p. 322.

107 William Campion, 'Christianity and politics', in *ibid.*, p. 462.

108 Illingworth, *Christian Character*, pp. 7–8, 88, 200–1. See also Wilfrid Richmond, *An Essay on Personality as a Philosophical Principle* (London: Edward Arnold, 1900), where he articulated his theory of 'philosophical socialism', arguing that personality was based in this divine capacity for fellowship, pp. 21–38 and *passim*.

109 Cheryl Walsh, 'The incarnation and the Christian socialist conscience in the Victorian Church of England', *Journal of British Studies* 34 (1995), 351–74; Peter d'A. Jones, *The Christian Socialist Revival* (Princeton NJ: Princeton University Press, 1968), ch. 5; David Newsome, 'The Assault on Mammon: Charles Gore and John Neville Figgis', *Journal of Ecclesiastical History* 17 (1966), 227–41; Richter, *Politics of Conscience*, pp. 122–9.

110 Alfred, Lord Tennyson, *In Memoriam*, section 45. It was quoted in William Wallace, 'Person and personality', in *Lectures and Essays on Natural Theology and Ethics* (Oxford: Clarendon Press, 1898); A. W. Momerie, *Personality: The Beginning and End of Metaphysics* (Edinburgh: Blackwoods, 1883), p. 53. For Tennyson's belief in the 'infinite whole', R. Douglas-Fairhurst, *Victorian Afterlives: The Shaping of Influence in Nineteenth-Century Literature* (Oxford: Oxford University Press, 2002), p. 268.

111 Quoted in Richmond, *Essay*, app. D.

2

The invention of the unconscious

Inward the course of empire takes its way (Frederic Myers)

The search for the self

The quest for the historical Jesus was not restricted to the universities or the established Churches. Across Britain and the United States, working-class radicals debated the historical basis of the Gospel records. Before George Eliot's translation of the *Leben Jesu* appeared, plebeian secularists had issued cheap pirated editions of Strauss's work. Their turn to historical enquiry was driven by a very different set of motives to those which animated Eliot and her ecclesiastical colleagues.[1] Some, including the Chartist ex-cobbler Thomas Cooper, believed that historical criticism would reveal the 'legendary incrustations' that had corrupted the true history of Christ.[2] Like Strauss and Eliot, he saw the critical method as a means to strip away 'the false, the idolatrous, and enslaving forms in which priestcraft clothes that glorious Galilean peasant'.[3] Others went much further. Cooper's erstwhile friend and colleague, the Chartist poet Gerald Massey, believed that Christ was no more than the sum of these fabulous accretions. He was 'made up from the features of various Gods, after a fashion somewhat like those "pictorial averages" portrayed by Mr Galton, in which the traits of several persons are photographed and fused into a portrait of a dozen different persons, merged into one that is not anybody'.[4] Massey saw Christ's personality as a thing of shreds and patches. It was an artificial creation 'formed from the sunken *debris* or dregs of ancient mythology'; a flotsam and jetsam of stories and legends that combined to create the false impression of an actual individual.[5]

Yet it would be wrong to see critical history simply as a destructive force. It also opened up the possibility of a new kind of psychological communion. When Cooper became a Baptist in 1859, his understanding of history was transformed.[6] It moved from being a critical method to become a kind of tangible force which would connect our lives with those of the departed through unbroken chains of influence.[7] In his very popular work, *The Bridge of History over the Gulf of Time* (1876), Cooper attempted to create a new sense of solidarity with the past, suggesting that personal memories and antique objects overlapped between the lives of the living and the dead to create an unbroken bond with the Gospel history of Christ.[8]

As we saw in the previous chapter, these competing approaches to history were bound up with different models of the self. The conflicting perspectives of the redeemed Cooper and the sceptical Massey were predicated upon different assumptions over the existence and nature of Christ's personality. This could be approached as an independent finite entity demanding critical recovery or as a concatenation of different myths that needed to be traced back to their independent traditions. These different approaches were not only dependent on different conceptualisations of Christ's personality as a historical object, but were also distinguished by contrasting ideas of the historian's own self.

In *The Bridge of History*, Cooper imagined his own personality as an entity entwined through memory and text with the personalities of the past.[9] It was a sense of connection that could take on much more intense and dramatic forms. In his defence of Christ's historical reality, Cooper was joined by allies who had obtained an even more intimate acquaintance with the past. From the 1840s, a number of writers claimed that the past was not only mediated through text and memory but could be approached directly through episodes of travelling clairvoyance, second sight or spirit possession, in which the boundaries between the self and the past were overcome.[10]

This chapter explores the tensions between these different ways of knowing the past and the conflicting understandings of selfhood that they entailed.[11] It is a conflict, I will show, that is sustained by different conceptualisations of death. These different conceptualisations determined both the form of the historical object and the imagined shape of the historian's insight.[12] As described in the previous chapter, Christ emerged as a historical character in the Christologies of the nineteenth century through reference to his carnal limitation. His being and consciousness were portrayed as entities bounded in the *kenosis* by death. Similarly, the authority of the historical text was itself dependent on an implicit understanding of the limits of the historian's self. Within the new professional discipline of history, interpretations only became accept-able if they could demonstrate that the interpreted object was somehow insulated from the infective or partisan concerns of the interpreter. Yet while the authority of the professional historian's self (like that of the kenotic Christ) might rest on its finite circumscription, alternative ways of historical knowing were also possible.[13] At the precise moment that the historical profession emerged, the clairvoyant and the medium were staking their own claims to historical authority: claims sustained by a very different and much more controversial presentation of the nature of selfhood and the boundaries of death.

This idea of a conflict over the boundaries of personality and mortality sounds obscure, yet it remains intrinsic to much of our everyday speech. From the melodramatic assertion that part of us has died at the end of a relationship through to the evangelical's claim that conversion has destroyed their old sin-ridden self, our speech is heavy with strategies for establishing the presence of death within the individual: a death which through these metaphors varies in its location and intensity. As the sociologist David Armstrong has claimed, 'It is necessary to be nomin-alist about death. Death is not a thing or event existing independently of human consciousness; it is simply the word given to a certain threshold, interface, space or point of separation. Discourse establishes by its analyses and interrogations a conceptual or cognitive space in which are crys-tallised objects, events, identities.'[14]

It is tempting to see Armstrong's claims about the relativity of death as yet another demonstration of our supposedly post-modern dismissal of the old cultural universals. Such a view, however, would be mistaken. An awareness of the presence and the mutability of death persisted throughout the popular and academic literature of the nineteenth century.[15] Death was seen as a protean phenomenon and its origins, extension and location were forever open to renegotiation.

In nineteenth-century literature, death is presented as a boundary that can extend beyond the limits of the flesh or divide the content of the physical frame. Popular Christian expositors of evolutionary theory, such as Henry Drummond, argued that death was situated outside the body, located in the relationship between the individual and the external world. Life, according to Drummond, is present only in so far as the agent is in correspondence or correlation with the environment. He believed that, 'All organisms are likewise living and dead – living to all within the circum-ference of their correspondences, dead to all beyond.'[16] These correspondences developed according to the attitude of the individual.

Those who maintained the right kind of relationship with the world escaped the limitations of their failing flesh.

In contrast with this idea that death could extend beyond the person, many practitioners argued that it could also extend through the body, dividing it in either time or space. The Protestant tradition of evangelical conversion insisted that a sin-ridden self could be extinguished and a new one reborn inside the same body.[17] Likewise death could be seen as creating new boundaries within an individual human frame. The accounts of railway spine or hysterical paralyses which pervade the contemporary psychological literature suggest that whole areas of the body, organs or limbs could be given up to death while the rest continues to live.[18]

There was no simple correspondence made between the end of the body and the termination of identity. The Victorian champions of medieval and oriental mysticism believed that the self could be extinguished while the body lived on. [19]In contrast to such mystical aspiration, a more anxious section of the Victorian population was haunted by the idea that the brain might continue to function long after the apparent failure of the flesh. There was a rich literature on the possibility of premature burial, and a small industry providing instruments through which the entombed but awakened individual could make contact with the outside world.[20]

It should now be evident that 'death is a relative term'.[21] Within Victorian society, its origin, intensity and location were all open to question and hence to social negotiation. As with the ending of a literary narrative, this negotiation was itself a political action, for it defined the scope and content of the individual's personality.[22] It designated the shape of memory, policing the boundary between the real and imagined past in much the same way as Strauss distinguished between history and myth. It revealed to people who they were, attaching them to a specific past and defining their future hopes. It was in the contest over the meaning and interpretation of death that modern notions of history and identity were defined in nineteenth-century Britain: a contest pursued through the new sciences of spiritualism and psychical research.[23]

Spiritualism and other forms of historical enquiry

From its first appearance in the middle of the nineteenth century, spiritualism was presented as a new science. Unlike the occult traditions which based their claims to authority on a knowledge of the ancient arcana, spiritualism was presented as a form of empirical investigation: its findings rested on a series of rational inferences from reproducible phenomena. It was an experimental method born from the accidental discoveries of two American sisters, Kate and Margaret Fox, who in 1848 had found that tapping and table rapping could be used to open up a discussion with the dead. In common with the new sciences of history and biblical criticism, spiritualism staked its claim to authority on an attempt to recover and represent the past. Like these disciplines, its methods were rooted in the abductive logic of detective work in which grand synthetic hypotheses were developed from the minutest hints and clues.[24] Whereas these last two disciplines authorised themselves through their privileged access to state documents or Hebrew texts, spiritualism maintained a 'democratic epistemology', arguing that the past could become available to any enquirer with the right procedure and attitude.[25] Its method, as the spiritualist Oliver Lodge argued, was simply a development of the everyday practice of reading, allowing 'a one sided communication with the past inhabitants of the earth'.[26]

The subject matter of spiritualism, like that of the discipline of history, was demarcated from ordinary knowledge by the presence of death. Historians demonstrated this presence through reference to the archive, which insulated documents from the living activities of politics or state administration.[27] In contrast, spiritualists relied on a series of practical techniques, using their bodies to try and demonstrate the distance between the inspired message and their personal concerns. Sometimes this was extremely easy. In the early experiments, messages were produced through knocking walls or rapping tables which obviously lay outside the medium's person.[28] At other times it was more complicated. In practices like automatic writing and trance speech, the inspired words of the speaking mouth or the moving hand could only be distinguished from the medium's subjective responses through a rhetorical performance which severed the familiar relationship between mortality and the body. Against the new disciplines of history and Christology, which had insisted that death insulated the individual body in time and space, spiritualist techniques were designed to demonstrate the fragility of this boundary – showing how death could be moved as easily as a veil or shroud to reveal a new identity.[29]

The technique of automatic writing developed during the first wave of spiritualist activity in the 1850s.[30] It was presented as a very limited form of possession in which spirits took over and controlled the writing hand. This was a minor local death: the medium maintained his or her own self-consciousness while being acutely aware of the new-found independence of his or her limbs. As one medium told the British investigator John Jones, 'I feel my hand and arm becoming buoyant like sea water; and if then I take up a pencil and have paper before me, my fingers, hands and wrists move, make words, write recipes, draw leaves and flowers, and mesmerise sick people, without the slightest volition of my own mind.'[31] The same sensation was well described by the Connecticut congressman Sidney Dean in a letter to William James:

> When the work is in progress I am in the normal condition, and seemingly two minds, intelligences, persons are practically engaged. The writing is in my own hand but the dictation is not of my own mind and will, but that of another, upon subjects upon which I can have no knowledge and hardly a theory; and I, myself, consciously criticise the thought, fact, mode of expressing it, etc., while the hand is recording the subject matter and even the words impressed to be written.[32]

The reality of this experience was also attested to by those spirits that apparently entered and possessed the medium. The following dialogue was reprinted in the anonymous volume, *Spirit Rapping in England and America*:

> Ques. Can you explain how you are able to write through a medium? Ans. I feel as though I enter into her for the time being, or as if my spirit entered into her. I am dismembered of my spiritual form and take hers . . . I have my spiritual form or body when I communicate by tapping or rappings, but to *write* my spirit must enter the medium, otherwise I am unable to control her will or muscles.[33]

The death produced in automatism divided the writing hand from the medium's body, undermining basic notions of authorship and personal responsibility. As many spiritualists were eager to make clear, they had no control over the content of these automatic writings, which were presented as the products of historical actors whose names authorised the texts. From beyond the grave, Thomas Paine, George Washington, Swedenborg, a clutch of Red Indian chiefs, Isaac Newton and the almost incessant Benjamin Franklin were quick to claim as their own the various philosophies, cosmologies and political systems produced through passive writers.

The experience of inspired speech was very similar to that of automatic writing. Once again, the encapsulated past was seen as entering the body of the medium through a form of limited death, in this case the occurrence of trance. As the British medium J. J. Morse argued, trance was 'a miniature representation of death ... a method by which you are enabled to solve the problem of death without dying.'[34] As with automatic writing, this experience was accompanied by feelings of help-lessness on the part of the conscious personality. The spirits claimed that they simply 'took power from the [medium's] organs of voice' and used it to their own purposes.[35] Emma Hardinge Britten, one of the most famous Anglo-American mediums, described her first trance engage-ment in terms that would now be understood as indicating mild dissociation:

> my last clear remembrance was of listening to a lovely quartette, beautifully sung by the 'Troy Harmonists', and then I had a dim perception that I was standing outside of myself, by the side of my dear father – dead – when I was only a little child but whose noble form I could plainly see close by me, gestic-ulating to, and addressing somehow, my second self, which was imitating him, and repeating all the thrilling words he was uttering.[36]

The authority of possessed speech, like that of historical writing, was achieved through the self-extinction of the medium who gave it voice.[37] As Roland Barthes argued, the historian, the spiritualist and the psychotic are all engaged 'in a radical censorship of the act of uttering', disclaiming their apparent involvement in the production of the text or speech.[38] The historian achieves this through repeated acts of attribution, refer-encing all of his or her statements back to an outside source, so that his or her own authorship seems to disappear. The possessed medium realises the same effect by continually shifting his or her identity during the seance or trance lecture, becoming, like the ventriloquist's dummy, a body spoken through rather than a speaking body.[39] Such acts create a narrative for which nobody assumes responsibility – a narrative which implies that it has been produced by the very spirit identity which it itself sustains.

The spread of spiritualism

The uptake of the new techniques of mediumship in Britain was contem-poraneous with the development of the new historical sciences in British universities and theological seminaries. Propagated by itinerant American mediums in the early 1850s, spiritualism found a ready audience among the British public.[40] It achieved a large following in West Yorkshire, where phrenology and primitive Methodism were already popular, and among London's educated bourgeoisie who had previously experimented with mesmerism and Swedenborgianism.[41] The speed with which spiritualism was taken up by these widely differing groups was impressive. In 1853, David Weatherhead founded the short-lived *Yorkshire Spiritual Telegraph*, and for a while Keighley became the spiritualist capital of Great Britain. Here the new practice made converts among the plebeian secularists and freethinkers so quickly that one writer in the *Westminster Review* was moved to complain: 'That in Bradford, Bingley and other Yorkshire towns there are secularists once notorious for believing nothing, now equally notorious for believing everything.'[42]

During the 1860s and 1870s spiritualism grew rapidly in popularity, with twenty periodicals and over 200 societies appearing across the country. Many of these clubs and papers had only the briefest existence, so it was almost impossible to estimate the number of spiritualist believers at any one time. Contemporary authors have hazarded guesses between 10,000 and 100,000, a disparity which reflects both the absence of any useful figures and the varying criteria for what constituted a spiritualist believer.[43]

The rapid growth of spiritualism was amenable to many explanations. In the writings of spiritualism's main protagonists, it has usually been seen as the natural progression of a self-evident scientific truth. Modern historians, however, have drawn attention to the radical implications of spiritualist practice, demonstrating how it served the popular agendas of feminism and socialism. The most obvious manifestation of the spirits' support for radical causes occurred in the trance addresses given by the many itinerant mediums who lectured across Britain and America. Through the mouths of Emma Hardinge Britten, J. J. Morse and Cora Tappan Richmond, spirits developed eloquent arguments in favour of class justice and female emancipation. It was clear that the theology of spiritualism developed in these addresses and through the spiritualist press reflected many of the older preoccupations of Owenite socialism.[44] The idea that all mankind was gradually progressing towards a spiritual estate (called 'Summerland') wherein class differences would be abolished, mapped onto Robert Owen's belief in the necessary movement of society towards an egalitarian utopia. Moreover, the ontology of spiritualism, which placed the personal reality of the individual beyond the materialistic differences of the world, provided a rationale for socialist action. From this perspective, as Logie Barrow has argued, socialism could be seen as an attempt to realise man's spiritual estate on earth, and spiritualism in turn provided both the rhetoric and the experimental proofs necessary to sustain the socialist project.[45]

Those same trance mediums who gave voice to radical causes were also vociferous in their espousal of the rights of women and, alongside their very public profession of the feminist project, there existed more subtle strategies through which the spirits came to aid women. As Alex Owen has argued, the domestic seance provided many women with a limited arena in which they could experiment with gender transgression. The possessed medium, as noted previously, abrogated personal responsibility for the words and actions that emanated from his or her body. Thus women, or at least female bodies, were able to assume masculine authority, and so dictate commands to friends or household members. Likewise, the possessed medium was granted a certain sexual licence, being able to indulge in verbal flirtation or, in the case of full form materialisation, actual physical contact and expression.[46]

The seance, in these accounts, appears as a form of ritualised transgression, like the medieval carnival, in which social roles and hence political authority were reversed within a limited space and across a limited period of time.[47] In carnival, this role reversal was tolerated by the civic authorities and sanctioned by tradition; in the seance, it was licensed through reference to the experimental authority of scientific spiritualism. Yet even in its scientific aspect spiritualism retained its carnivalesque implications, for its researches were predicated upon a confusion of the empirical and the transcendental. Moreover, these domestic investigations of the spiritual realm confounded the distinction between the laboratory and the home, reducing science to a part of everyday life. Likewise, the fact that sublime messages were relayed through shop-girls or ordinary tables, collapsed the division between the sacred and the profane.[48] In its investigation of the boundaries of the personal, spiritualism disrupted the boundaries of the social.

Spiritualism thus presented a direct challenge to the fundamental notions of identity on which nineteenth-century society was based. Against that bounded finite personality described in the previous chapter, spiritualism offered the hope that personal history and its constraining death could be transcended. In the act of communion with the dead, a double movement was initiated in which the spirit narrative entered the medium and the medium moved outside his or her own personal history. The casual incarnations of the seance room disrupted the medium's life narrative, creating gaps or spaces which could not be recovered through mainstream historical or psychological means. The temporary nature of these episodes prevented their intellectual colonisation, for such mobile identities could not be captured and surrendered to psychological expertise.[49] Spirit possession was a technique for getting out of history; it freed the individual from the constraints of his or her personal identity, creating a transient space in which the project of identity itself became impossible.

Spiritualism and the scientists

Given the various political challenges implicit in spiritualist practice, its mixed reception among members of the professional scientific community is perhaps unsurprising. Although a handful of famous scientists did convert to spiritualism, most notably Alfred Russel Wallace, William Crookes and Oliver Lodge, the responses of the vast majority of scientists fell somewhere on a scale between indifference and outright hostility.[50] The attitude of manifest indifference was perhaps best expressed by Thomas Henry Huxley who, on being invited by the Dialectical Society to investigate the phenomena of spiritualism, acidly responded: 'The only good that I can see in demonstration of the truth of "Spiritualism" is to furnish an additional argument against suicide. Better live a crossing sweeper than die and be made to talk twaddle by a "medium" hired at a guinea a *séance*'.[51] Huxley's position of studied indifference was shared by many of his colleagues, but a small group of physicians and alienists pursued a more active campaign against the spiritualist project, pathologising its physical phenomena and criticising the evidential basis of spiritualist testimony.

This campaign centred around the notion of the human will which in the nineteenth century was taken as the central criterion of mental health. This in part was an artefact of psychiatry's long involvement in judicial practice but it was also connected to the discipline's professional agenda.[52] At one level, the apparent absence of will in the asylum patient allowed progressive physicians to abandon the old language of mental introspection in any discussion of the sufferer's condition, and deploy instead mechanical descriptions developed in physiological science. Moreover, this failure of the patient's rational volition was presented as an argument for his or her surrender to the physician's pastoral control.[53] From this perspective, spiritualism appeared as a discipline for the cultivation of mental pathology. Its rhetoric of self-abandonment and surrender to external forces described the classic symptoms of insanity. The mediumistic trance which had heralded the intervention of the spirits was seen as a demand for the intervention of psychiatrists. Both these groups, spirits and psychiatrists, predicated their claims to control upon a failure of the individual's volition.

The common rationale of spirits and psychiatrists is less curious than it immediately appears. As we have already seen, the authority of both these parties relied on the collapse of the boundary between the spirit and the flesh, which allowed not only for a physiological description of mental states but also for the occult interpretation of physical actions. These new descriptions were predicated on the appearance of trance or automatism.[54] Again, this is unsurprising since their common understanding of these states had developed out of a common set of examples and interpretations produced in mesmeric practice half a century before.[55] The trance was, for spiritualists, 'a miniature representation of death'; for psychiatrists and neurologists, 'a mode of partial, or maybe complete death' resulting in the dissolution of the nervous system.[56]

In spite of these structural similarities, psychiatrists and spiritualists maintained very different assessments of the moral status of automatism. For psychiatrists, automatism was, 'a reduction of mental function to the plane which obtains in the lowest developments of animal life'.[57] The voluntary induction of such a state, they argued, could lead to permanent mental disease. The American neurologist, William Hammond believed that trance was one of the 'precursors of organic disturbance in the brain or spinal cord, leading to paralysis, epilepsy or mental derangement'.[58] These different interpretations drew upon much older Christian associations: the spiritualist idea of flesh being subsumed by a heavenly spirit appeared as a miniature or individual Pentecost; the medical model of the flesh overriding the conscious will resurrected the Adamic vision of a carnal revolt against the command of God.

Despite these different assessments of the phenomena of mediumship, the structural similarities of the two sciences ensured a constant slippage between them of their common terms.[59] 'Automatism', as we have already seen, provided an obvious example of this kind of translation, with both spiritualists and psychiatrists benefiting from its new associations. A more strategic subversion of psychiatric language involved the concept of 'hallucination'. This concept was used by alienists like Henry Maudsley and physiologists like W. B. Carpenter to describe and undermine the supernatural visions of seers and mystics. Devoid of any objective validity, the hallucination was presented as a demented production of a diseased brain.[60] However, such a definition could easily be subverted. The aristocratic spiritualist Roden Noel argued that hallucinations 'have an objective reality since they are 'outside me', in the sense that they are in the body'.[61] Moreover, he claimed, 'that when a madman, or a delirious person, has what we may call 'hallucinations of sense' . . .

it is difficult to prove that whereas our precepts have objective validity, and *are external to our individual selves,* his are no such thing.'[62] A different approach was taken by the French philosopher of mysticism Ernest Recejac, who understood Maudsley's argument for the non-objectivity of visions as justification of their reality as spiritual phenomena.[63] Psychiatry thus provided both a vocabulary and a diagnostic framework for the historical practices of spiritualism. Although its vocal attacks were often effective, the language of morbid pathology could only really sustain the idea of temporary death in life upon which the medium's claim to historical insight relied.

The claims developed in spiritualist practice sat uneasily with the insights generated by the other sciences of Victorian Britain. Although spiritualism may have presented itself, according to the American neurologist and hostile critic George Miller Beard as 'an attempt to apply the inductive method to religion; to make faith scientific; to confirm the longings of the heart by the evidence of the senses', the miraculous productions of the seance room seemed to demonstrate the inconsistency of the natural world.[64] As the mediums produced extraordinary facts which fell outside the rules of historical discourse, their evidence, like that of the biblical miracles, began to be treated as a demonstration of the fallibility of human witnesses rather than the limits of natural law. Their reports were no longer seen as simple representations of real events which could easily be assimilated into the scientific canon. Rather, they were themselves difficult or complicated texts demanding a hermeneutic examination.

As in biblical criticism, the necessity of a hermeneutic approach to popular testimony was justified through reference to its embeddedness in the personal life of the author. Popular testimony was seen as a corrupted form of representation which mixed experimental evidence with the witness's social and psychological interests.[65] Critical psychiatrists and mental physiologists saw such testimony as another example of spiritualist transgression: a transgression in which the boundary between observer and observation was broken down.[66] W. B. Carpenter argued that popular testimony was infected by the presence of what he called 'expectant attention'.[67] This was a concept that had first been articulated by the physicist Michael Faraday who argued that phenomena such as table turning or spirit rapping could be attributed to unconscious muscular actions in the bodies of the seance participants.[68] These muscular actions effectively mimicked the anticipated behaviour of spirits since they were the unconscious embodiments of the spiritualist's own excited anticipations. Carpenter extended the logic of Faraday's argument, claiming that expectant attention could infect the mind as well as the muscles, producing 'mental prepossessions' and 'spectral illusions'. Through its operation, the division between the observer and the observed was broken down. The spiritualist, Carpenter claimed, was no longer capable of representing reality, rather the reality he or she reported was an unconscious representation of his or her own mystical preoccupations.[69]

Carpenter's demand for the medical policing of testimony was taken up by his fellow scientists. Beard argued that human witness was compromised since the average individual continually oscillates between a normal condition and the trance state.[70] In this trance state, once again, the boundary between the self and its representations is dissolved:

> In trance man becomes an automaton; the coordinated action of the faculties called the will is displaced by a series of mental and muscular movements as purely automatic as the beating of the heart or the opening of a flower. In this state objective or subjective become confounded: there is, indeed, no true objective life; the brain absolutely creating objects, persons, experiences, or mutilating and transforming all impressions made upon it.[71]

This confusion of the subjective life and the objective world renders the major part of human testimony worthless. Amateur witness could never furnish the natural sciences with empirical evidence; instead, Beard declares, 'The first step in all the sciences has always been the rejection of average human testimony. If we accept what people say, there can be no scientific knowledge of any kind.'[72]

Beard's position was roundly endorsed by the English alienist Henry Maudsley. Maudsley was adamant in his claim that the prerogative of testimony belonged to professional scientists alone. He argued that the arrangement of the nervous system is such that reported sensations could never be freed from the corrupting influence of dominant ideas.[73] As Maudsley quipped, 'The common saying that "seeing is believing" may then be applied in a double sense – not alone in the understood sense that we believe by what we see, but also in the sense that we see by what we believe.'[74]

At one level, as S. E. D. Shortt has convincingly argued, these writings can be seen as a professionalising attempt to claim 'epistemological sovereignty' in the reporting of empirical evidence.[75] Viewed from a modern perspective informed by psychoanalysis, they take on a very different significance. The dissolution of the boundary between self and objective experience transforms the content of popular testimony: it is no longer a representation of real events, but has become an unconscious confessional, revealing the hidden obsessions and desires of the witness's mind.[76] Spiritualists and plebeian scientists who claimed authority by demonstrating the transparency of their selves before the natural or spiritual world were now confronted by the unconscious return of this self in their speech or writings. Furthermore, the psychologist of testimony could be seen as taking over the prerogative of spiritualism; drawing a death through the medium's discourse, marking out the point where personal fantasy ended and objective reality began. Thus the psychologist or mental physiologist became an exegete, engaged in a hermeneutic practice to discover the real author of experiences and events. This hermeneutic turn was to be foundational to the work of the first explorers of the subliminal, Edmund Gurney, Frederic Myers and their colleagues in the Society for Psychical Research.

The politics of psychical research

The Society for Psychical Research (SPR) was founded in the spring of 1882, through the efforts of the Dublin physicist Professor W. F. Barrett, and the Finchley spiritualist Edmund Dawson Rogers.[77] It was an eclectic organisation. Members were drawn from among the elite spiritualist circles of London and, after the election of the moral philosopher Henry Sidgwick as the Society's President, a committed group of young academic investigators from Trinity College, Cambridge.[78] Under Sidgwick's guidance, the new society publicly allied itself to an uncommitted or agnostic form of investigation, a strategy which further endeared it to the English establishment.[79] In the 1880s the SPR could proudly count two bishops, nine Fellows of the Royal Society, one past and one future prime minister and many writers (including Ruskin and Tennyson) among its members.[80]

Despite the SPR's intellectual and social position, it has been persistently identified by many commentators with the contemporaneous wave of plebeian and popular spiritualism that swept the British Isles. The London doctor Ernest Hart derided its activities as a form of 'new witchcraft'; the folklorist Edward Clodd condemned its philosophy as a form of 'bastard supernaturalism' and the *Pall Mall Gazette* argued that this new interest in the marvellous was evidence of a mental atavism, whose indulgence was reducing the nation's intellect to a more primitive state.[81] Such interpretations are, I think, mistaken. Although the overarching rationale of the Society was an experimental investigation into the possibility of the soul's survival of physical death, the vast corpus of its work was concerned with a more immediate form of immortality: the persistence of the individual personality during the minor deaths of automatic writing, epilepsy, hysteria and apparent possession.

This concern with mortality was, as I have already argued, intrinsically political. One aspect of this political dimension has been explored by modern historians such as Richard Noakes, Roger Luckhurst, John Cerullo, Frank Miller Turner, John Perry Williams and Brian Wynne.[82] They argue that the SPR's attempt to extract experimental proofs for the existence of eternal life and spiritual nature was motivated by its members' desire to find a vehicle for their conservative values. This argument could well hold true. Certainly many of the central protagonists of psychical research were deeply concerned with ethical and spiritual questions. John Maynard Keynes summed up Sidgwick's life, saying: 'He never did anything but wonder whether Christianity was true and prove that it wasn't and hope that it was.'[83] Edmund Gurney, another Trinity scholar and the SPR's first Honorary Secretary, had published articles on vivisection and the ethics of pain.[84] Frederic Myers, whose massive contribution to psychical research came to set the agenda of the Society as a whole, was also deeply disturbed by the implications of agnosticism. Combining a romantic temperament with almost unconscionable snobbery, he at first refused any involvement with an activity that smacked of spiritualism, claiming that it would be equivalent to 're-entering by the scullery window the heavenly mansion out of which I had been kicked by the front door'.[85]

As a form of interpretation, the approach which connects psychical research to a conservative agenda will be, by now, quite familiar – for it resurrects that nineteenth-century critique which was used to problematise the notion of popular testimony. According to sociologists like Wynne and Cerullo, the Victorian science of psychical research was guided by unconscious or only half-conscious motives which informed the apparently neutral activities of investigation and theory formation. Against the scientist who declares his transparency before nature, these modern critical historians insist on the logical priority of the self and its social interests. This hermeneutic strategy, which dissolves the tacit boundary between memory, aspiration and reported experience, was, I shall argue, itself partly developed in the practice of psychical research.[86]

The second political dimension associated with the SPR's concern with immortality will again be familiar: it is the idea that death defines the content of the self and the parameters of our forensic responsibility.

The original protagonists of psychical research seem to have been well aware of this political dimension and of the social threat contained within the spiritualist negotiation of death.[87] The early papers published in the Society's *Proceedings* and *Journal* repeatedly attacked this popular contestation of identity, berating the medium's false assumption of authority and the threat to modern thinking that it contained. Such criticism was well warranted for, as Gurney argued, if the spiritualist rhetoric of possession and self-annihilation was admitted, there was 'no manner in which our faith in the continued identity of persons concerned, or ultimately of our own, [could] be sustained'.[88] Myers was quick to join in the attack, concentrating on the micropolitical threat inherent in spiritualist rhetoric. In a paper read before the Society in 1885, he singled out:

> certain spiritualists who decorate their strings of sermonising platitudes with the imagined authorship of Abraham or Abraham Lincoln, or Isaac, or Isaac Newton, or Isaac Commenius, or Jacob, or Jacob Bohme, according to fancy – as readily as a street seller labels his ices vanilla or pineapple . . . Perhaps beneath there may lurk nothing better than our own small selves; and those oscillations may have no greater amplitude than between one and another centre of our own irregularly developed brains.[89]

Myers reiterated his point in a discussion of the psychological significance of automatic writing. He complained that this phenomenon had been unjustly ignored because of the 'earnestness with which certain spiritualists have claimed such writings as the work of Shakespeare, Byron and other improbable persons. The message given has too often fallen below the known grammatical level of those eminent authors and the laugh thus raised has drowned the far more instructive question as to *whence* in reality the automatic rubbish came.'[90]

The dangers of spiritualist belief were remarked on in the Society's first major literary production, *Phantasms of the Living*, published in 1886. *Phantasms* was presented as a scientific study of 'crisis apparitions' – visions of distant dying individuals experienced by their family or friends at the moment of death. [91] Although such visions had traditionally been attributed to the actions of newly disembodied spirits, Gurney and Myers proposed a more subtle explanation. They argued that these were hallucinations triggered by cortical lesions and extraordinary episodes of thought transference.[92] Myers believed that their new model, based on concepts of nervous sensitivity and the SPR's newly developed concept of 'telepathy', challenged the hegemony of spiritualistic interpretation and exposed the political dangers which arose when individuals made false inferences from such apparently supernatural experiences:

> The men who claim to have experienced them have not been content to dismiss them as unreasonable or unimportant. They have not relegated them to the background of their lives as readily as the physiologist has relegated them to a few paragraphs at the end of a chapter. On the contrary they have brooded over them, distorted them, misinterpreted them. Where the savants have minimised, they have magnified and the perplexing modes of marvel which textbooks ignore have become as it were the ganglia from which all kinds of strange opinions ramify and spread![93]

The tone of these writings and the criticisms they contain alienated the great majority of the SPR's spiritualist members. By the middle of the 1880s, the Society's meetings were characterised by a persistent internecine warfare between the occult and academic wings of the organisation.[94] Edmund Dawson Rogers, who had been instrumental in the formation of the Society, twice attempted to resign from its Council in 1884, complaining to readers of *Light* that the SPR was 'studying the mere bones and muscles [of spiritualism], and [has] not penetrated to the heart and soul'.[95] Other contributors to *Light* soon joined the fray: the pseudonymous 'X' indicted the SPR for employing telepathy as a catch-all explanation for every mediumistic phenomenon.[96] In 1886 the crisis reached a head with the publication by Mrs Henry Sidgwick of a critical paper on the slate-writing medium William Eglinton.[97] Its tone and Eglinton's outraged response led to the mass resignation of the Society's most prominent spiritualist members.[98]

Given the political strategy implicit in the work of Gurney and Myers, this mass resignation should probably be seen as a setback. Myers believed that the correct way to combat the challenge inherent in spiritualist practice was through a system of re-education or indoctrination into the logic of psychical research. Spiritualism was a danger, he insisted, because its adherents made false inferences as to the origins of mediumistic phenomena; its subversive content was an artefact produced through the mistaken use of historical reasoning. For this subversive content to be removed, it was necessary that spiritualists learn a new analytic, reinterpreting the gifts of mediumship as the unconscious products of their own minds.

> if a man tells you that the spirit of Shelley writes through him, and recommends free love, it is of no use to answer that it is all nonsense and very wrong. The man thinks you know nothing about it, and sticks

to his Shelley and his free love more triumphantly than ever ... To prevent a graphic automatism from being a source of mental danger, it is necessary, not that it be repressed and sneered at, but that it should be openly practised and understood. When thus treated, there is, as far as I know, no cause for grave anxiety of any kind in connection with any of that group of phenomena [i.e. automatic writing] which we are now discussing.[99]

The education which Myers proposed went to the very heart of the spiritualist enterprise, for it aimed to remove that death or narrative discontinuity upon which the whole notion of possession was predicated.

Everyday immortality: the making of the subliminal self

By turning to the language of hypnotism and mesmerism, Gurney and Myers drew upon a body of work which had been fielded against supernatural phenomena since the end of the eighteenth century. Early authorities such as Franz Anton Mesmer and John Elliotson had suggested that anomalous episodes of clairvoyance or possession could be attributed to the flow of invisible forces around a magnetised individual, provoking inspired performances.[100] Yet by the middle of the nineteenth century this conceptual machinery had been largely abandoned. Practitioners such as the Manchester surgeon James Braid argued that the phenomena of trance were simply the effects of physical changes in the nervous system of the subject.[101] Trance states and unconscious performances were not produced by magnetised fluids but by the direction of attention. Supernatural episodes such as possession or clairvoyance did not mark the death of the self: rather, they revealed the boundaries of consciousness; boundaries which could be adjusted and rearranged through hypnotic interventions.[102]

It is easy to see how the philosophies of mesmerism and hypnotism appealed to Gurney and Myers. They offered both a language for reconceptualising spiritualistic experience – such episodes revealed the edge of consciousness rather than the death of the personality – and a possible technology (hypnotism) for undoing such episodes of self-annihilation. In his introduction to *Phantasms of the Living*, Myers writes warmly of the psychological possibilities of hypnotism: 'Here is a psychical experiment on a larger scale than was ever before possible; that we have at length got hold of a handle which turns the mechanism of our being: that we have found a method of shifting the threshold of consciousness, which is a dislocation as violent as madness, a submergence as pervasive as sleep and yet is waking sanity.'[103] The language Myers uses is comparable to the spiritualist assessment of trance but the results it generated were far more mundane. Whereas the medium's ecstatic transport revealed the persistence of the spirit beyond the boundary of death, the hypnotic trance simply revealed the persistence of personality beyond the boundaries of consciousness. Thus the initial task of the psychical researchers was the demonstration or perhaps the constitution of a characteristic personality within the hypnotised subject, and the connection of this personality to the individual's waking consciousness.

In the 1880s this was a quite radical manoeuvre. The uneasy and largely unwitting alliance of spiritualists and psychiatrists had long agreed that the suspension of consciousness was equivalent to the death of the self. Both these groups, as we have already seen, considered trance behaviour to be purely automatic, whether produced through the reflex actions of the body or the intervention of exterior spirits. In a series of experiments designed by Gurney, this viewpoint was directly challenged.[104] His experiments had two main objects: first, to demonstrate the presence of the will in the hypnotised subject; and second, to reveal the persistence of trance memory in the waking state.[105] In a collection of papers published in the newly established journal *Mind*, and the SPR's own *Proceedings*, Gurney reported how subjects in a state of hypnotic paralysis attempted to retrieve proffered sovereigns, with fruitless results.[106] The will was present but the flesh was weak.[107] In a further set of experiments, Gurney hypnotised subjects and presented them with information which he would ask them to repeat upon waking. Again, this information could not be retrieved until Gurney issued a pre-agreed hypnotic command or engaged the subject in some semi-hypnotic activity such as automatic writing.[108] These demonstrations suggested that hypnotic memories persisted within the individual, existing as streams of thought concurrent with the ordinary consciousness of our waking lives.[109]

The analytic developed in Gurney's work had a twofold effect. At one level, it reduced the metaphysical drama of ecstasy and possession to an intra-psychic event. Those mediumistic operations which had taken place outside the person, beyond the boundary of death, could now be seen as internal phenomena, occurring outside consciousness but within the individual's body and mind. At a second level, Gurney's experiments on will and memory in the hypnotic state revealed that this field beyond the edge of consciousness was not the haunt of astral forces or invading spirits, but rather demonstrated the same forms of will and memory

which characterised the waking consciousness. It was, in short, a subliminal *self* and its investigation would become the central aim of Myers's
work. As William James wrote:

> *What is the precise constitution of the Subliminal* – such is the problem
> which deserves to figure in our Science hereafter as the *problem of Myers*;
> . . . But Myers has not only propounded the problem definitely, he has also
> invented definite methods for its solution. Post hypnotic suggestion, crystal
> gazing, automatic writing and trance speech, the willing game, etc., are
> now thanks to him, instruments of research, reagents like litmus paper or
> the galvanometer for revealing what would otherwise be hidden.[110]

Myers's 'instruments of research' were, for the most part, borrowed
from the practices of plebeian spiritualism, but the method by which
they were deployed was quite different. Whereas the medium's trance
episodes and automatic productions were intended to generate knowledge
from outside the individual, Myers arranged his investigations so that
they would continually reflect and reinforce the known character of the
subject under investigation. As James noted:

> [Myers] took a lot of scattered phenomena, some of them recognised as
> reputable, others outlawed from science, or treated as isolated curiosities;
> he made series of them, filled in the transitions by delicate hypotheses or
> analogies, and bound them together in a system by his bold inclusive concep-
> tion of the Subliminal Self, so that no one can now touch one part of the
> fabric without finding themselves entangled in it.[111]

Through his subversion and combination of the spiritualist technologies, Myers transformed a space that had existed beyond the person
into a new psychological domain. The temporary incarnations produced
in spiritualist practice were rendered permanent in his new arrangement, providing new spaces for investigation and control. Myers's rhetoric
transformed the seance room from a theatre of the spirits into a laboratory of the subliminal. The thousands of trance messages and automatic
scripts produced across Western Europe and America and the miracles
which had disrupted the historical record now served as testimony for
the existence of the subliminal consciousness.[112] What had been celebrated as evidence of life after death was revealed as an argument for a
more mundane form of immortality – the persistence of the medium's
personality throughout the minor deaths of automatism, ecstasy and
possession.

The subliminal self as a narrative trap: three studies

The early mission of psychical research was thus concerned less with immortality than with establishing the biographical continuity and integrity of the living individual. As Gurney made clear, the psychical researcher had to follow any clue which might connect the supernatural or inspired performances of a possessed medium with the known character they had left behind. Writing in 1886, he argues, 'If the superiority of men to brutes depends on personality, and if personality depends essentially upon memory, then those who desire that man's dignity should be maintained, and that personality should be continuous, can hardly afford to despise the smallest fact of memory which exhibits the possibilities of union and comprehension as triumphing over those of disruption and dispersion.'[113]

Demonstrating the 'possibility of union' was a narrative art. Whereas previously a spirit persona had been projected from the minor clues contained in the automatic message, the psychical researchers now attempted to reconstruct a narrative identity which reflected the known aspects of the medium's life history.[114]

An early example of this kind of narrative strategy was provided by Myers in his analysis of a series of automatic scripts produced by his pseudonymous friend Mr 'A'. Using a planchette, the subject 'A' had automatically written a series of anagrams, puzzles which he originally understood as being the productions of an alien intelligence. Upon translation, the initial anagrams were revealed as a collection of aphorisms on abstract topics. These maxims seemed quite distinct from 'A's usual beliefs, one declaring that 'Life is the less able', another that 'Every life yes is'. The phrases' authorship was originally claimed by 'Clelia', a female spirit still waiting to be born. However, in the fourth session the writing suddenly denied the existence of Clelia and instead claimed to be a product of 'unconscious cerebration'. 'A' later corroborated this theory (with some reservations). He related the first phrase (given above) to the spiritualist literature he had recently been reading, the second to his study of Spinoza (who had claimed that life was an affirmation of the deity).[115] As 'A' reported to Myers: 'Upon the first day I became seriously interested; on the second puzzled; on the third I seemed to be entering on novel experiences half awful and half romantic; upon the fourth the sublime entered very painfully into the ridiculous.'[116] Myers gave a more excited assessment, calling it the first time that 'a sane and waking man' had held a 'colloquy with his own dreams'.[117]

The progression from spiritual inspiration to a kind of mundane *sartori* was also experienced by Professor Herman Hilprecht, whose story achieved an exemplary status in the science of psychical research.[118] Hilprecht was the Professor of Assyrian at the University of Pennsylvania, and in the spring of 1893 had been working upon the descriptions of a collection of inscribed fragments recovered from the temple of Bel at Nippur. Two sketches of some agate pieces, which had once apparently been finger rings, particularly perplexed him. One bore the cuneiform characters 'KU' so he hesitantly ascribed it to the Babylonian king Kurigalzu. The other fragment remained unclassifiable. Dissatisfied with his researches, he gave up his work and fell exhausted into a deep sleep. That night he dreamt that he had met one of the ancient Nippur priests, who led him to the treasure chamber of the Bel temple. There he was informed that the agate fragments, which he had believed to be individual finger rings, were once in fact part of the same votive cylinder. This cylinder, sent by King Kurigalzu to the temple, had been cut into three parts when the king ordered a pair of agate earrings for the statue of Ninib. When he awoke, Hilprecht recorded the dream and then rushed to compare sketches of the fragments. They did indeed join, the original inscription of the votive cylinder reading: 'To the god Ninib, son of Bel, his lord, has Kurigalzu, pontifex of Bel, presented this.'[119]

Hilprecht's dream appeared to be a graphic and deeply romantic example of spirit inspiration. He had been presented with six pieces of novel information: the correspondence of the fragments; their existence as a votive cylinder; its presentation by King Kurigalzu; its dedication to Ninib; its transformation into earrings; the location of a treasure chamber on the south-east side of the temple. Each of these conjectures was further confirmed when Hilprecht visited the Imperial Museum at Constantinople and inspected the agate fragments in person. However, as the American psychologist William Romaine Newbold pointed out, each one of these new pieces of information could also be produced through the process of analysis that Hilprecht employed every day.[120] The common elements of the fragments, he argued, would have brought them together in a subconscious association, from which their origin and inscription could have been deduced. The origin of the final piece of information, the location of the treasure house, seemed more mysterious until it transpired that Hilprecht had been told about the treasure chamber by the archaeologist John S. Peters some five years previously. Once again the occult source of information was revealed as nothing darker than the lacunae produced by the individual's lapse in memory.

It is easy to see how Hilprecht's dream appealed so deeply to the psychical researchers. The reunification of mysterious fragments held deep within a hidden treasure house could be seen as an allegory for the project of psychical research as a whole. Moreover, the mundane explanation of the dream priest's occult pronouncement provided symbolic demonstration of the psychologist's right to minister over the sacred. This secularising imperative provided the motivation for the post-office clerk and SPR enthusiast Frank Podmore in his investigation of Morell Theobald's possessed domestic servant, Mary.

Morell Theobald was one of the most famous spiritualists in England. A wealthy London accountant, his home became a veritable haven for the spirits, with family members and staff engaged in various forms of mediumship.[121] In 1882 he appointed Mary as a replacement cook and she soon manifested a strong clairvoyant ability, attracting new spirit visitors to the household. Such gifts endeared her to the family, excusing the laziness and unpunctuality she demonstrated in her work – indeed the spirits even aided her directly, with unseen agencies daily preparing the breakfast and laying the grate. Spirit messages in English, German, Old French, Latin, Greek, Hebrew and Raratongan appeared about the house, the authorship often being claimed by a Persian poet, Saadi.

In 1884 Theobald invited Podmore and a fellow SPR researcher, Frank Hughes, to investigate the phenomena. They soon dismissed most of the physical productions of the spirits. Breakfasts and fires remained unprepared under their supervision and the spirit messages that appeared written high on walls or ceilings seemed consistent with their having been written by someone standing on a chair or armed with a pencil attached to a broom. The spirit Saadi's poetical works and autobiographical fragments were traced to an article in Part 6 of *Chambers Repository of Instructive and Amusing Tracts*.[122] This secondary material which once would have attested to the historical reality of the spirit was now seen as evidence of its production by a living human being.

These exposures of poltergeist hauntings, spirit inspirations and pseudo-possessions would seem to be the natural conclusion to the psychical researchers' scientific investigations. However, it should by now be apparent that our idea of the natural is open to question. The belief that an individual's life should demonstrate narrative continuity and integrity is, as we have seen, a reflection of a particular negotiation of death which came to predominate in the nineteenth century. The narrative continuity which each of the authors introduced into his case studies is an aesthetic production. As Hayden White has argued with regard to the historian's work:

> The facts do not speak for themselves, but . . . the historian speaks on their behalf, and fashions the fragments of the past into a whole whose integrity is in its *re*presentation . . . Novelists might be only dealing with imaginary events whereas historians are dealing with real ones but the process of fusing events, whether imaginary or real, into a comprehensible totality capable of serving as the *object* of representation is a poetic process . . . These fragments have to be put together to make a whole . . . and they are put together in the same way that novelists put together figments of their imaginations to display an ordered world, a cosmos, where only disorder or chaos might appear.[123]

Like the historical narrative, the subliminal self was an aesthetic and contested production. It had no pre-given form; rather its shape and contents were produced in the various confrontations which took place between the SPR and the spiritualist community. It was a fluid item, its intellectual substance developing in the different contests in which it was fielded as an explanation. Given this versatility, it is no surprise that many contemporary commentators were flummoxed by the question of what the subliminal self actually is. Gerald Balfour in his 1906 address to the SPR, confessed: 'I have never yet succeeded in forming a clear idea of what Myers means by the subliminal self', a failure that was shared by many others.[124] While James might have lamented the vague conception of the subliminal used by Myers in *Human Personality*, the English academic psychologists William McDougall and G. F. Stout went further, lambasting the theory's incoherence.[125]

One can sympathise with Stout and McDougall in their perplexity. The subliminal self which emerges in Myers's writings is a tattered patchwork of ideas. It is portrayed, at different times, as an ordered hierarchy, a loose coalition of streams of consciousness and an animal colony. In contrast to our modern, psychoanalytic conception of the unconscious as a unitary phenomenon, Myers argued that the individual is subject to a 'fissiparous multiplication', inhabited by smaller transitory personalities which are in turn possessed by multiple and fragmentary selves. These minor personalities and selves are not mere unconscious characters or memories, but exist as concomitant streams of consciousness, each one endowed with a separate awareness of its own.[126]

Yet Myers believed that the true mission of psychology was to bring each of these subliminal selves under the direction and control of their waking leader. He collapsed psychological and political metaphors, equating 'the incipient disintegration of personality [with] the anarchy of competing groups without a ruler'.[127] Accordingly, he argued that the difference between 'the sage and the dement' lay in the ability of the one to marshal the uprushes of subliminal selves under his or her conscious control, while the other surrendered will and memory to the subliminal region:

> the difference being that in the case of the man of genius, the group of cells which contributes to the orator the brilliant metaphor, to the mathematician the flash of insight into the inter-relation of formulae is working under the orders of the conscious centre. While in the insane case the group of models cells which suggests to the nursery maid 'kill the baby' is working independently of the conscious centre – is hypertrophied into a self assertion which ill befits its essential incompleteness and irrationality.[128]

The synthesising activity of genius bears an uncanny resemblance to the psychical researcher's narrative art. The association and attachment of subliminal fragments of information through the intervention of a conscious and controlling subject was (as we have seen) the political aim and activity of Podmore, Gurney and Myers.

Towards the end of his life, Myers became convinced of the reality of spirit communication.[129] Through the mediumship of the American psychics Mrs Piper and Mrs Thompson, Myers received messages from Gurney and from his own dead lover, Annie Marshall.[130] The emotional claim of these communications was further reinforced by the intellectual appeal of the spiritualist arguments contained in the work of Stainton Moses. Moses, an Oxford-educated Anglican clergyman, was viewed as an impeccable witness by the SPR hierarchy; his personal notebooks, detailing his possession by a small host of spirits guided by the control, 'Imperator' (the prophet Malachi), were passed on to Myers when Moses died.[131]

The conversion apparently engendered by these emotional and intellectual attractions seems to threaten the political task of psychical research. To admit the reality of possession (as was noted previously) threatened to undermine the continual identity or 'everyday immortality' of ordinary individuals. Within Myers's revised schema, however, the structure of the subliminal self remains in place and it continues to fulfil a political function. It operates as a kind of filter for the sacred, combining extracarnate communications with the fragmentary memories and desires of the individual's past. Thus possession and inspiration still required expert intervention in order to separate the personal from the spiritual. As Myers argued, the vast majority of possessing spirits should be seen 'simply as a number of parasitical existences who perhaps rise into individualisation by their contact with our own spirits', rather than 'a Gabriel, a Plato, a Beelzebub or Napoleon'.[132] The political mission of psychical research, as we shall see in the following chapter, developed from the government of the human to the ministry of the divine.

Myers's final acceptance of the reality of eternal life presented the project of psychical research with a new set of philosophical problems. The denial of death undid that boundary which rendered the individual sensible and intelligible, erecting a new and irrevocable tension between the poles of identity and immortality. Certainly, the tropes and explanations produced in the confrontation between spiritualism and psychical research militated against the idea that self could transcend the boundaries of death: its spiritual excursions were simply adventures within the many-layered space of the deathbound individuality. There was, however, another perspective through which even this political aspect of Myers's project could be seen as self-defeating. His investigation and renegotiation of the meaning and location of death contributed towards the same heady nominalism that characterised the spiritualist conception of the person. This sustained reflection undermined the notion of a 'natural' personality, revealing instead the artifice involved in the investigation and production of the self. It was a problem that returned to haunt the SPR's co-workers in Switzerland, France and America.

The career of the subliminal self

The confrontation between the spiritualist and the psychologist was repeated in seances and consulting rooms throughout Europe and North America. In most of these countries there was soon established a vigorous native tradition of psychical research.[133] The rhetoric of the subliminal was also taken up at another site, however, which was to prove far more significant. This was the medical investigation into hysteria, another form of behaviour which disrupted the individual's relationship with the past.[134]

The homology between the hysteric's loss of control and the spiritualist's domination by external forces had, as we have seen, long been insisted upon by proselytising psychiatrists. The examples of paralyses and forgetting which divided the hysterics' bodies and minds were analogous with that meeting between the personality and death which the spiritualists encouraged. Hysteria like spiritualism was a technique for getting out of history, for severing the connection between the body and the past.

In resurrecting the nineteenth-century identification of spiritualism with hysteria, there is a danger that we will reintroduce the political strategy upon which this identification was predicated. Within the terms of this argument, spiritualism and hysteria existed in an unhappy symbiosis. Spiritualism received a pathological connotation from its association with hysteria, while those individuals blighted by hysteria were accused of the same kind of self-serving cynicism with which spiritualists were charged. The belief that hysteria operated as a strategy for self-promotion persists in modern critiques of psychiatry. Thomas Szasz's interpretation of hysteria as a goal-directed language has been taken up by critics on left and right, framing narratives which reduce both psychiatry and illness to a mutual contest for domination and control.[135] As we have already noted in regard to modern historical explanations for the emergence of psychical research, such arguments remain implicated in the structures they seek to explain.

The pre-eminent nineteenth-century exponent of narrative explanations for hysterical behaviour was Jean-Martin Charcot.[136] Whereas British alienists insisted that hysteria was for the most part a mercenary sham, Charcot believed that its origins lay in the history of the individual.[137] It emerged, he claimed, through a combination of psychical trauma and hereditary degeneration: concepts which anchored the hysteric's behaviour in his or her physical past. The psychical trauma was usually attributed by Charcot to an original act of violence, from the knife wounds and workplace injuries that incapacitated his male patients to the minor household accidents suffered by the females.[138] Likewise degeneration, in the eyes of European commentators, was usually seen as a form of fleshly inheritance – it was the ancestor's past made physical in the subject's body.[139] The narrative path of Charcot's diagnostic explanations always terminated within the confines of the human frame.

Although Charcot's hysterical patients may have been divorced from the world around them, their illness could be traced back firmly to an all too human past. The boundary or death which Charcot drew around his patients' illnesses was not a simple rhetorical production. It had a material if superficial existence, being displayed upon the flesh of the hysterical body. The creation of this visual aspect required a massive social effort. Charcot and his followers catalogued the various forms of the hysterical attack and mapped the distribution of anaesthesias across the patient's skin.[140] Later more complex techniques were deployed, such as 'faradisation' in which an electric current was passed through the hysteric's body. This had originally been developed to demonstrate the loss of physical sensitivity, but it soon created a series of more useful side effects such as localised bleeding or discoloration. Through experiment and investigation the hysteric's body was revealed as a patch-work of disconnected stigmata and anaesthesias. The inner divisions of the hysterical mind were displayed for all to see across the frame of the suffering patient.[141]

Seen from the perspective of medicine and morbid pathology, the pattern of these anaesthesias had a slightly disturbing implication, for they followed the lines of a folk neurology coalescing around the limbs or the ovaries (which had long been imagined as the seat of hysteria) rather than the 'true' nerve endings traced out by modern science.[142] They demonstrated the psychical rather than the physical basis of the illness. This demonstration became even more disturbing when viewed from the perspective of Catholic demonology or modern spiritualism,[143] for it revealed the very human limitations of the invading spirit's knowledge: its automatism and anaesthesias reproduced the everyday beliefs of the mundane world. Moreover the visual force of this image also mitigated against the rhetoric of possession. The divisions made visible were, after all, contained within the constraining boundary of the human frame. There was no outer cause for these divisions; they were generated internally. The stigmata which had once pointed beyond the self towards an encounter with the divine now directed attention inwards, towards the hysteric's physical and emotional past. The patient's body stood in mute testimony to the internalising analytic of modern science.

Charcot's reinterpretation of stigmata went beyond the bodies of his individual patients into the body of history. He scrupulously collected historical images of ecstasy and demon possession and reclassified them according to his own psychiatric nosology.[144] In 1883, Charcot's student, Désiré Bournville, began the republication of a series of Catholic works on demonology, introducing each volume as an unrecognised case of hysteria.[145] In 1887, Charcot, in collaboration with Paul Richer, extended his project, publishing *Les démoniaques dans l'art*, a collection of posses-sion images culled from the history of art.[146] This predilection for retrospective diagnosis took on an almost obsessive quality. When the American surgeon C. F. Withington visited Charcot in 1879 he found the neurologist's study bedecked with prints of exorcisms and possessed individuals.[147]

For modern commentators such as Jan Goldstein and Mary James, this concern with 'retrospective diagnosis' can be seen as part of a two-pronged professionalising strategy.[148] On one level, the demonstration of hysteria's continuous presence throughout history granted a certain reality and permanence to what had been seen as an eminently protean disease. Against the frequent accusations that hysteria was simply a hypnotic artefact manufactured by the physicians of the Salpêtrière, Charcot could point to its immutable form across history. On another level, the scientist's insistence that possession episodes were really examples of hysteria exposed the frailty of clerical knowledge and the medical dangers attendant upon its exercise. Such priestly misdiagnosis was an argument for the extension of medical and scientific authority into education and pastoral care, promoting a strategy of laicisation and secularisation that was characteristic of the Third Republic. In addition to the professionalising strategy which Goldstein and James have identified, we can suggest an analogy with the project of psychical research. Retrospective diagnosis, like the narrative strategies of Gurney and Myers, operated as a technique for filling in the gaps in history. Those ahistorical episodes of ecstasy and possession were rewritten into the body of the historical record. The past of individual bodies was used to complete the lacunae in the body of the past.

This concern with the visualisation of hysteria was shared by Charcot's one-time student and follower Pierre Janet.[149] Like his teacher, he had traced the pattern of anaesthesias and paralyses in his patients, treating them as a fleshy mnemonic for the psychic state. Moreover, he extended this study to the fields of vision and memory, describing the contractions and negative hallucinations which disrupted the hysteric's sight and the systematised amnesias which prevented the recall of certain words or events.[150] His model developed, like Charcot's, around the idea of psychical or hysterical traumas dividing the consciousness from certain areas of the mind or the body.

Janet went beyond Charcot, however, in his conceptualisation of these excluded areas of memory and will. Whereas Charcot had simply written off such areas as passive and unconscious, Janet's investigations into hypnotic somnambulism and apparent possession led him to a position closer to that of Gurney and Myers. In his first case study of the Le Havre somnambulist Leonie, Janet first posited the existence of a telepathic rapport between the subject and the hypnotist. Later he discovered that Leonie's purposive actions in her hypnotised state stemmed from 'Leontine', another personality created in previous entrancements by itinerant mesmerists. This personality was also conscious of all Leonie's actions. The existence of this continuous but obscure memory and its realisation in willed action pushed Janet towards a dynamic conception of the subconscious mind.

In his first major publication, *L'automatisme psychologique*, published in 1889, Janet developed a historical model of psychological automatism. Whereas healthy voluntary action involved a reaction to one's present circumstances, Janet believed that automatism involved the reproduction of outdated responses to an event in the individual's long-forgotten past. This temporal model was combined with the spatial metaphors developed by Gurney and Myers. The waking present consciousness contracted to reveal other consciousnesses trapped around old experiences and ideas. These alternate consciousnesses existed in a kind of narrative reverie, as Janet noted: 'it is always the same monotonous story which the patient resumes at this point where she has been interrupted and unceasingly begins over again'.[151]

Like the English psychical researchers, Janet was engaged in an attack on anachronism. He wanted to restore the lives of his patients to an intelligent, ordered narrative. His patients, the peasantry and bourgeoisie around Le Havre, were beset by mystical phenomena.[152] In one case, Achille, a travelling salesman, had returned to his home one evening bereft of the capacity for speech. This affliction continued for a number of days until a deeper, hoarser voice emerged from his body claiming to be the Devil. Despatched to Salpêtrière, Achille came under the care of Janet, who used distraction and automatic writing to establish a rapport with the demon. It soon transpired that the demon originated in a recent act of infidelity. Janet's technique revealed the mundane historical origin of this supernatural invasion; the spirit confessed to his own traumatic birth and divulged the secret path that would lead to reintegration. Therapy, for Janet as for Myers, involved a process of synthesis or, as Janet termed it, 'presentification'. Those alternate consciousnesses that had been rooted in the endless reverie of the past were collapsed into an awareness of the present. This model, particularly in its application to supernatural phenomena, revealed the irony inherent in hysteria. A form of behaviour through which individuals divorced themselves from the past now became symptomatic of their enthralment to history.

This process of retrieving the possessed patient's identity through a mixture of hypnosis, trickery and imaginative narration received its most detailed demonstration in Switzerland. Here the psychophysiologist Théodore Flournoy and the trainee psychiatrist Carl Jung produced case studies of mediumship which were to become classics of the psychical researcher's art.[153] Inspired by the work of James and Myers, Flournoy had searched for a medium who would introduce him not so much to the world of the spirits as to the hidden realms of the subliminal.[154] After some years spent searching among the amateur spirit circles of bourgeois Geneva, he was introduced to Hélène Smith, a young shop assistant and sometime Martian, Marie Antoinette and Indian princess.[155]

Flournoy's encounter with Smith was remarkable, not so much for the form it took – for it followed the pattern of detection and disenchantment familiar from British psychical research – but because of the wealth of complex material which Smith's spirit personalities produced. Under the guidance of a domineering control named Leopold, Smith became a mouthpiece for her past and future incarnations.[156] In her first cycle studied by Flournoy, her spirit was taken up to Mars by the alien, Astané. From this vantage point there followed a succession of strange images: descriptions of Martian botany, society and engineering; introductions to various Martian dignitaries; and, eventually, a fully fledged Martian language. The 'Hindoo' cycle involved Flournoy more directly. Smith's Indian incarnation, the Princess Simandini, claimed to be the eleventh wife of Sivrouka, a rajah of Tchandraguiri and previous incarnation of Flournoy himself. The marriage, though blessed by the undying devotion of Sivrouka, was still a source of some regret, for the young princess had been removed from her real home among the Arab peoples. The final cycle appeared on more familiar territory as the entranced medium re-enacted scenes from her brilliant life as Marie Antoinette.

The movement between these incarnations, the weight of evidence that they produced and the intelligence of Leopold, her spirit guardian, taxed Flournoy's ingenuity to its very limit. The fluid identities which attached themselves to Hélène Smith eluded easy categorisation. Under the guidance of the spirit Leopold, Smith's incarnations continually transformed themselves, so escaping accusations of inconsistency or artifice. She evacuated the linguistic terrain familiar to her audience and substituted it with a glossolalic landscape to which only she had access. From these strange lands she was able to construct, or perhaps discover, a new history and identity for both herself and others. Again, as with the Anglo-American spiritualists before her, this new land lay beyond the authority of experts.

Flournoy's task, like that of Podmore and Myers before him, was to find a link between her acknowledged life narrative and the stories of her alternative incarnations.[157] The Martian descriptions were written off as the entranced resurrection of a childhood fantasy. The population of Mars and its exotic dwellings were simply a more exalted version of those 'castles in the air' constructed by every child. Likewise the Marie Antoinette figure was traced to a more recent romantic identification.[158] It was the figure of Simandini which caused Flournoy the most trouble. Her Sanskrit pronouncements, circulated among local linguists, were verified as having (in part at least) an Indian origin. Moreover the precise information which Simandini gave regarding her existence at the palace of Tchandraguiri in 1401 was initially confirmed. As one anonymous orientalist wrote in response to Flournoy's query:

> Was [Smith's story of Simandini] a romance? Certain details cause me to doubt it. A romancer so careful in regard to local colouring to introduce into his narrative Indian words, would not have given the title of the prince under the Sanscrit form *Nayaka*, but would have used the vulgar form naïk; he would not have made the wife, in speaking to her husband call him by his name Sivrouka (as Hélène constantly does in this somnambulism). I have no recollection of having read anything of this kind and I know of no work of fiction from which the story might have been taken.[159]

Flournoy was forced into a new search for sources which would confirm the mundane origin of this extraordinary information. Eventually, after a search of the popular histories and romances, he discovered an early nineteenth-century work on the history of India.[160] The six volumes, written by an ill-regarded scholar, De Marles, contained a single reference to a rajah, Sivrouka Nayaka residing at Tchandraguiri in 1401. To Flournoy this discovery, which could be seen as providing independent testimony for Simandini's pronouncements, instead demonstrated the scope and power of the subliminal mind. Despite the fact that only two copies of De Marles's work existed in Geneva (and one of those in a private library), Flournoy insisted upon a forgotten encounter between the medium and this work. As he proclaimed in a deliberate misquotation of the spirit-seer Aksakoff, '*I refuse to admit that it could have come through occult means. I believe it was by some natural process*.'[161] Yet Flournoy need not have turned to twisted paraphrases to justify his project, for his principles could have been found in the programmes of biblical criticism developed by Strauss and Renan just a few decades before.

Flournoy developed a new concept to explain this process: 'cryptomnesia', the entry of hidden knowledge from the subliminal during the moment of trance.[162] Through this concept, the mental territory articulated by the spiritualist was once again inverted. Instead of the wide vistas of metempsychotic memory open to the medium's investigation alone, there appears the ever-increasing province of the subliminal – a territory cut off from the consciousness of the spiritualist yet open to the authority of the psychologist.[163]

The form of this encounter was to be repeated many times. In consulting rooms across Europe and North America, mediums and patients who somehow resisted history, who in moments of illness or inspiration fell outside the familiar boundaries of personality, were coaxed back into their old incarnations through the psychologist's or the psychical researcher's narrative art. In Switzerland, Flournoy's young colleague, Jung, established his professional credentials by tracing the historical origins of his cousin Helen Preiswerk's possessed identities.[164] In Boston, psychologists such as William James and psychotherapists such as Morton Prince won wide audiences for their vexed interrogations of their patients' multiple personalities.[165] They were consumed as popular detective stories, 'shilling shockers' in which every ruse was used to recover the true history of the individual.[166]

It should now be clear that the subconscious or unconscious self was not a pre-existent entity discovered by mesmerists and psychical researchers; it was something constructed in the nineteenth-century struggles over the historical status of the supernatural. Professional history and psychotherapy were arguments for a particular version of the self and a particular negotiation with death. Although much of Freud's work would develop later, the implication for psychoanalysis is clear. As Thomas Mann's character Settembrini instructs his protégé in *The Magic Mountain* (1924):

> Analysis as an instrument of enlightenment and civilization is good, in so far as it shatters absurd convictions, acts as a solvent upon natural prejudices, and undermines authority . . . But it is bad, very bad, in so far as it stands in the way of action, cannot shape the vital forces, maims life at its roots. Analysis can be a very unappetizing affair, as much so as death, with which it may well belong – allied to the grave and its unsavory anatomy.[167]

Just as the mystics and spiritualists made their own pact with death to disavow the past or access a certain history, so too did the analysts make an alliance with the grave. This alliance allowed the psychologist to exclude all those elements, ranging from anomalous phenomena to hypnotic suggestions, that threatened the integrity of the finite individual.[168] Against Freud's proclamation that his discovery of the unconscious has challenged the integrity of man, we can see how it operates instead as a technology for restoring man's threatened unity. The internalisation of death, developed in spiritualism and psychical research, reinforced the atomism of the individual. It led to transformation of the individual's eschatological orientation. He or she no longer looked beyond the self for an encounter with the divine; instead, there was an introspective turn towards a new layer of imagined history. As shall be seen in the next chapter, in the new psychology of religion, the sacred – which had once stood outside the individual – was relocated within the field of memory.

Notes

1 J. R. Beard, *Voices of the Church in Reply to Dr D. F. Strauss* (London: Simpkin Marshall, 1845), p. ix; J. McClintock and C. E. Blumenthal, 'Translators preface', in A. Neander, *The Life of Jesus Christ in its Historical Connexion* (London: H. G. Bohn, 1851), pp. 12–13; Timothy Larsen, 'Biblical criticism and the crisis of beliefs: D. F. Strauss's *Leben Jesu* in Britain', in Larsen (ed.), *Contested Christianity: The Political and Social Contexts of Victorian Theology* (Waco: Baylor University Press, 2004), pp. 43–58, 201–4.

2 T. Cooper, 'Critical exegesis of the gospel history at the Literary Institution, Tottenham Court Road', *Cooper's Journal or Unfettered Plain Thinker for Freedom and Truth* 1 (1850), pp. 12, 26, 58–9, 105–8, 121–3, 138–88; Cooper, *The Life of Thomas Cooper*, ed. John Saville (Leicester: Leicester University Press, 1971), p. 363.

3 [T. Cooper], 'Mr Cooper's orations', *Reasoner* 3 (1847), 507.

4 Gerald Massey, *The Historical Jesus and the Mythical Christ* (New Southgate: privately printed, 1887), p. 9. For similar statements, see: J. M. Peebles, *Jesus: Man, Myth or God* (London: J. Burns Progressive Library, 1878); John Denham Parsons, *Our Sun God or Christianity before Christ* (London: The Author, 1895).

5 G. Massey, *The Logia of the Lord: Or Prehistoric Sayings Ascribed to Jesus the Christ* (New Southgate: privately printed, 1887), p. 24. The idea that Christ's person was simply a concatenation of myths dated from the much older works of David Hume, Charles Volney, Godfrey Higgins and William Drummond. It had long been lampooned by orthodox ministers, Richard Whately, *Historic Doubts Relative to Napoleon Bonaparte* [1819], ed. Richard Pomeroy (London: Scolar Press, 1985); G. V. Smith, 'The fallacy of the mythical theory of Dr Strauss, illustrated from the history of Martin Luther, and from actual Mahomedean myths of the life of Jesus Christ', in Beard, *Voices*, ch. 8. Smith's essay was largely an abridged translation of Würm's *Auszüge aus der schrift das Leben Luther's kritich bearbeitet von Dr Casuar, Mexico, 2836* (Tübingen, 1837).

6 Cooper, *Life*, pp. 380–1.

7 On the development of the language of historical influence, R. Douglas-Fairhurst, *Victorian Afterlives: The Shaping of Influence in Nineteenth-Century Literature* (Oxford: Oxford University Press, 2002), pp. 151–69.

8 T. Cooper, *The Bridge of History over the Gulf of Time* (London: Hodder and Stoughton, 1876); Larsen, *Contested Christianity*, pp. 113–20, 213–17.

9 Mark Salber Phillips, 'Distance and historical representation', *HWJ* 57 (2004), 123–41.

10 For example, William Howitt, 'Anti-Christian spiritualism', *Spiritual Magazine* (January 1879), 6; Florence Theobald, *Spirit Messages on the Nature of Christ's Person* (London: E. W. Allen, 1887); 'Arcanus', *Modern Christianity and Modern Spiritualism Judged by the Teachings of Jesus Christ* (London: J. Burns, 1890); J. M. Peebles, *Jesus: Man, Myth or God* (London: J. Burns Progressive Library, 1878), pp. 29–32.

11 On the forms of selfhood projected by different forms of history, see: H. White, *The Content of the Form* (Baltimore: Johns Hopkins University Press, 1987), pp. 87–8.

12 See the suggestive remarks of Michel de Certeau, 'Surin's melancholy', in *Heterologies: Discourse on the Other* (Minneapolis: University of Minnesota Press, 1989), pp. 101–18, esp. p. 112; Jacques Ranciere, *The Names of History: On the Poetics of Knowledge*, trans. Hassan Melehy (Minneapolis: University of Minnesota Press, 1994).

13 Bonnie Smith, *The Gender of History: Men, Women and Historical Practice* (Cambridge MA: Harvard University Press, 1998), pp. 103–5, 130–55.

14 David Armstrong, 'Silence and truth in death and dying', *Social Science and Medicine* 74 (1987), 655.

15 There is now a burgeoning literature on historical conceptions of death, see: Philippe Ariès, *The Hour of our Death* (London: Peregrine Books, 1987), esp. ch. 10; Michael Wheeler, *Death and the Future Life in Victorian Literature* (Cambridge: Cambridge University Press, 1992). On the centrality of death in Victorian popular culture, see: Thomas Laqueur, 'Bodies, death and pauper funerals', *Representations* 1 (1983), 109–31. For an invaluable contemporary discussion, see: Hereward Carrington and John R. Meader, *Death: Its Causes and Phenomena* (London: William Rider, 1911), esp. pt 2.

16 Henry Drummond, *Natural Law in the Spiritual World*, 33rd edn (London: Hodder and Stoughton, 1897), pp. 171–2. On Drummond, see: George Adam Smith, *The Life of Henry Drummond* (London: Hodder and Stoughton, 1899).

17 2 Corinthians 5.17. For a contemporary commentary, Canon Ryle, 'Regeneration', in Edward Garbett (ed.), *Evangelical Principles* (London: William Hunt and Co., 1875). For background, M. H. Abrams, *Natural Supernaturalism: Tradition and Revolution in Romantic Literature* (London: Oxford University Press, 1971), pp. 47–8.

18 On railway spine, see: Ralph Harrington, 'On the tracks of trauma: railway spine reconsidered', *Social History of Medicine* 16 (2003), 209–23. For hysterical paralyses see below, p. 56–9.

19 On this specific point, see: J. H. Leuba, 'The state of death', *Am. J. Psychology* 14 (1903), 397–403; Ethel Puffer, 'The loss of personality', *Atlantic Monthly* 85 (1899), 195–204. For a review of the contemporary literature on this subject: [Anon.], 'Modern mysticism', *Quarterly Review* 190 (1899), 79–102.

20 Carrington and Meader, *Death*, chs 3 and 4; Thomas M. Madden, 'On morbid somnolence and death trance', *Medical Magazine* 6 (1897), 857–62, 922–9; William Tebb and E. P. Vollum, *Premature Burial and How it May be Prevented* [1896] (London: Swann Sonnenschein, 1905); [Anon.], 'What is death?', *The Spectator* (29 December 1896), 933–4; William See, 'The extreme rarity of premature burial', *Popular Science Monthly* 17 (1880), 526–30.

21 The phrase is Henry Drummond's (*Natural Law*, pp. 152, 155).

22 Walter Benjamin, *Illuminations* [1955] (London: Fontana Press, 1992), p. 93; Peter Brooks, *Reading for the Plot* (Oxford: Clarendon Press, 1984), pp. 22ff.

23 The history of modern spiritualism that follows will mainly be restricted to an examination of some of its structural implications for ideas of history and personality. There already exist excellent histories of nineteenth-century British spiritualism. For the institutional and biographical aspects of the spiritualist movement, see: Janet Oppenheim, *The Other World: Spiritualism and Psychical Research in England, 1850–1914* (Cambridge: Cambridge University Press, 1985) and Alan Gauld, *The Founders of Psychical Research* (London: Routledge and Kegan Paul, 1968). For the relationship of spiritualism to plebeian culture, see: Logie Barrow, *Independent Spirits: Spiritualism and English Plebeians, 1850–1910* (London: History Workshop/ Routledge and Kegan Paul, 1986). For the feminist implications of the spiritualist project: Alex Owen, *The Darkened Room: Women, Power and Spiritualism in Nineteenth-Century England* (London: Virago, 1989). For the connections of spiritualism to other sciences: John Peregrine Williams, 'The making of Victorian psychical research: an intellectual elite's approach to the spiritual world' (Ph.D. dissertation, University of Cambridge, 1984); Richard Noakes, 'Cranks and visionaries: science, spiritualism and transgression' (Ph.D. dissertation, University of Cambridge, 1998).

24 On the novelty of this method, see: T. H. Huxley, 'On the method of Zadig: retrospective prophecy as a function of science', *Nineteenth Century* 7 (1880), 929–40; Carlo Ginzburg, 'Morelli, Freud and Sherlock Holmes: clues and scientific method', *HWJ* 9 (1980), 7–36. On inference as the criterion of historical practice, R. G. Collingwood, *The Nature of History*, ed. J. Van de Dussen (Oxford: Oxford University Press, 1994), pp. 251–3, 261–3.

25 The phrase is Logie Barrow's, see, 'Democratic epistemology: mid-nineteenth-century plebeian medicine', *Society for the Social History of*

Medicine Bulletin 29 (1981), 25–9. For an example of spiritualist rules and procedure, see: James Burns, 'How to investigate spiritual phenomena', in *Report on Spiritualism, of the Committee of the London Dialectical Society*, new edn (London: James Burns, 1881), appendix; Thomas R. Hazard, *Mediums and Mediumship* (London: James Burns, n.d.).

26 Oliver Lodge, 'How should spiritualists regard scientific men?', *Borderland* 4 (1897), 166. On Oliver Lodge and his interest in spiritualism, see: John D. Root, 'Science, religion and psychical research', *Harvard Theological Review* 71 (1978), 245–53.

27 Antoinette Burton, 'Thinking beyond the boundaries: empire, feminism and the domains of history', *Social History* 26 (2001), 60–71; Carolyn Steedman, 'The space of memory: in an archive', *History of the Human Sciences* 11 (1998), 65–83; Steedman, *Dust* (Manchester: Manchester University Press, 2000), ch. 4.

28 On the role of furniture in spiritualist practice, Daniel Cottom, 'On the dignity of tables', *Critical Enquiry* 14 (1988), 765–83.

29 On trance, see: A. Winter, *Mesmerized: Powers of Mind and Body in Victorian Britain* (Chicago: Chicago University Press, 2001), pp. 117–30.

30 Sonu Shamdasani, 'Automatic writing and the discovery of the unconscious', *Spring: A Journal of Archetype and Culture* 54 (1993), 100–31.

31 John Jones, *The Natural or the Supernatural, or Man, Physical, Apparitional and Spiritual* (London: H. Balliere, 1861), p. 260.

32 William James, *Principles of Psychology* 1 [1890] (London: Dover, 1950), p. 395.

33 Adin Ballou quoted in [Anon.], *Spirit Rapping in England and America: Its Origins and History* (London: Henry Vitzetelly, 1853), p. 70; 'Julia' [William Stead], 'Automatic handwriting', *Borderland* 3 (1896), 340–1.

34 J. J. Morse, *Practical Occultism: A Course of Lectures through the Trance Mediumship of J. J. Morse* [1888] (Manchester: Two Worlds, 1925), pp. 10, 12. On Morse, see: Morse, *The Mysteries of Mediumship* (London: Progressive Literature Agency, 1894).

35 W. H. Harrison, *Spirit People* (London: Spiritualist Newspaper Office, 1875), p. 35.

36 Quoted in Owen, *Darkened Room*, p. 212.

37 On the relationship between personality and authority in the sciences, see: Barry Barnes, 'On authority and its relationship to power', in John Law (ed.), *Power, Action and Belief* (Keele: University of Keele, 1986).

38 Roland Barthes, 'The discourse of history', trans. Stephen Bann, in Elinor Schaffer (ed.), *Rhetoric and History: Comparative Criticism: A Yearbook* III (Cambridge: Cambridge University Press, 1986), p. 14. The parallel has attracted a lot of attention from literary critics, see: Helen Sword, *Ghostwriting Modernism* (Ithaca: Cornell University Press, 2002), pp. 158–66; A. S. Byatt, *Possession* (London: Virago, 1991), p. 116. Arnold Toynbee claimed

that all great historical work originated in an episode of ecstatic communion with the dead (*A Study of History*, X, (Oxford: Oxford University Press, 1954), pp. 130–8).

39 cf. Michel de Certeau, *The Writing of History* (New York: Columbia University Press, 1988), p. 258; Steve Connor, *Dumbstruck: A Cultural History of Ventriloquism* (Oxford: Oxford University Press, 2002), esp. pp. 368–9.

40 Again, I am relying on the spiritualists' own representation of the discipline's development. Logie Barrow (*Independent Spirits*, ch. 1) has suggested that some form of indigenous British spiritualism may well have developed outside the American tradition.

41 For a contemporary account of Swedenborgian activity in London: C. M. Davies, *Heterodox London, or Phases of Free Thought in the Metropolis* (London: Tinsley Bros., 1874), pp. 90–115.

42 [William Binns], 'Religious heresies of the working classes', *Westminster Review* n.s. 21 (January 1862), 89, quoted in Barrow, *Independent Spirits*.

43 Both Oppenheim, *The Other World*, pp. 49–50, and Owen, *Darkened Room*, p. 25, argue for this broad estimate of the spiritualist population. Gauld, *Founders*, p. 77, and Barrow, *Independent Spirits*, p. 97, place the figure at nearer 10,000. On the elasticity of the term 'spiritualist', see: C. M. Davies, *Mystic London, or Phases of Occult Life in the Metropolis* (London: Tinsley Bros., 1876), pp. 365ff.

44 J. F. C. Harrison, *Robert Owen and the Owenites in Britain and America* (London: Routledge Kegan Paul, 1969).

45 Barrow, *Independent Spirits*, ch. 6; Barrow, 'Socialism in eternity', 37–69.

46 Owen, *Darkened Room*, esp. ch. 8, and her essays: 'The other voice: women, children and nineteenth-century spiritualism', in C. Steedman, C. Unwin and V. Walkerdine (eds), *Language, Gender and Childhood* (London: Routledge and Kegan Paul, 1985); 'Women in nineteenth-century spiritualism: strategies in the subversion of femininity', in J. Obelkevich, L. Roper and R. Samuels (eds), *Disciplines of Faith* (London: History Workshop/Routledge, 1987); Judith R. Walkowitz, 'Science and the séance: transgressions of gender and genre in late Victorian London', *Representations* 22 (1988), 3–29. For a comparable treatment of American spiritualism, see: Ann D. Braude, *Radical Spirits: Spiritualism and Women's Rights in Nineteenth-Century America* (Boston: Beacon Press, 1989). For a contemporary view of clairvoyant activity as an escape from the confines of everyday life, see: F. Podmore, *Modern Spiritualism* II (London: Methuen, 1902), pp. 323f.; H. G. Wells, 'Peculiarities of psychical research', *Nature* 51 (6 December 1894), 121.

47 P. Stallybrass and A. White, *The Politics and Poetics of Transgression* (London: Methuen, 1986).

48 On this sacrilegious aspect of spiritualism, see: Cottom, 'Dignity of tables'. On the confusion of the empirical and the transcendental in spiritualist practice, see: June Macklin, 'A Connecticut Yankee in Summerland', in

V. Crapazano and V. Garrison (eds), *Case Studies in Spirit Possession* (New York: John Wiley, 1977), pp. 71–4.

49 De Certeau, *Writing of History*, pp. 258–66; Paul Virilio, *Aesthetics of Disappearance* (New York: Semiotexte, 1991), pp. 9–39.

50 For a general overview of the scientific responses to nineteenth-century spiritualism, see: Richard Noakes, 'Natural causes? Spiritualism, science, and the Victorian supernatural', in Nicola Bown, Carolyn Burdett and Pamela Thurschwell (eds), *The Victorian Supernatural* (Cambridge: Cambridge University Press, 2004), pp. 23–43.

51 [Dialectical Society], *Report on Spiritualism, of the Committee of the London Dialectical Society* [1871] (London: James Burns, 1881), p. 230.

52 R. Smith, *Trial by Medicine: Insanity and Responsibility in Victorian Trials* (Edinburgh: Edinburgh University Press, 1981).

53 Michael Clark, 'The rejection of psychological approaches to menial disorder in late nineteenth-century English psychiatry', in Andrew Scull (ed.), *Madhouses, Mad-doctors and Madmen* (London: Athlone, 1981); Janet Oppenheim, *Shattered Nerves* (Oxford: Oxford University Press, 1991), pp. 43f.

54 For psychiatric models of trance, see James Crichton-Browne, *Cavendish Lectures on Dreamy Mental States* (London: Balliere, Tindall and Cox, 1895).

55 On the spiritualist debt to mesmerism, see: Adam Crabtree, *From Mesmer to Freud: Magnetic Sleep and the Roots of Psychological Healing* (New Haven: Yale University Press, 1993), ch. 10; Ann Taves, *Fits, Trances and Visions: Experiencing Religion and Explaining Experience from Wesley to James* (Princeton, NJ: Princeton University Press, 1999), pp. 131–76.

56 Morse, *Practical Occultism*, p. 10; James Anderson, 'Epilepsies and Insanities', in Daniel Hack Tuke (ed.), *Dictionary of Psychological Medicine* [1892] repr. (New York: Arno Press, 1976), p. 450; J. C. Howden, 'The religious sentiment in epileptics', *JMS* 18 (1873), 493–4. Beard and James used the chandelier model of consciousness (fully lighted – waking; all burners low – sleep; only one burner on – trance; all burners extinguished – death: G. Beard, *The Nature and Phenomena of Trance* (New York: Putnam's Sons, 1881), p. 1; W. James, *On Exceptional Mental States* [1896], ed. E. Taylor (Amherst: University of Massachusetts Press, 1984), p. 18.

57 Henry Rayner MD, 'Automatic writing, III', *BMJ*, (16 December 1893), 1338; see also, [Anon.], 'Mr Stead and automatic writing', *BMJ*. (4 November 1893), 1015; [Anon.], 'Automatic writing, II', *BMJ* (2 December 1893), 1225–6; Charles Kidd in *Dialectical Society*, pp. 254–5. For a summary of such views, see: Podmore, *Spiritualism* II, ch. 6; J. P. Williams, 'Psychical research and psychiatry in late Victorian Britain: trance as ecstasy or trance as insanity', in W. F. Bynum, R. Porter and M. Shepherd (eds), *The Anatomy of Madness*, vol. I, *People and Ideas* (London: Routledge, 1985), pp. 233–54, esp. pp. 239–42.

58 William Hammond, *Spiritualism and Allied Causes of Nervous Derangement* (London: H. K. Lewis, 1876), p. 118.

59 On this slippage, see: Michel de Certeau, *Practice of Everyday-Life* (Berkeley: University of Berkeley Press, 1984), pp. xi–xxii; B. Barnes, 'On the implications of a body of knowledge', *Knowledge: Creation, Diffusion, Utilisation* 4 (1982), 95–110.

60 H. Maudsley, 'Emmanuel Swedenborg', *JMS* 15 (1869), 170–96, 417–36; Maudsley, 'Hallucinations of the senses', *Fortnightly Review* n.s. 24 (1878), 370–86; *Pathology of the Mind*, 3rd. edn (London: Macmillan, 1895), pp. 78f.

61 Roden Noel, 'Spiritism and other theories', *Light* (21 November 1885), 568. Roden Noel (1834–94) had served as Groom of the Privy Chamber but resigned his commission because of his growing republican sympathies, see A. W. Brown, *The Metaphysical Society: Victorian Minds in Crisis* (Princeton NJ: Princeton University Press, 1968), pp. 154–5.

62 Roden Noel, 'Rival theories', and 'Rival theories again', *J.SPR* 2 (1886), 270; see also Noel, 'Hallucination, memory and the unconscious self', *J.SPR* 2 (1886), 158–70.

63 E. Recejac, *Essay on the Bases of the Mystic Knowledge*, trans. Sara Carr Upton (London: Kegan Paul, Trench, Trübner and Co., 1899), pp. 155–8. Recejac was drawing on Maudsley's *Physiology of Mind*. He went on to argue (pp. 155–8) that men should cultivate mono-ideism since it is equivalent to the mystic practice of concentration.

64 George Beard, 'The psychology of spiritism', *North American Review* 129 (1879), 65. For Beard, see: Charles Rosenberg, 'The place of George Miller Beard in American psychiatry', *Bulletin of the History of Medicine* 36 (1962), 245–59.

65 George Miller Beard, 'A new theory of trance and its bearing on human testimony', *Journal of Nervous and Mental Diseases* 4 (1877), 1–47; Beard, 'The scientific study of human testimony', *Popular Science Monthly* 13 (1878), 54–64, 173–83; T. H. Huxley, 'The value of witness to the miraculous' [1889], in *Lectures and Essays* (London: Watts and Co., 1931), pp. 119–41

66 Henry Maudsley, *The Physiology and Pathology of Mind*, 2nd ed. (London: Macmillan and Co., 1868); Maudsley, *Natural Causes and Supernatural Seemings* (London: Kegan Paul, Trench and Co., 1886); Wilhelm Wundt, 'Spiritualism as a scientific question', trans. Edwin D. Mead, *Popular Science Monthly* 15 (1879), 577–93.

67 William Carpenter, 'Electrobiology and mesmerism', *Quarterly Review* 93 (1853), 501–7. For general introductions to this concept, see: R. Noakes, '"Instruments to lay hold of spirits": technologizing the bodies of Victorian spiritualism', in I. R. Morus (ed.), *Bodies/Machines* (Oxford: Berg, 2002); Roger Luckhurst, 'Passages in the invention of the psyche: mind-reading in London, 1881–84', in Roger Luckhurst and Josephine McDonagh (eds), *Transactions and Encounters: Science in Victorian Culture* (Manchester: Manchester University Press, 2002), pp. 117–50.

68 'Professor Faraday on table moving', *Athenaeum* 1340 (2 July 1853), 801–3.

69 W. B. Carpenter, 'On the fallacies of testimony in relation to the super-natural', *Contemporary Review* 27 (1876), 279–95; Carpenter, *Mesmerism, Spiritualism, &c. Historically and Scientifically Considered* (London: Longmans, Green and Co., 1877); Carpenter, *Principles of Mental Physiology*, 6th edn (London: Kegan Paul, Trench and Co., 1888), pp. 630–4.

70 On Beard's relationship to Carpenter, see: George Beard, *The Study of Trance, Muscle Reading, etc.* (New York: n.p., 1882), pp. 23–4.

71 Beard, 'Psychology of spiritism', 68; see also, Beard, 'Scientific study of human testimony', 179–80.

72 Beard, 'A new theory of trance', 42. Cf. Collingwood, *Nature of History*, pp. 256–7.

73 Maudsley, *Physiology and Pathology of Mind*, ch. IV, esp. pp. 105–15.

74 H. Maudsley, *Common Errors in Seeing and Believing* (London: Sunday Lecture Society, 1881), p. 7.

75 S. E. D. Shortt, 'Physicians and psychics: the Anglo-American medical response to spiritualism', *Journal of the History of Medicine and Allied Sciences* 39 (1984), 339–55.

76 For examples of the unquestioning implication of the self in modern discussions of testimony, see: Paul Ricoeur, 'The hermeneutics of testimony', *Anglican Theological Review* 61 (1979), esp. sect. 2; Shoshana Felman and Dori Laub, *Testimony: Crises of Witnessing in Literature, Psychoanalysis and History* (London: Routledge, 1992).

77 On Barrett, see: *Who Was Who II (1916–1928)* (London: A. and C. Black, 1992), p. 158. On Rogers, see: E. D. Rogers, *Life and Experiences of Edmund Dawson Rogers, Spiritualist and Journalist* (London: Office of Light, n.d.). On the Society's formation: Podmore, *Spiritualism* II, pp. 159ff.; W. F. Barrett, 'Some reminiscences of fifty years psychical research', *Proc.SPR* 34 (1924), 280–7; E. D. Rogers, 'The origin of the SPR', *Light* (9 September 1893), 429–30.

78 On Henry Sidgwick, Knightsbridge Professor of Moral Philosophy at the University of Cambridge, see: D. G. James, *Henry Sidgwick, Science and Faith in Victorian England* (Oxford: Oxford University Press, 1970); Arthur and Eleanor Sidgwick, *Henry Sidgwick: A Memoir* (London: Macmillan, 1906).

79 Henry Sidgwick, in [SPR], *Presidential Addresses to the Society for Psychical Research, 1882–1911* (Glasgow: Robert Maclehose for the SPR, 1912), pp. 1–6; 'Objects of the society', *Proc.SPR* 1 (1882–3), 3–4.

80 These were respectively: William Boyd Carpenter, Bishop of Ripon; Harvey Goodwin, Bishop of Carlisle; John Couch Adams, Professor of Astronomy at Cambridge; William Barrett; Oliver Lodge; A. Macalister; Lord Rayleigh, physicist; Balfour Stewart, Professor of Physics at Owens College, Manchester; J. J. Thompson, Cavendish Professor at Cambridge; John Venn, logician and fellow of Caius College, Cambridge; W. E. Gladstone; Arthur Balfour and, among the authors, J. A. Symonds and Charles Lutwidge Dodgson.

81 Ernest Hart, 'The revival of witchcraft', *Nineteenth Century* 33 (1893), 347–68; Hart, *Hypnotism, Mesmerism and the New Witchcraft* (London: Smith Elder and Co., 1898); Edward Clodd, 'Presidential address', *Folklore* 6 (1895), 78–80; [Anon.], 'Psychical research', *Pall Mall Gazette* (21 October 1882), 4–5; Maudsley, *Natural Causes*, pp. 175–6.

82 Roger Luckhurst, *The Invention of Telepathy* (Oxford: Oxford University Press, 2002), pp. 70–3, 109–12; John Cerullo, *The Secularization of the Soul* (Philadelphia: Institute for the Study of Human Issues, 1982), ch. 3; Frank Miller Turner, *Between Science and Religion* (New Haven: Yale University Press, 1974), chs 2, 5; Williams, 'The making of Victorian psychical research', intro. and *passim*; Williams, 'Psychical research and psychiatry', pp. 235–9; Brian Wynne, 'Physics and psychics: science, symbolic action and social control in late Victorian England', in B. Barnes and S. Shapin (eds), *Natural Order* (London: Sage Publications, 1979).

83 Quoted in Oppenheim, *The Other World*, p. 111.

84 E. Gurney, 'An epilogue to vivisection', *Cornhill Magazine* 45 (1882), 191–9; Gurney, 'A chapter on the ethics of pain', *Fortnightly Review* 36 (1881), 778–96. On Gurney, see: Trevor Hall, *The Strange Case of Edmund Gurney* (London: Duckworth, 1964). Hall's claim that Gurney committed suicide after discovering deceit among his hypnotic performers has been widely contested, see: Alan Gauld, 'Mr Hall and the SPR', *J.SPR* 43 (1965–6), 53–62.

85 F. W. H. Myers, *Fragments of Inner Life* [1893] (London: SPR, 1961), p. 15. On Myers, see: Turner, *Between Science and Religion*, ch. 5; on his snobbery, see Gauld, *Founders*, p. 331.

86 On the problems associated with the ascription of interests, Steve Woolgar, 'Interests and explanations in the social study of science', *Social Studies of Science* 11 (1981), 365–94.

87 Simon Schaffer has argued that the SPR is part of the 'British intellectual police', its aim being to combat the subversive investigations of spiritualism, 'Cleaning up', *London Review of Books* (1–14 July 1982), 10.

88 E. Gurney, 'Peculiarities of certain post-hypnotic states', *Proc.SPR* 4 (1886–7), 321.

89 F. Myers, 'Further notes on the unconscious self, pt 2', *J.SPR* (March 1886), 225; see also E. Gurney 'Problems of hypnotism', *Proc.SPR* 2 (1883–4), 270–7.

90 F. Myers, 'Automatic writing or the rationale of planchette', *Contemporary Review* 47 (1885), 235, 248.

91 E. Gurney, F. W. H. Myers and F. Podmore, *Phantasms of the Living*, 2 vols (London: SPR and Trübner and Co., 1886). On the writing of *Phantasms*, see: Gauld, *Founders*, pp. 160ff.; Cerullo, *Secularization*, pp. 92–3. On Podmore, post-office clerk and Fabian socialist, see Hall, *Edmund Gurney*, app. A.

92 This interpretation was widely publicised, Gurney and Myers, 'Apparitions',

Nineteenth Century 15 (1884), 791–815; 'Visible apparitions', *Nineteenth Century* 16 (1884), 68–95, 851–2. 'Telepathy' (both the word and the concept) was invented by Myers, Luckhurst, *Invention of Telepathy*.

93 Gurney et al., *Phantasms*, p. lviii; see also, F. Myers, 'Automatic writing II', *Proc.SPR* 3 (1885), 1 64, esp. 3, 33, 62; Myers, 'Automatic writing III – physiological and pathological analogies', *Proc.SPR* 4 (1885–7), 212; Myers, 'Automatic writing IV – the daemon of Socrates', *Proc.SPR* 5 (1888–9), 525. W. F. Barrett, 'Letter to *Light*', *J.SPR* (1886), 229; F. Podmore, *Studies in Psychical Research* (London: Kegan Paul, Trench, Trübner and Co. Ltd, 1897), p. 18.

94 For a chronology of this conflict, see: Richard Barnett, '"A scientific sprit": negotiating knowledge in the Society for Psychical Research, 1882–1888' (M.Sc. dissertation, University of London, 2003).

95 E. Rogers, 'The SPR and the CAS', *Light* (3 February 1883), 54.

96 'X', 'The telepathic theory', *Light* (14 March 1885), 121; 'X' (28 March 1885), 148; George Wyld, 'The telepathic theory', *Light* (28 March 1885); 'Telepathy and the SPR', *Light* (11 April 1885), 170. See also A. R. Wallace's belated response to the publication of *Phantasms*: 'Are there objective apparitions?', *The Arena* (1891), repr. A. R. Wallace, *Miracles and Modern Spiritualism* (London; George Redway, 1896), pp. 231–54.

97 Mrs H. Sidgwick, 'Mr Eglinton', *J.SPR* 2 (1886), 282–334; Sidgwick, 'The charges against Mr Eglinton', in *ibid.*, 467–9.

98 Podmore, *Spiritualism* II, ch. 2; Cerullo, *Secularization*, pp. 73–5; Oppenheim, *The Other World*, pp. 139–40.

99 Myers, 'Automatic writing', 32. Cf. Myers's letter to Wilfrid Ward where he claimed to have experienced so many minor ecstasies and epiphanies that they no longer held any special significance for him: Masie Ward, *The Wilfrid Wards and the Transition* (London: Sheed and Ward, 1934), pp. 366–7.

100 Alan Gauld, *A History of Hypnotism* (Cambridge: Cambridge University Press, 1992), pp. 3, 234–40, 246–7; Winter, *Mesmerized*, pp. 38–40.

101 On Braid, see: James Milne Bramwell, 'James Braid, surgeon and hypnotist', *Brain* 19 (1895), 90–153; Gauld, *Hypnotism*, pp. 279–88; Crabtree, *Mesmer to Freud*, pp. 155–62.

102 The clearest articulation of this position occurred in the work of the German writers Eduard von Hartmann and Carl du Prel: E. von Hartmann, *Philosophy of the Unconscious* [1869] (London: Kegan Paul, Trench, Trübner, 1931); du Prel, *The Philosophy of Mysticism* [1885], 2 vols (London: George Redway, 1889). For a fuller discussion of their work, see: R. Hayward, 'Popular mysticism and the origins of the new psychology, 1880–1910' (Ph.D. dissertation, Lancaster University, 1995).

103 Gurney et al., *Phantasms*, pp. xlii–xliii; F. Myers, 'On telepathic hypnotism and its relation to other forms of hypnotic suggestion', *Proc.SPR* 4 (1886–7), 185; Myers, 'Multiplex personality', *Proc.SPR* 4 (1886–7), 496–514. Myers describes hypnotism as a form of 'psychical vivisection', a view shared by

continental researchers, e.g. Beaunis, Forel and Kraft-Ebing, see, A. Moll, *Hypnotism, including a Study of the Chief Points of Psychotherapeutics* [1889], 3rd edn, trans. Arthur Hopkirk (London: Walter Scott, 1899) p. 333.

104 This challenge was discussed by Arthur Pierce and Frank Podmore, 'Subliminal self or unconscious cerebration', *Proc.SPR* 7 (1892), 317–32.

105 For discussions of Gurney's experiments in hypnosis, see: Gauld, *Hypnotism*, pp. 389–93; T. W. Mitchell, 'The contribution of psychical research to psychotherapeutics', *Proc.SPR* 45 (1938–9), 175–86; F. Myers, 'The work of Edmund Gurney in experimental psychology', *Proc.SPR* 5 (1888–9), 359–73; Williams, 'The making of Victorian psychical research', ch. 7, sect. 2. Hall (*Edmund Gurney*) has suggested that Gurney's experimental results were produced through his subject's deliberate deceit.

106 On the establishment of *Mind*, see: Frank Neary, '"A question of peculiar importance": George Croom Robertson, *Mind* and the changing relationship between British psychology and philosophy 1876–1920', in G. Bunn, A. D. Lovie and G. Richards (eds), *Psychology in Britain: Historical Essays and Personal Reflections* (Leicester: British Psychological Society, 2001).

107 E. Gurney, 'Problems of hypnotism', *Proc.SPR* 2 (1883–4), 265–92; Gurney, 'Further problems of hypnotism', *Mind* 12 (1887), 212–32, 397–442.

108 E. Gurney, 'Peculiarities of certain post-hypnotic states', *Proc.SPR* 4 (1885–7), 268–323; Gurney, 'Recent experiments in hypnotism', *Proc.SPR* 5 (1888–9), 3–17.

109 I have omitted from this brief discussion Gurney's attempt to demonstrate the operation of a mesmeric influence in the trance state, see: E. Gurney and F. Myers, 'Some higher aspects of mesmerism', *National Review* 5 (1885), 581–703; Gauld, *Founders*, app. A.

110 William James, 'Frederic Myers' service to psychology' [1901], repr. *Essays in Psychical Research* (Cambridge MA: Harvard University Press, 1986), p. 196; also James, 'Review of *Human Personality and its Survival of Bodily Death*', in *ibid.*, pp. 211–12; also Théodore Flournoy's review of same, *Proc.SPR* 18 (1903), 46.

111 James, 'Frederic Myers', p. 195. Myers was often criticised for constructing his model of the inner life or soul from what were largely regarded as abnormal phenomena, see: Nicholas Murray, *Manifold Personality* (Columbia: n.p., [1888]); Paul Carus, 'The soul in science and religion', *Monist* 16 (1906), 220.

112 On the use of psychical research in making sense of historical anomalies, Gurney et al., *Phantasms*, p. xlvi; F. Podmore, *Apparitions and Thought Transference* (London: Walter Scott, 1893), p. 373; C. C. Massey 'The influence of psychical research on the dominant culture', *Light* Supp. (24 October 1885), pp. 519–22.

113 E. Gurney, 'Stages of hypnotic memory', *Proc.SPR* 4 (1886–7), 531.

114 This rhetorical operation did predate the foundation of the SPR:

W. Hammond recounts a spiritualist patient whose messages from Pascal were traced to a memoir she had been reading, *Spiritualism*, pp. 195–6; W. Hammond, *The Physics and Physiology of Spiritualism* (New York: Appleton, 1871), pp. 28–35.

115 F. Myers, 'On a telepathic explanation of some so-called spiritualistic phenomena', *Proc.SPR* 2 (1884), 226–37; the same material was covered in Myers, 'Automatic writing II', 24f.; Myers, 'Rationale of planchette', 240–3.

116 Myers, 'Telepathic explanation', 226. A similar process of self-realisation is described by Charles Hill Tout, 'Some psychical phenomena bearing upon the question of spirit control', *Proc.SPR* 7 (1892), 309–16.

117 Myers, 'Automatic writing II', 24.

118 W. Romaine Newbold, 'Subconscious reasoning', *Proc.SPR* 12 (1896), 11–20; Théodore Flournoy, *Spiritualism and Psychology* (New York: Harper Brothers, 1911), p. 131; Andrew Lang, *The Book of Dreams and Ghosts* (London: Longmans Green and Co., 1897), pp. 19–23; Podmore, *Studies*, pp. 382–4; F. Myers, *Human Personality and its Survival of Bodily Death*, 2 vols (London: Longmans Green and Co., 1903), 1, pp. 375–9; it has recently reappeared in a popular work by Brian Inglis, *The Power of Dreams* (London: Paladin/Grafton Books, 1988), pp. 36–7, 60–1.

119 Newbold, 'Subconscious reasoning', 14–15. For a discussion, Rhodri Hayward, 'Policing dreams: history and the moral uses of the unconscious', *HWJ* 49 (2000), 143–60.

120 Newbold, 'Subconscious reasoning', 17. For Newbold (1865–1926), see: *AmericanDB* VII, pp. 448–9.

121 Morell Theobald, *Spirit Workers in the Home Circle* (London: T. Fisher Unwin, 1887); Owen, *Darkened Room*, ch. 5.

122 Podmore, *Spiritualism* II, pp. 91–4.

123 Hayden White, *Tropics of Discourse: Essays in Cultural Criticism* (Baltimore: Johns Hopkins University Press, 1978), p. 125. Some modern philosophers do argue that the world, or lived experience, does indeed have a narrative structure: David Carr, *Time Narrative and History* (Bloomington: Indiana University Press, 1986); Noel Caroll, 'Interpretation, history, and narrative', *Monist* 73 (1990), 134–66.

124 G. Balfour, in [SPR], *Presidential Addresses*, p. 267; Gauld, *Founders*, pp. 293–7; Oppenheim, *The Other World*, pp. 262–3.

125 James, 'Review', pp. 211–15; G. F. Stout, 'Mr F. W. H. Myers on *Human Personality and its Survival of Bodily Death*', *Hibbert Journal* 2 (1903), 44–64. W. McDougall, [Review of *Human Personality and its Survival of Bodily Death*], *Mind* n.s. 12 (1903), 513–28, who commented that Myers had found the subliminal self too difficult a concept to explicate, so had introduced it implicitly through repeated examples (515).

126 James, *Principles*, ch. 6; F. Myers, '*The Principles of Psychology*', *Proc.SPR* 7 (1891–2), 111–33.

127 F. Myers, 'Further notes on the unconscious self III', *J.SPR* 2 (1886), 241; Myers, 'Multiplex personality', 506–7.

128 Myers, 'Further notes, III', 238; F. Myers, 'The subliminal consciousness. Ch. III: The mechanism of genius', *Proc.SPR* 8 (1893), 333–61; Myers 'The subliminal consciousness. Ch. VI: The mechanism of hysteria', *Proc.SPR* 9 (1893–4), 3–25; Myers, *Human Personality*, chs 2 and 3; James, *Mental States*, pp. 149–65. The murderous nursery maid is probably an allusion to the case of Martha Brixey, see: Smith, *Trial by Medicine*, pp. 155–7.

129 In *Human Personality*, Myers dates this transformation between 1888–1901, pp. 189–90. He apparently remained convinced long after his own death. In seances with Madams Piper and Thompson, his spirit informed fellow psychical researchers of the reality of eternal life, and as late as 1971 produced automatic scripts through a Cornish schoolteacher on the subject of immortality: Helen Dallas, *Mors Janua Vitae* (London: William Rider and Son, 1910); Oliver Lodge, *The Survival of Man* (New York: George H. Doran Co., 1920), pp. 288–312; Kenneth Richmond, *Selected F. W. H. Myers Scripts* (London: Central Association of Spiritualists, 1972).

130 On Annie Marshall's affair with Myers, see: Gauld, *Founders*, pp. 117–24; on her post-mortem communications, see *ibid.*, pp. 322–5. Marshall operates as a kind of 'dark lady of the sonnets' throughout Myers, *Fragments*. On Mrs Piper, see: Anna M. Robbins, *Past and Present with Mrs Piper* (New York: Henry Holt, 1921).

131 F. Myers, 'The experiences of W. Stainton Moses – 1', *Proc.SPR* 9 (1893–4), 245–353; and pt 2 in *Proc.SPR* 11 (1895), 24–113; Myers, *Human Personality* II, pp. 223–36. A. W. Trethewy, *The Controls of Stainton Moses* (London: Hurst and Blackett, n.d.).

132 F. Myers, 'The subliminal consciousness VII: motor automatism', *Proc.SPR* 9 (1893–4), 71. The same position was held by William James, *Mental States*, pp. 91–2; James, *Varieties of Religious Experience* [1902] (London: Fontana Library, 1960), pp. 242, 411.

133 On the international uptake of psychical research, see: Hayward, 'Popular mysticism', ch. 2, sect. 5.

134 Since hysteria has been such a protean disease, across both time and academic discussion, what follows should be seen as a strictly limited exploration, concentrating on just one single aspect of the disease. For an overview of the literature on hysteria, see: Mark Micale, 'Hysteria and its historiography', *History of Psychiatry* 1 (1990), 33–124. On the protean nature of the disease: Chris Alam and H. Merskey, 'The development of the hysterical personality', *History of Psychiatry* 3 (1992), 135–65.

135 T. Szasz, *The Myth of Mental Illness* (London: Paladin, 1973). For a useful critique of Szasz's agenda, see: Peter Sedgwick, *Psycho-Politics* (London: Pluto, 1982), ch. 6. For a critique of the recent feminist and post-modernist investment in hysteria, see: Beret Strong, 'Foucault, Freud and French feminism: theorising

hysteria as theorising the feminine', *Literature and Psychology* 35 (1989), 10–26.

136 The following discussion of Charcot's work is limited to his visual approach and his work on the supernatural. For general introductions to Charcot's work, see: Ruth Harris, 'Introduction', in J. M. Charcot, *Clinical Lectures on Diseases of the Nervous System* [1889] (London: Tavistock/Routledge, 1991); A. R. G. Owen, *Hysteria, Hypnosis and Healing* (London: Dobson, 1971). For his relationship with his female patients: Mary James, 'The therapeutic practices of Jean-Martin Charcot (1825–1893), in their historical and social context' (Ph.D. dissertation, University of Essex, 1989); Martha Noel Evans, *Fits and Starts: A Genealogy of Hysteria in Modern France* (Ithaca: Cornell University Press, 1991), ch. 1. On Charcot's extension of the hysteria diagnosis to men and its subsequent refinements: Mark Micale, 'Jean-Martin Charcot and the theory of hysteria in the male', *Medical History* 34 (1990), 363– 411.

137 For the British argument, see: Robert Brudenell Carter, *On the Pathology and Treatment of Hysteria* (London: John Churchill, 1853).

138 Mark Micale, 'Hysteria male/hysteria female: reflections on comparative gender construction in nineteenth century medicine', in Marina Benjamin, *Science and Sensibility: Essays on Gender and Scientific Enquiry 1780–1945* (London: Basil Blackwell, 1990).

139 On degeneration, see: Daniel Pick, *Faces of Degeneration, a European Disorder, c. 1848–c. 1918* (Cambridge: Cambridge University Press, 1989); Sander Gilman, *Degeneration: The Dark Side of Progress* (New York: Columbia University Press, 1992).

140 Désiré M. Bournville, *Iconographie photographique de la Salpêtrière* (Paris: Bureaux de Progrès Médical, 1876–80).

141 Diane Sadoff, 'Experiments made by nature: mapping the hysterical body', *Victorian Newsletter* 81 (1992), 41–4; Ian Hacking, *Rewriting the Soul: Multiple Personality and the Sciences of Memory* (Princeton NJ: Princeton University Press, 1995), pp. 180–2.

142 Charcot, *Clinical Lectures*, nos 19 and 20.

143 Charcot's writing on modern spiritualism was fairly limited, see his, 'Hysteria and spiritism', *Boston Medical and Surgical Repository* 59 (1888), 65–8; Charcot, *Clinical Lectures*, no. 8.

144 Sarah Ferber, 'Charcot's demons: retrospective medicine and historical diagnosis in the writings of the Salpêtrière school', in Marijke Gijswijt-Hofstra, Hilary Marland and Hans de Waardt (eds), *Illness and Healing Alternatives in Western Europe* (London: Routledge, 1997), pp. 120–40; Mary James, 'Hysteria and demonic possession', in Basiro Davey, Alastair Gray and Clive Seale (eds), *Health and Disease: A Reader*, 2nd edn (Basingstoke: Open University Press, 1995), pp. 55–61.

145 The contents of this *Bibliothèque démoniaque* are listed in Owen, *Hysteria*, p. 247.

146 Published in Paris by Delahaye and Lecrosnier.

147 C. Withington, 'A last glimpse of Charcot at the Salpêtrière', *Boston Medical and Surgical Journal* 89 (1893), 207, in James, 'Therapeutic practices of Charcot', 15.

148 Jan Goldstein, 'The hysteria diagnosis and the politics of anticlericalism in late nineteenth-century France', *Journal of Modern History* 54 (1982), 209–39; James, 'Jean-Martin Charcot', chs. 5 and 6.

149 Again this discussion of Janet is limited to his work on possession. For fuller discussions, see: Henri Ellenberger, *The Discovery of the Unconscious* (London: Harper Collins, 1996), ch. 6; Onno van der Hart and Barbara Friedman, 'A reader's guide to Pierre Janet', *Dissociation* 2 (1989), 3–16. For Janet on the visualisation of hysteria, see: *The Mental State of Hystericals* [1901] (Washington DC: University Publications of America, 1977), pp. 1–11.

150 Janet, *Mental State of Hystericals*, pp. 30–1, 68–73. On amnesia, pp. 78–91.

151 *Ibid.*, p. 202. This argument drew on the massive French medical literature on nostalgia and amnesia. See Mark Roth's articles, 'Remembering forgetting: *maladies de la mémoire* in nineteenth-century France', *Representations* 26 (1989), 49–68; and 'Dying of the past: medical studies of nostalgia in nineteenth-century France', *History and Memory* 3 (1991), 5–29.

152 See for instance the case of Achille described in P. Janet, 'Un cas de possession et l'exorcisme moderne', *Bulletin de l'Université de Lyon* 8 (1894), 41–57; and the case of Meb, Janet, 'Un cas de phénomène des apports', *Bulletin de l'Institut Psychologique International* 1 (1900–1), 329–35; see Janet, *L'automatisme psychologique: essai de psychologie expérimentale sur les formes inférieures de l'activité humaine* (Paris: Alcan, 1889), pt 3; Janet, 'Le spiritisme contemporain', *Revue Philosophique* 33 (1892), 413–42; Janet, 'Introduction' to J. Grasset, *Le spiritisme devant la science* (Paris: Montpellier, 1904).

153 Théodore Flournoy, *From India to the Planet Mars* [1899], ed. S. Shamdasani (Princeton: Princeton University Press, 1994); Carl Jung, 'On the psychology and pathology of so-called occult phenomena', *Collected Works* 1 (London: Routledge and Kegan Paul, 1957), pp. 3–89.

154 On Flournoy (1854–1920), see: Edouard Claparède, 'Théodore Flournoy, sa vie et son œuvre', *Archives de Psychologie* 18 (1921), 1–125.

155 On this earlier search, see: *ibid.*, 35f.. The results of these investigations were reported in Flournoy, 'Genese de quelques pretendus messages spirites', *Revue Philosophique* 47 (1899), 144–58. On the initial search for Hélène Smith, see: Shamdasani, 'Introduction' to Flournoy, *India to the Planet Mars*, pp. xviii–xx.

156 The form of Smith's possession was quite distinct from that pioneered in Anglo-American spiritualist practice. A follower of Alan Kardec, she believed that the medium drifted between his or her past or future lives, rather than simple possession by wandering spirits. On Kardec, see: Leslie Shepherd (ed.), *Encyclopaedia of Occultism etc.* II (Detroit: Gale Research Co., 1984),

pp. 713–14; F. Podmore, *Naturalisation of the Supernatural* (London: Methuen, 1908), ch. 10.

157 Podmore and Myers were both highly impressed with Flournoy's study: F. Myers, 'Pseudo-possession', *Proc.SPR* 15 (1900–1), 384–415; Podmore, *Spiritualism* II, pp. 315–22. For the comparable American response: James Hyslop, 'From India to the planet Mars', *North American Review* 171 (1900), 734–47.

158 Terry Castle has recently argued that Smith's Marie Antoinette spirit persona can be seen as the unconscious product of a lesbian legitimation fantasy, see: 'Marie Antoinette obsession', *Representations* 38 (1992), 1–38.

159 Flournoy, *India to the Planet Mars*, p. 185.

160 J. Lacroix de Marles, *Histoire générale de l'Inde* (Paris, 1828).

161 Flournoy, *India to the Planet Mars*, p. 190. Italics in original.

162 On cryptomnesia: T. Flournoy, *Spiritism and Psychology* (New York: Harper Bros., 1911), pp. 172–3, 204–6; Ian Stevenson, 'Cryptomnesia and parapsychology', *J.SPR* 52 (1983), 1–30; Harry Trossman, 'The cryptomnesic fragment in the discovery of free association', *Psychological Issues* 34/35 (1976), 229–53.

163 The colonial metaphor comes from Hyslop, 'From India to the planet Mars', 734.

164 Carl Jung, 'On the psychology and pathology of so-called occult phenomena', in Herbert Reed, Michael Fordham and Gerard Adler (eds),*Collected Works*, vol. I, *Psychiatric Studies* (London: Routledge and Kegan Paul, 1957), pp. 3–89; Jung, *Zoifinga Lectures (1896–99): Collected Works Supplementary Volume*: A (Princeton NJ: Princeton University Press, 1983) and his later more tempered account in 'On spiritualistic phenomena' [1905], in *Collected Works*, vol. XVIII, *The Symbolic Life* (Princeton NJ: Princeton University Press, 1976), pp. 293–308. There is an excellent account of Jung's investigations into spiritualism by: F. X. Charet, *Spiritualism and the Foundation of C. G. Jung's Psychology* (Albany: State University of New York Press, 1993).

165 Morton Prince, *The Dissociation of Personality*, ed. Charles Rycroft (Oxford: Oxford University Press, 1978). For an excellent discussion, Ruth Leys, 'The real Mrs Beauchamp: gender and the subject of imitation', in J. Butler and J. Scott (eds), *Feminists Theorise the Political* (London: Routledge, 1992).

166 The 'shilling shocker' jibe was made by Wilfred Trotter, see Rycroft 'Introduction' to Prince, *Dissociation*, p. viii; [Anon.], 'Four women in one body', *Current Literature* 40 (1906), 439–43.

167 Thomas Mann, *The Magic Mountain* [1924] (London: Penguin, 1988), p. 222.

168 On the exclusion of hypnotic suggestion and the possibility of mimetic identification, see: Leon Chertok and Isabelle Stengers, *A Critique of Psychoanalytic Reason* (Stanford: Stanford University Press, 1992).

3

The soul governed

The human soul is made of paper (Michel Tournier, *The Erl-King*)

The body of numbers

When William James sniffed nitrous oxide in the spring of 1882, he resurrected and transformed an experimental gesture which had been central to the practice of Christian mysticism. For centuries, Western ecstatics had attempted to transcend the boundaries of the human personality, and thus approach a knowledge of the divine life through the employment of ascetic and meditative techniques. The writings of Père Surin, Madame Guyon and Catherine of Genoa give minute and often horrifying descriptions of these methods: Surin crippled himself jumping from a window into the River Garonne; Catherine starved herself; while Mme Guyon (perhaps the most extreme of all the mystics) removed her own teeth, wore briars and licked the wounds of lepers.[1] These privations were at once symbols of, and attempts to encourage, a meeting between the body and death. The conflict between the desire of the flesh and the will to the divine divided the mystic self, introducing the cosmic into the body.

James eschewed the traditional privations of the mystics. Instead he introduced the transcendental nasally, using nitrous oxide to produce an 'anaesthetic revelation'.[2] This technique apparently equalled the success of the older forms of mysticism for, as James reported, he felt himself at once subsumed within a cosmic oneness which obliterated all sense of self.[3] As he explained some years later: 'The keynote of [this experience] is invariably a reconciliation. It is as if the opposites of the world, whose contradictoriness and conflicts make all our difficulties and troubles, were melted into unity.'[4]

Despite this experience, James remained profoundly suspicious of his apparent achievement of transcendence. Like the psychical researchers and the kenotic Christologists, he was committed to the integrity of the individual.[5] In his *Principles of Psychology* (1890), James insists that 'No psychology . . . can question the existence of personal selves. The worst a psychology can do is so to interpret the nature of these selves as to rob them of their worth.'[6] Likewise, in his ethical writings he criticises the idea of a monistic communion, arguing that such an ideal undoes the individual's personal motivation and blinds him or her to the presence of evil. This suppression of the self challenges James's celebration of 'the strenuous life' in which the individual realises his or her potential through unremitting physical and intellectual efforts.[7]

James departed from the Christian mystics in his interpretation of his transcendental apprehension. Whereas they had believed that the self was extinguished at the moment of ecstatic communion, James insisted that the ecstatic moment resulted from the finite and limited individual's partial identification with the divine. It was an insight which revealed the integrity of the personality and its potential for growth. This partial form of identification was similar, James thought, to the Catholic experience of the Eucharist: 'Even the Catholic will tell you that when he believes in the identity of the wafer with Christ's body, he does not mean in all respects – so that he might use it to exhibit muscular fibre, or a cook make it smell like baked meat in the oven. He means that in the one sole aspect of nourishing his being in a certain way, it is identical with and can be substituted for the very body of his redeemer.'[8]

The shared imagery points, perhaps, to a deeper analogy between James's project and the practice of Christian mysticism. Both mysticism and the new psychology were techniques for transforming hidden, introspective knowledge into public language.[9] The mystics had communicated the inner presence of the divine through the body. Wracked by stigmata and paralyses, the mystical figure achieved a kind of personal Eucharist, substituting his or her own flesh for the absent body of Christ.[10] Similarly, the new psychologists tried to reveal the lost or subliminal inner life of man, but in place of hidden processes of growth and ideas obscured from the waking consciousness, the new psychologists substituted a body of knowledge constructed through statistical techniques and experimental investigation.

The new psychology of the unconscious emerged in the liminal spaces produced by the plebeian mystics' refusal of history, yet – as James's experiments demonstrated – it soon took on a life of its own, colonising all those invisible aspects of personality that had previously existed beyond the boundaries of historical representation. The human soul which, as we have seen, is defined in the theology of St Paul in opposition to the carnal limits of the temporal self, was now presented as a kind of invisible history, containing all the manifold aspects of individual and racial past. Through the new logic of psychology, pastoral work was transformed. It no longer ministered the individual's relationship to the divine; rather, it was concerned with his or her expression of a deep and forgotten past. This transformation of the pastoral received its clearest expression in the new discipline of the psychology of religion.

The psychology of religion

The invention of the psychology of religion as an academic discipline was a largely American phenomenon.[11] It appeared in the 1880s, almost as soon as the first departments of psychology were established. Some authors have attributed this geographical and temporal specificity to the deeply religious character of the American population, with practitioners arguing that the discipline arose in response to the spiritual crisis or 'psychic fragmentation' suffered by the United States as it entered the modern era.[12] The large-scale movement of the population from the land into urban centres undermined the traditional structures of pastoral authority based within the community and the home. The psychologists presented themselves as the new ministers to this socially and spiritually uprooted state.[13]

A more useful explanation for the sudden growth of the psychology of religion can be found in the work of John O'Donnell, Kurt Danziger and Nikolas Rose.[14] These authors have drawn attention to the emergence of psychological expertise within administrative practices, particularly those practices concerned with children and education. Certainly the new psychology was intimately concerned with pedagogy. The connection is emphasised by psychologists as diverse as William James, G. Stanley Hall, John Dewey, George Albert Coe and the British academic James Sully. Each of these authors found it necessary to address specifically the problems of modern education.[15] They presented the discipline as a new attempt to integrate intellectual and practical concerns. Although Hall himself may have complained that 'business conspires with Bethel to bring mental philosophy into general disfavour', these were in fact the mundane forces which constituted the very essence of the new psychology.[16] Hall's own career at Johns Hopkins was launched with a series of papers on the moral and religious training of children.

The effectiveness of such instruction, he argued, was wholly dependent upon psychological knowledge. 'It should', Hall claimed, 'be written over the door of every institution for higher religious education: "Let no one enter here who does not know psychology."'[17] In an attempt to fulfil his own demands, he founded a journal of education, the *Pedagogical Seminary*, in 1891, and sponsored a series of congresses on the child in conjunction with the National Education Association.[18]

The new psychology based its appeal to pedagogy on a presentation of the child as a complex of historical forces demanding expert interpretation and control. The most straightforward of these forces, the individual's habits, had long been a concern of British psycho-physiologists, who presented habit as a mechanism through which action and emotion could be physically inscribed upon the nerves. Maudsley and Carpenter believed that the nervous system would develop around the points of its most frequent exercise.[19] The doctrine contained the seeds of the pedagogic project, for it became possible (in theoretical terms at least) to transform the whole of an individual's life through a handful of strategic childhood interventions. The task of future discipline was delegated to the plasticity of human nature. As James recognised, 'Habit is thus the enormous flywheel of society, its most precious conservative agent. It alone is what keeps us within the bounds of ordinance and saves the children of fortune from the envious uprisings of the poor . . . It keeps different social strata from mixing . . . it is well for the world, that in most of us, by the age of thirty, the character has set like plaster and will never soften again.'[20] The implication of this psychological insight is clear. As James continues, education under the auspices of new psychology must '*make our nervous system our ally instead of our enemy: we must cultivate the right habits*'.[21]

The method of cultivation proposed by many psychologists differed little from the centuries-old procedures employed by ordinary schoolmasters. Many advocated the reformation of the child's personality or nervous system through a system of corporal discipline. George Albert Coe, a Methodist pedagogue and a pioneer author in the psychology of religion, argued that 'Children should not be shielded from the painful consequences of foolish conduct. There is an educative value in bruises, cuts, burns, even in the scratches and blows from other children. One of the worse situations in which a child can be placed is a home that so shields him from pain that he fails to learn the fact of law, both mental and social, and the correlative fact that self-restraint is essential to the largest freedom.'[22]

The same approach was espoused by G. Stanley Hall. Hall argued that it was probably better 'not to repress one nascent bad act in some natures, but let it and the punishment ensue, for the sake of Dr Spanckster's tonic'. As he explained, 'Dermal pain is not the worst thing in the world, and by judicious knowledge of how it feels at both ends of the rod, by flogging and being flogged, far deeper pains may be forfended. Insulting defiance, deliberate disobedience, ostentatious carelessness and bravado are diseases of the will, and in very rare cases of Promethean obstinacy, the severe processes of breaking the will is needful, just as in surgery it is occasionally needful to rebreak a bone wrongly set, or deformed to make it better.'[23] Hall's pedagogical strategy was not simple reckless sadism. He accompanied his endorsement of physical punishment with a series of minute statistics detailing the penalties imposed by a Swabian schoolmaster, Hauberle, across the course of his career. Over fifty years the energetic teacher had inflicted 911,527 blows with a cane; 124,010 with a rod; 20,989 with a ruler; 136,715 by hand; 10,295 blows to the mouth; 7,905 clips on the ear and a total of 1,115,800 slaps on the back of the head.[24]

This deep concern with the recording and assessment of disciplinary action points to a significant role for the corporal regime. For in their mapping of the effects of punishment and their faith that habit would eventually repay the educational investment in the infant, the psychologists granted a historical albeit subconscious continuity to the inner life of the child.[25] According to the new psychologists, this was a dramatic achievement. Until the latter half of the nineteenth century, American theologians had portrayed the child as naturally depraved: it was a soulless creature and as such existed beyond the bounds of spiritual government.[26] The idea of habit undid this boundary, binding the child into the adult life. The historical sense and subjective continuity of the child were not natural endowments but were achieved, in this pedagogic regime, through the physical training of the body.[27]

The government and sustenance of this historical soul marked the second point of fusion between psychology and pedagogics. The child's life became an object of close surveillance, its religious and moral development was recorded, creating normative models and giving insight into the most effective forms of ethical intervention. Hall, first at Johns Hopkins and then at Clark, pioneered a system of questionnaire forms which were distributed through teachers to school pupils. Children were examined for their religious experiences and theological preconceptions, and the results combined to provide information on the nature and development of the infant soul.[28] These early pedagogic investigations were soon claimed as the origin of the psychology of religion.[29]

The emergent personality which the new psychologists so carefully documented was a fragile phenomenon. Its existence was both a natural development and a social production. As George Coe argued, 'personality implies self-knowledge and self control . . . education is intended to assist the child to realise himself as a person . . . we are persons only through acts of self discrimination, self criticism, and choice that are strictly our own. There is a sense in which personality or selfhood may be said to be self attained rather than bestowed.'[30]

In the American psychology of religion, the growth of personality was imagined as a kind of ongoing *kenosis*. It was a movement from an indeterminate state of being to a defined sense of personality through repeated acts of self-limitation.[31] The unconsciousness that was forsaken in this process was not so much divine, however; rather, it encompassed the knowledge and wisdom of the child's racial history:

> Individual experience is so partial, so limited – heredity with its vague masses of ancestral reminiscence is vaster than any individual life or mind can express – and the frequent sense of being exceptional or strange suggests that what we call consciousness is froth or a drossy syllabub, and there is a larger subliminal existence, a *natura non naturata* of the soul that is doomed to remain a dim region because the light that might illuminate the whole obscurely, had to be concentrated in some part, and because personality so involves limitation.[32]

As with the Christologist's gloss on the Temptation, personality, according to the psychologists of religion, could only be achieved through an ongoing regime of self-control. As Coe said: 'To be a person is not merely to act from a law that is within and to impose this law upon external material: it is also to take possession of the law, to be a lawgiver to oneself, and to have self knowledge and to exercise self control . . . Capricious indulgence of desire ends in slavery.'[33]

Hall's identification of the divine unconsciousness with the racial life located the moral drama of self-control within a political framework. The authentic nature of man lay outside his personal desires within the goals and aims of society as a whole. Thus the pedagogic concern with the production of a true self was also an attempt to realise a far deeper political rationality. It aimed to fashion the child in the image of the wider society as a whole.[34]

The culmination of this process occurred in adolescence. The pedagogues insisted that during this period the child's attention be directed outwards, onto his or her relationship with the wider society.[35] This was seen as the optimal moment for psychical intervention, since it was during this time that the emergent ego was most vulnerable to external influences. Hall drew on the psychological language of Myers and Janet to justify this assertion:

> Assuming that personality is compound and made up of many elements . . . into which disease, trauma, hypnotism, may partially resolve it, as seen in the phenomenon of multiplex personality, we must regard the adolescent as especially characterised by a loosening of the bonds between the manifold factors of our ego, somatic and psychic, or else by a sudden and independent growth of single elements which leaves the former associative bonds relatively weakened, or perhaps by both together.[36]

This period of adolescent crisis could take on biblical proportions. Discussing puberty in the second volume of *Adolescence*, Hall likens the process to a kind of 'psychic Fall' in which the 'old unity and harmony with nature is broken up; the child is driven from his paradise and must enter upon a long viaticum of ascent and conquer a higher kingdom of man for himself, break out a new sphere and evolve a more modern story to his psycho-physical nature . . . The old level is left forever. Perhaps the myth of Adam and Eden describes this epoch.'[37]

In American psychology of religion, the self and the social world coincide around the disintegrating figure of the adolescent. The isolated ego produced through religious instruction and corporal punishment is fused with the wider environment. In sociological and psychological terms, adolescence marks the integration of the racial and the individual lives. In pedagogical terms, it marks a transition from external or parental control of the child to the internal self-discipline of the adult. Within both these models, adolescent conversion becomes a subject of paramount importance, since it is the most obvious manifestation, both psychically and culturally, of the switch between the old and the new life. As Hall stated, the 'chief fact of genetic psychology is conversion'.[38]

Pedagogy and statistical investigations underwrote the success of the psychology of religion. They allowed it to take a local rhetoric, the psychical researchers' reassessment of spiritual phenomena as subliminal, and apply it to the population as a whole. In place of that micropolitical significance which characterised Gurney and Myers's confrontations with the plebeian spiritualist, the new psychology of religion aimed at a generalised politic of the spiritual life. It neither limited itself spatially to a few mystical individuals, nor restricted itself tempo-rally to a few supernormal episodes within their subjects' otherwise everyday lives: it claimed a universal significance. This transformation, which substituted statistical unities for the lost spiritual unities of the population, was encapsulated in the works of Edwin Diller Starbuck and James Henry Leuba, two authors widely recognised as the original pioneers of the psychology of religion.[39]

The Clark school of religious psychology

The claims of the psychology of religion were predicated upon the idea that the fragmentary episodes of the religious life could be turned into a coherent object capable of supporting investigation and intervention. Drawing on the rhetoric of the subliminal self, the early psychologists of religion argued that the discrete events which characterised the reli-gious life – moments of insight, epiphanies or conversions – could be seen as minor expressions of a continuous religious consciousness which persisted below the threshold of perception. Yet American psychologists departed from the English psychical researchers in the methods they adopted in their attempts to recover this lost consciousness. Although Gurney and Myers had used statistical techniques in their early investi-gation of *Phantasms of the Living*, their exploration of the subliminal had depended for the most part on individual instances of hypnosis and automatic writing.[40] The Americans, in contrast, insisted that the general characteristics of the unconscious could only be revealed through the collective investigations of statistics. As Hall, the champion of this new programme, exclaimed: 'by tabulation, comparison etc. the fragments [of the soul life] may be ordered and systematised [so] as [to] together furnish a basis of illation to the larger unconscious life, on which consciousness floats, to sound and dredge it, explain the tides and currents, map its depths and shadows, study the known and the unknown, and better learn to navigate it'.[41]

Inspired by Hall, the early psychologists of religion turned to the schoolroom questionnaire and the statistical table in their attempt to trace the features and the cartography of the human soul. Hall's erst-while pupil, Edwin Diller Starbuck, regarded by many as the founder of the psychology of religion, began his enquiry in 1895 by sending out over 1,000 forms to college students and church members asking for details of their personal religious growth and their experience of conver-sion.[42] He requested details of childhood temptations; formative experiences; patterns of worship; the subject's physical and mental state preceding conversion; the nature of the conversion experience; relapses; and changes in the respondent's physical, moral and intellectual outlook wrought by his or her spiritual rebirth.

From 200 initial responses, he gleaned 137 that were usable. Starbuck collated these replies on 'enormous specially ruled charts' in order to 'lessen the personal equation'.[43] The process allowed him to reduce the manifold experience of the religious life into a series of generalised norms. The various averages thus produced were taken as indications of an underlying law. As Starbuck noted in his discussion of the age of conversion: 'the dice seem to be loaded, that is there seem to be determining elements that make the numbers accumulate in certain years'.[44] The effect of such investigations was to reveal the religious life of the individual as a continuous and legible terrain. This terrain no longer stood beyond or outside the everyday life of the person, but was demonstrably linked to his or her biological and social function. In contrast to the death-bound division claimed in the evangelical model of conversion, Starbuck's method revealed the mundane connections of the human soul.

Starbuck worked hard to produce a map of the interior life which would mirror the prevailing social mores of twentieth-century America. First, he divided his raw data according to the sex of the subject. From this he was able to demonstrate a small sex difference in the age of conversion. Women experienced two waves of conversion at 13 and 16, while the normal male converted at 16, with small wavelets at 12 and 19. Moreover, despite the fact that his figures revealed more men converting in revivals than women, Starbuck persistently claimed that 'feeling plays a larger part in the religious life of females while males are more controlled by intellection and volition'.[45] Thus he claimed that in childhood, girls concentrated upon the subjective and emotional aspects of religion, whereas boys were only interested in its external form and the routine of sacred observance. Likewise, he insisted that in adolescence women expressed their religious doubts in the form of morbid fears, while men dwelt upon intellectual and doctrinal problems.[46] Such gender differences, Starbuck believed, revealed the physical basis of the religious life. Citing the work of the Scottish psychiatrist Thomas Clouston and the English sex psychologist Henry Havelock Ellis, Starbuck argued for an intimate connection between the religious consciousness and individual sexuality, claiming that the soul life reflected both gender difference and the transformative influence of puberty.[47] Starbuck's methods and conclusions were replicated in the work of J. H. Leuba – so closely, indeed, that Starbuck accused his colleague of plagiarism.[48]

The statistical unities generated by Starbuck's method thus hooked religious consciousness into the biological and social life of the individual. His assertion that the spiritual life could be seen 'as an irradiation of the reproductive instinct' reinforced a reductionist argument which had been in common currency since the mid-nineteenth century.[49] It opened up a narrative path, soon pursued by a whole gaggle of polemicising psychologists, which connected all religious emotions with the physiology of sex.[50] This strategy once again placed the religious life beneath the jurisdiction of physiologically informed psychologists; for as Theodore Schroeder (one of the most notorious proponents of this position) asserted, it was from our sexual desire that the whole of modern religion had been mistakenly inferred.[51]

The significance of Starbuck and Leuba's connection of religious conversion and adolescent sexuality went beyond its pedagogical or rhetorical function. In Protestant theology, conversion had been seen as a moment of grace, its form and timing brought about through the will of God. This supernatural quality was emphasised in the colloquial language of the converts. Evangelical authors drew upon St Paul's idea of conversion as 'a putting off of the old man' and the 'putting on of the new' to emphasise the idea of the death of the self. As with the spiritualist strategies detailed in chapter 2, it was a method for achieving the closure of the individual's life narrative, and as such was portrayed as being beyond the subject's influence or control. Starbuck's approach to conversion and his use of the rhetoric of the subliminal self can be seen, once again, as a strategy for reintegrating the subject into his or her sanctioned life history. The moment of grace was no longer a movement beyond the threshold of the personality; rather, it was an internal switch into a previously unconscious section of the subject's knowledge and memory.[52] Drawing on the language of James's *Principles*, Starbuck beautifully summed up this new view of conversion: 'The new "stream of consciousness" sweeps things before it and the old sins are washed away.'[53] It was a baptism in the stream of the secondary consciousness. The adventures of the spiritual life which once had taken place beyond the bounds of knowledge and representation were, through a kind of statistical Eucharist, reformed as a body of numbers. The cartography of the human soul had been traced in paper.[54]

William James and the theology of the subliminal self

If Hall, Starbuck and Leuba had produced a new and domesticated version of the religious life, then James's *Varieties of Religious Experience* could be regarded as its first proper theology. James's work was predicated upon the proposed identity of the spiritual and the psychological life. James recognised the common basis of psychology and religion, insisting that 'both admit that there are forces seemingly outside of the conscious individual that bring redemption to his life. Nevertheless psychology, defining these forces as "subconscious", and speaking of their effects, as due to "incubation", or "cerebration", implies that they do not transcend the individual's personality; and herein she diverges from Christian theology, which insists that they are direct supernatural operations of the Deity.'[55]

This sense of common context supplies the intellectual framework for the volume as a whole. In twenty lectures given under the aegis of the Gifford bequest at Edinburgh University, James systematically analysed literary reports of faith, conversion, saintliness, mysticism and possession. These analyses were arranged along two scales, for as James argued, 'phenomena are best understood when placed within their series, studied in their germ and their overripe decay, and compared with their exaggerated and degenerated kindred'.[56] The first axis follows a familiar religious progression, gradating experiences between the mundane and the sacred. In the early chapters of the work, James demystifies the traditional idea of religious experience by demonstrating its connection with the uncanny emotions of everyday life. The fleeting sense of presence which haunts ordinary men is for James an incipient form of that divine presence celebrated by St Theresa or Dionysius the Areopagite. Those unsettling moments of *déjà vu* reported in the writings of John Addington Symonds or Alfred, Lord Tennyson are, for James, a glimpse not only of the future but of that state of cosmic consciousness described by Sufis and Hegelians.[57] This serial presentation, which had in part been pioneered in the work of Frederic Myers, has a twofold purpose. On a pedagogical level, it provided James's audience with a ready key for understanding the mystical through reference to their own experience. On a metaphysical level, it undid that boundary which had separated the mystical from the normal events of the mental life. It created a kind of rhetorical immortality, allowing the extension of the psychological project from the human into the divine.

The second axis structuring the *Varieties* is normative. Between the twin poles of 'the sick soul' and the 'religion of healthy mindedness', James constructs a pragmatic scale of religious emotion, judging each individual experience by its adaptiveness to the needs of modern life. The 'sick soul', he wrote, possesses a consciousness crystallised around the ideas of personal sin and a vengeful God. It is thus alienated from both the external world and the internal self. James illustrates this dual form of alienation through the autobiographies of John Bunyan and Leo Tolstoy. While at the height of his personal success and literary fame, Tolstoy became imbued with a deep suspicion of the world. His everyday actions and opinions suddenly seemed a groundless dumb charade. It was as if he had lived his life drunk and woken up sober. James diagnosed Tolstoy's experience as one of anhedonia, a condition first described by the French psychologist Théodule Ribot.[58] In contrast to analgesia, where the afflicted enjoys a general insensibility to pain, the anhedonic is robbed of the ability to perceive pleasure. Separated from any meaningful connection with the outside world, Tolstoy's consciousness remained trapped beneath the threshold of misery.[59]

James believed that Tolstoy's predicament was mirrored by the spiritual crisis of John Bunyan. Whereas Tolstoy was alienated from the outer world, Bunyan had become separated from his inner self. Under the influence of Calvinist theology, the divine became convinced of his own spiritual unworthiness. As he wrote in his confessional, *Grace Abounding to the Chief of Sinners*: 'I was more loathsome in my own eyes than was a toad.'[60] Again, James is quick to diagnose Bunyan's condition: 'He was a typical case of the psychopathic temperament, sensitive of conscience to a diseased degree, beset by doubts, fears and insistent ideas, and a victim of automatisms, both verbal and sensory.'[61]

Following the pragmatic criteria of his normative framework, James judges the sick soul harshly: 'What can be more base or unworthy', he complains, 'than the pining, puling, mumping mood, no matter by what outward ills it may have been engendered? What is more injurious to others? What is less helpful as a way out of difficulty? It but fastens and perpetuates the trouble which occasioned it, and increases the total evil of the situation. At all costs then we ought to reduce the sway of that mood; we ought to scout it in ourselves and others, and never show it tolerance.'[62]

To counteract the stupefying effects of this religious attitude, James advocates what he terms 'the religion of healthy mindedness'. This disposition embraces both self and world within a joyful unity; it inures the individual to pain, engendering a heady optimism. For James, the clearest contemporary realisation of this attitude appeared in the figure of Walt Whitman.[63] Whitman, poet and sensualist, had been studied by the Canadian psychiatrist Richard Bucke, who saw his unbridled love for man, beast and nature as an expression of a new form of cosmic consciousness. Whitman's spiritual understanding surpassed those stages of enlightenment achieved by St Paul and the Buddha, for he had managed to integrate his cosmic vision with a grounding in American common sense. As Bucke exclaimed: 'It may be that Walt Whitman is the first man who, having Cosmic Consciousness very fully developed, has deliberately set himself against being thus mastered by it, determining, on the contrary, to subdue and make it the servant along with simple consciousness, self consciousness, and the rest of the united individual SELF.'[64]

James attributes this achievement to Whitman's 'systematic expulsion from all his writings of all contractile elements. The only sentiments he allowed himself to express were of the expansive order.'[65] Whitman's method was the cultivation of the personal consciousness; this cultivation was achieved through the mystical refusal to recognise those boundaries which defined the modern self.

This mystical strategy was also used by the American 'mind-cure' and faith healing movements which sprang to prominence in the last decade of the nineteenth century. Mixing spiritualism, popular psychology and mystical theology, they advanced the idea that the individual could cure personal ills (both physical and mental) if he or she surrendered into union with God. As one exponent wrote, 'The underlying cause of all sickness, weakness or depression is the *human sense of separateness* from that Divine Energy which we call God. The soul which can feel and affirm in serene but jubilant confidence as did the Nazarene: 'I and my Father are one', has no further need of healer or of healing. This is the whole truth in a nutshell.'[66] For James, this emphasis on practical therapeutics and the cultivated expansion of consciousness qualified the new movements as religions of healthy mindedness.

At one level, James's advocacy of the religion of healthy mindedness seems to embrace that same mystical doctrine of self-surrender that he rejects in his writings on pluralism. Certainly, he recognised that the mind-curer's therapeutic practice belonged within the much older Lutheran tradition of self-surrender. It was a profoundly 'anti-moralistic method . . . Passivity, not activity; relaxation, not intentness, should now be the rule.'[67] Such a method sat unhappily with James's ethic of the strenuous life. When viewed through the framework of his pluralistic philosophy, however, the incoherence between the strenuous life and the religion of healthy mindedness disappears. Pluralism (as we noted earlier) denied the idea of a universal monism, insisting instead on the sanctity of the individual. Within this system, the moment of self-surrender involved a union with the subliminal rather than with the external world. Instead of eliminating the self, as the mystics had believed, James considered that self-surrender expanded and reinforced the personality. It allowed the conscious self to draw upon the hidden resources of its subliminal spirituality. James endorsed Starbuck's view 'that to exercise the personal will is still to live in the region where the imperfect self is the thing most emphasised. Where on the contrary, the subconscious forces take the lead, it is more probably the better self *in posse* which directs the operation. Instead of being clumsily and vaguely aimed at from without, it is then itself the organising centre.'[68]

The subliminal thus underwrites the normative framework of the *Varieties*. The 'sick soul' is damned, not so much because of its alienation from the self and the world, but because it remains separated from the various strands of subliminal consciousness. It mirrors those hysterical consciousnesses studied by Myers and Janet. As James wrote in an earlier article: 'The original sin of the hysteric mind . . . is the contractions of the field of consciousness.'[69] In contrast, the healthy-minded religions and those who reached a condition of saintliness enjoyed the fruits of a union with their subliminal selves. Their expansive vision earned James's approbation:

> Your great organising geniuses are men with habitually vast fields of mental vision, in which a whole program of future operations will appear dotted out at once, the rays shooting far ahead into definite directions of advance. In common people there is never this magnificent inclusive view of a topic. They stumble along, feeling their way, as it were, from point to point, and often stop entirely. In certain diseased conditions consciousness is a mere spark, without memory of the past or thought of the future, and the present narrowed down to some one simple emotion or sensation of the body.[70]

James's normative framework is thus predicated on that same rhetorical move which characterised Myers's *Human Personality*. It was a manoeuvre which transformed the self-denying strategies of popular mysticism and traditional religion into an exploration and celebration of the depth and extent of the subliminal consciousness. Whereas previous psychiatrists could only despair at the mystic's apparent celebration of pathological and self-destructive phenomena, James's hermeneutic allowed him to interweave his own pluralistic ethic with the traditional assessment of religious experience.[71]

The similarity between the *Varieties* and Myers's work goes deeper. In his later essays, Myers did not deny the existence of a spiritual realm but instead employed his notion of the subliminal consciousness to mediate between the divine and the human. Spiritual phenomena were thus surrendered to psychological authority. James repeats the same manoeuvre. Throughout the *Varieties*, he is careful not to deny the possibility of spiritual agency. In his second Gifford lecture on the subject of conversion, James argues that: 'The notion of a subconscious self certainly ought not at this point of our enquiry to be held to *exclude* all notion of higher penetration.'[72] Likewise, in his lecture on saintliness, he suggests: 'If the grace of God miraculously operates, it probably operates through the subliminal door.'[73] For James (as for Myers) the subliminal operated as a testing grid:

> It is evident that from the point of view of their psychological mechanism, the classic mysticism and these lower mysticisms spring from the same mental level, from that great subliminal or transmarginal region of which science is beginning to admit the existence, but of which so little is really known. That region contains every kind of matter: 'seraph and snake' abide there side by side. To come from thence is no infallible credential. What comes must be sifted and tested, and run the gauntlet of confrontation with the total context of experience, just like what comes from the outer world of sense. Its value must be ascertained by empirical methods, so long as we are not mystics ourselves.[74]

James cites the opinion of the Scottish theologian John Caird:

> Religion must indeed be a thing of the heart; but in order to elevate it from the region of subjective caprice and waywardness, and to distinguish between that which is true and false in religion, we must appeal to an objective standard. That which enters the heart must first be discerned by the intelligence to be *true*. It must be seen as having in its own nature a *right* to dominate feeling, and as constituting the principle by which feeling must be judged.[75]

The organising frameworks of the *Varieties* are thus constructed around the extremes of religious experience; their subject matter, as Hall ungraciously put it, is 'the yellow literature of religious biography'.[76] It was an opinion shared by many of the contemporary psychologists of religion.[77] Whereas they had used experimental techniques to uncover the normal religious consciousness, James reverted to literary biography in his discussion of religious 'freaks and spores'. It was a stylistic retrogression, yet it reinforced, and in some ways even defined, the discipline as a whole.

James's reference to the extremes of religious behaviour has a twofold effect: first, it supports that concept of the normal religious consciousness developed in the early pedagogical writings on the psychology of religion. Although actual discussion of this normal consciousness is conspicuously missing from James's work, it still operates implicitly as a kind of absent cause, defining the nature of extremity and likewise receiving its own definition through the investigation of abnormal experience. Second, in his use of such exotic examples, James increases the ambit of the subliminal consciousness. It now encapsulates the transcendental realm, becoming an effective explanation across a massive variety of terrains:

> the transmarginal or subliminal region . . . is obviously the larger part of each of us, for it is the abode of everything that is latent and the reservoir of everything that passes unrecorded or unobserved. It contains, for example, such things as all our momentarily inactive memories, and it harbors the springs of all our obscurely motivated passions, impulses, likes, dislikes, and prejudices. Our intuitions, hypotheses, fancies, superstitions, persuasions, convictions, and in general all our non-rational operations, come from it. It is the source of our dreams and apparently they may return to it. In it arise whatever mystical experiences we may have, and our automatisms, sensory or motor; our life in hypnotic and 'hypnoid' conditions, if we are subject to such conditions; our delusions, fixed ideas, and hysterical accidents, if we are hysteric subjects; our supernormal cognitions, if such there be, and if we are telepathic subjects. It is also the fountainhead of much that feeds our religion. In persons deep in the religious life, as we have now abundantly seen – and this is my conclusion – the door to this region seems unusually wide open.[78]

The substitution of the subliminal for the transcendental returns the phenomena of religious experience to the narrative of personal history. Those small episodes through which individuals tried to escape the constraining frame of identity now demarcated the authoritative space of the new psychology. In the studies of prayer, inspiration, visions and revivalism which followed the publication of *Varieties*, the sacred drama of the religious life was played out inside the theatre of the individual mind. In the writings of the psychologists, religious experiences which had marked the limits of history now heralded the beginnings of ignorance in the consciousness of the modern subject.

The sexual history of hellfire

The power of this new rhetoric achieved its clearest exposition in the psychological commentaries on revivalism and the new evangelicalism. Revivalism had long been a target for psychiatric and medical intervention. Its main tenet – the surrender of the self to emotion and impulse and the scenes of disorder that its doctrines engendered – marked it out as a particular social threat.[79] This concern was not only limited to the secularising scientists: it was shared by a whole group of ministers and theologians who recognised and often suffered from the political challenge inherent in its doctrines.[80] Indeed, it was partly to counter this threat that the pioneer psychologists of religion advertised their services.[81] Starbuck, in his original volume, quoted David Starr Jordan, the President of Stanford University, on the necessity of discriminating between the different forms of religious revival. Jordan had complained that 'because revivals of religion have been productive of endless good under wise hands, is no reason why revivals of hysteria, of sensationalism and sensualism should not receive the rebuke they merit . . . It is certain that chronic religious excitement is destructive to higher life.'[82] Starbuck himself recognised two troubling aspects of revival phenomena. They could undo the higher inhibitory centres of the human brain and, additionally, they might subvert or undermine the natural growth of the religious consciousness.

Starbuck and Jordan's position was endorsed by George Coe. Discussing the revivalist's dogma of conversion through grace, Coe suggested that 'it is not less dangerous to religion than it is obnoxious to psychology', for it placed the facts of religious experience outside the realm of rational analysis.[83] The correct response, he urged, for psychologists and laymen was to reject such transcendentalising rhetoric and insist on the psychological continuity of the subject. This strategy, as we have already seen, was made possible by the assumption of the subliminal self.

In the *Varieties*, James maintains a similar position, insisting that the sense of personal transformation, and the motor automatisms enjoyed by revival converts, can easily be ascribed to the actions of the subconscious mind.[84] This discursive manoeuvre opened a narrative path which connected the atemporal event with the individual's history. Again, these narrative paths were usually developed around a normative framework. Frederick Morgan Davenport, perhaps the foremost writer on religious revivalism, insisted that most of its phenomena could be attributed to an uninhibited recrudescence of the individual's racial memory. Drawing on the psychological theories of the crowd developed by the French author Gustave Le Bon, Davenport argued that revival phenomena were atavisms from an earlier age.[85] Their perpetrators, he argued, were women, children, 'Negroes' and Celts: groups which lacked the ability to maintain self-control. 'These people', Davenport complains, 'with their visions and hallucinations . . . their sense of impotence in the hour of decision, and their tendency to abject self-surrender are a human type on its way to perfection. A careful dynamic study would find them mentally immature, rationally and volitionally imperfect, and I for one cannot believe that the feet of the supernatural deliberately chose to tread in the slime of the subliminal, the lower mystical marshlands of the human spirit, while avoiding the sunlit hills of full rational consciousness.'[86]

Davenport's narrative strategy, which contextualises spontaneous phenomena within the history of the race, was supplemented by a second, erotogenetic argument. Many authors, inspired by the scenes of unbridled passion unleashed during revival services, insisted that these events must have their origin within the evangelical audience's repressed sexuality. As the American sociologist W. I. Thomas wrote in 1907:

> The appeal made during the religious revival to an unconverted person had psychologically some resemblance to the attempt of the male to overcome the hesitancy of the female. In each case the will is set aside and strong suggestive means are used; and in both cases the appeal is not of the conflict type, but of an intimate, sympathetic and pleading kind. In the effort to make a moral adjustment, it consequently turns out that a technique is used which was derived originally from the sexual life, and the use, so to speak, of the sexual machinery for a moral adjustment involves, in some cases, the carrying over into the general process of some sexual manifestations. The emotional forms used and the states aroused are not entirely stripped of their sexual content.[87]

The racial and sexual narratives attached to revival phenomena carry a deeper implication. Although their authors worked hard to map the events of crowd evangelism back into their subjects' life histories, the sexual and racial imagery they use insinuates an external source for these occurrences. Thomas's comparison of conversion and seduction revealed the revival process as another example of the psychological concept of 'suggestion'. Suggestion had been defined by Boris Sidis as 'the intrusion into the mind of an idea; met with more or less opposition by the person; accepted uncritically at last; and realised reflectively almost automatically' – a definition which seemed to easily encompass the techniques of evangelical conversion.[88] Sidis himself was quick to claim spontaneous awakenings of revivalism as products of pathological suggestion: 'Religious revivalism is a social bane, it is far more dangerous to the life of society than drunkenness. As a sot man falls below the brute, as a revivalist he sinks below the sot . . . In the morbid condition of the body politic, the toxic germs of religious mania, the poisonous microbes of the revivals past, once more find a favourable soil.'[89]

The equation was commonplace, yet it threatened the whole enterprise of new psychology.[90] For, viewed from this perspective, the revivalist service went beyond the mere germination of a 'yeasty subconscious'; rather, its suggestive techniques return the subject to a state of childhood plasticity, undoing the complex web of history and identity woven by pedagogy and psychology. In the 'social contagion' of religious awakening, the individual is dissolved into a mimetic medium reforming around alien and revolutionary ideas.[91] The sources of the spiritual life were located beyond the horizons of the individual biography, in the adventures of language and society. As we shall see in the next chapter, the paper soul – so carefully constructed by the new psychologists – could be quickly consumed within the hellfire sermons of evangelical revivalism.

Notes

1 These mystics maintained a persistent hold on the Victorian imagination: Max Nordau, *Degeneration* (London: William Heinemann, 1911); Baron F. von Hugel, *The Mystical Element of Religion, as Studied in St Catherine of Genoa etc.* (London: J. M. Dent and Sons, 1908); T. T. Allen, *Autobiography of Mme Guyon* (London: Kegan Paul, 1898); [Anon.], 'Autobiography of a mystic', *Church Quarterly Review* 47 (1898), 180–207; H. Collins (ed.), *Spiritual Letters of Father Surin* (London: Art and Book Co., 1893). On the fascination that mysticism held for the fin de siècle literary imagination, see: Christina Mazzoni, 'Hysterical pregnancies and virgin births', (Ph.D. dissertation, Yale University, 1991).

2 The phrase was invented by James's friend and mentor, the narcotic philosopher Benjamin Paul Blood, see: *The Anaesthetic Revelation* (Amsterdam NY, 1873). On James's friendship with Blood: R. B. Perry, *The Thought and Character of William James* II (London: Humphrey Milford, [1935]), pp. 225–35, 658–61. For the influence of Blood on James's thought, see: William James, 'A pluralistic mystic', *Hibbert Journal* 8 (1909–10), 739–59.

3 William James, *Varieties of Religious Experience* (London: Fontana, 1960), pp. 373–4; James, [The subjective effects of nitrous oxide] appended to 'On

some Hegelisms', *Mind* 7 (1882), 206–8. See also James's endorsement of a similar report in, 'Consciousness under nitrous oxide', *Psychological Review* 5 (1898), 194–6.

4 James, *Varieties*, p. 374.

5 John Dewey argues that James abandoned his commitment to the self in his later writings, 'The vanishing subject in the philosophy of William James', *J. Phil.* 37 (1940), 589–99. See however Milic Capek's responses, 'The reappearance of the self in the last philosophy of William James', *J. Phil.* 38 (1941), 526–44.

6 William James, *Principles of Psychology* 1 [1890] (London: Dover, 1950), p. 226 and chs 9 and 10 *passim*. See also, James, 'The importance of individuals' [1890], repr. *The Will to Believe* (Cambridge MA: Harvard University Press, 1979), pp. 190–5.

7 William James, 'The absolute and the strenuous life' [1907], repr. *The Writings of William James*, ed. J. J. McDermott (Chicago: Chicago University Press, 1977), pp. 847–50; James, *Varieties*, pp. 401f.. For a good exposition of James's notion of the strenuous life, see: Don S. Browning, 'William James's philosophy of the person: the concept of the strenuous life', *Zygon* 10 (1975), 162–74; Browning, *Pluralism and Personality* (Lewisburg: Bucknell University Press, 1980), esp. chs 1, 10 and 11.

8 James, 'On some Hegelisms', 200.

9 This relationship has been explored by Michel de Certeau, *The Mystic Fable*, trans. M. B. Smith (Chicago: University of Chicago Press, 1992), pt 1; de Certeau, 'Mysticism', *Diacritics* 22 (1992), 11–25.

10 On the connection between the Eucharist and mysticism, Michel de Certeau, 'Surin's melancholy', in *Heterologies: Discourse on the Other*, trans. B. Massumi (Minneapolis: University of Minnesota Press, 1986), pp. 107f..

11 E. L. Schaub, 'The psychology of religion in America during the past quarter century', *Journal of Religion* 6 (1926), 115f.; Théodore Flournoy, 'Observations de psychologie religieuse', *Archives de Psychologie* 2 (1903), 34; Benjamin Beit-Hallahmi, 'Psychology of religion 1880–1930: the rise and fall of a psychological movement', *J.Hist.Behav.Sci.* 10 (1974), 84–90. On Germany, see: David Wulff, 'Experimental introspection and religious experience: the Dorpat school of religious psychology', *J.Hist.Behav.Sci.* 21 (1985), 131–50. In France the approach to religion remained largely psychiatric, e.g. E. Murisier, *Les maladies de sentiment religieux* (Paris: Felix Alcan, 1901).

12 James Bissett Pratt, 'The psychology of religion', *Harvard Theological Review* 1 (1908), 436; Peter Homans, 'Psychology and religion movement', in M. Eliade (ed.), *Encyclopaedia of Religions* X (New York: Macmillan, 1987), p. 69.

13 G. Hall, 'Moral education and will training', *Pedagogical Seminary* 2 (1892), 73; G. A. Coe, *Education in Religion and Morals* (New York: Fleming H. Revel, 1904), pp. 272–82.

14 J. O'Donnell, *The Origins of Behaviorism* (New York: New York University Press, 1985); K. Danziger, *Constructing the Subject* (Cambridge: Cambridge University Press, 1987); N. Rose, *The Psychological Complex* (London: Routledge Kegan Paul, 1985); Rose, *Governing the Soul* (London: Routledge, 1989).

15 C. J. Karrier, *The Individual, Society and Education* (Urbana: University of Illinois Press, 1986), chs. 4 and 5; Danziger, *Constructing the Subject*, ch. 8; O'Donnell, *Origins of Behaviorism*, pp. 151–8. On the child study movement: K. Stevens, 'Child study', in Foster Watson (ed.), *Encyclopaedia and Dictionary of Education* 1 (London: Pitman's, 1921), pp. 309–10; Sara E. Wiltse, 'A preliminary sketch of the history of child study in America', *Pedagogical Seminary* 3 (1895), 189–212. For its practical application in Britain: Carolyn Steedman, 'The mother made conscious', *HWJ* (1985), 49–63.

16 G. S. Hall, 'Philosophy in the United States', *Mind* 4 (1879), 90.

17 G. S. Hall, *Adolescence* 1 (London: Stanley Appleton, 1905), p. 326.

18 O'Donnell, *Origins of Behaviorism*, p. 143; Dorothy Ross, *G. Stanley Hall: The Psychologist as Prophet* (Chicago: Chicago University Press, 1972), ch. 15; Sara Carolyn Fisher, 'The psychological and educational work of G. Stanley Hall', *Am. J. Psychology* 36 (1925), esp. 20–49; C. J. Karrier, *The Individual, Society and Education*, 2nd edn (Urbana: University of Illinois Press, 1986), pp. 150–9.

19 R. Smith, *Inhibition: History and Meaning in the Sciences of Mind and Brain* (London: Free Association Books, 1992), pp. 142–62.

20 James, *Principles* 1, pp. 121, 122 and ch. 4 *passim*. For a summary of this chapter and its origins: John C. Malone, 'William James and habit: a century later', in M. Johnson and T. Henley, *Reflections on the Principles of Psychology after a Century* (Hillsdale: Lawrence Erlbaum Associates, 1990), pp. 135–68. See also, W. James, *Talks to Teachers* [1899] (London: Longmans, 1917), ch. 8. James illustrated the role of habit in this work by regurgitating most of this chapter from his *Principles*. On habit in education, see: Paul Radestock, *Habit and its Importance in Education* (Boston: D. C. Heath, 1886); G. L Rowe, *The Role of Habit in the Science of Education* (London: Methuen, 1907).

21 James, *Principles* 1, p. 122; James, *Talks to Teachers*, p. 68.

22 Coe, *Education*, pp. 139–40. For Coe (1862–1951), see his autobiographical essay: 'My own little theatre', in Vergilius Ferm (ed.), *Religion in Transition* (London: Macmillan, 1937), pp. 90–125; H. Shelton Smith, 'George Albert Coe: revaluer of values', *Religion in Life* 22 (1952–3), 46–57, and the special issue of the *Journal of Religious Education* 47 (March–April 1952) devoted to Coe's life and work.

23 Hall, 'Moral education and will training', 81; G. Hall, 'A study of anger', *Am. J. Psychology* 10 (1899), pp. 16–91.

24 Hall, 'Moral education and will training', fn. 82. The figures also appeared in Radestock, *Habit*, p. 92.

25 The language of investment is James's: To educate the nervous system 'is to fund and capitalise our acquisitions and live at ease upon the interests of the fund'. (*Talks to Teachers*, pp. 66–7).

26 On the natural depravity of children: Coe, *Education*, ch. 4. The change is usually dated to Horace Bushnell's publication of *Christian Nurture* in 1844. On Bushnell, see: Dugald MacFadyean, 'Bushnell', in *ERE* III, pp. 44–6.

27 On the role of punishment in the achievement of a historical consciousness, see: M. Foucault, *Discipline and Punish* (London: Penguin, 1979), p. 29.

28 G. Hall, 'Moral and religious training of children', *Princeton Review* 9 (1882), 26–48; Hall, 'Early sense of self', *Am. J. Psychology* 9 (1898), 351–95; Earl Barnes, 'The theological life of a child', *Pedagogical Seminary* 2 (1892), 442–8. See also E. D. Starbuck's later paper: 'The child-mind and child religion', *Biblical World* 30 (1908), 30–8, 101–12; Starbuck, Part II, *Biblical World* 31 (1909), 8–22. For a British equivalent, James Sully, *Studies of Childhood* (London: Longmans Green and Co., 1895), pp. 120–32, 506–13.

29 Georges Berguer, 'Revue et bibliographie générales de psychologie religieuse', *Archives de Psychologie* 14 (1914), 23; Pratt, 'Psychology of religion', 435f.; Pryns Hopkins, 'A critical survey of the psychologies of religion', *Character and Personality* 6 (1937), 17; Schaub, 'Psychology of religion', 125; Beit-Hallahmi, 'Psychology', 85; James Heisig, 'Psychology of religion', in Mircea Eliade (ed.), *Encyclopaedia of Religions* X (New York: Macmillan, 1987), p. 59; David Wulff, *The Psychology of Religion* (New York: Praeger, 1992), pp. 42–3: Hendrika Vande Kemp, 'G. Stanley Hall and the Clark School of religious psychology', *American Psychologist* 47 (1992), 290.

30 Coe, *Education*, p. 119 and chs 7 and 8 *passim*; G. Coe, *The Religion of a Mature Mind* (London: Fleming H. Revell, 1902), pp. 25–33, 73–107. The argument was based in the Christological insistence upon the contingency of selfhood (see above, ch. 1).

31 This idea of an infant evolution from a state of selflessness to moral self-consciousness was common among American psychologists: J. M. Baldwin, *Mental Development in the Child and the Race* (London: Macmillan, 1895); Baldwin, 'The genesis of the ethical self', *Philosophical Review* 6 (1897), 225–42; C. L. Herrick, 'The dynamic concept of the individual', *J.Phil.* 1 (1904), 373–8; J. Dashiel Stoops, 'The moral individual', *J.Phil.* 3 (1905), 141–8. For a British example, see Sully, *Childhood*, pp. 109–20.

32 Hall, 'Sense of self', 282.

33 Coe, *Education*, pp. 99, 93.

34 Stoops drew on Plato's equation of state government and inner government to argue that the movement from sense experience to volition was analogous to the movement from the labouring to the executive classes ('Moral individual', 142f.). Cf. M. Foucault, 'On governmentality', *Ideology and Consciousness* 6 (1979), 5–22; Foucault, 'Omnes et singulatim: towards

a criticism of political reason', in S. McMurrin (ed.), *The Tanner Lectures on Human Value* (Utah: University of Utah Press, 1982); Foucault, *History of Sexuality* III, *The Care of the Self* (Harmondsworth: Penguin, 1990).

35 John Dewey, 'The place of religious emotion' [1886], repr., Dewey, *The Early Works, 1882–1898* I, ed. Jo Ann Boydston (Carbondale: Southern Illinois University Press, 1975), pp. 90–2; G. Coe, *The Spiritual Life* (New York: Eaton and Mains, 1902), pp. 71–87.

36 Hall, *Adolescence* 1, p. 242; Hall, 'Moral and religious training', 45; W. H. Burnham, 'A study of adolescence', *Pedagogical Seminary* 1 (1891), esp. 183–4; J. Dashiel Stoops, 'The psychology of religion', *J. Phil.* 2 (1905), 514–18. For medicine, see: John M. Fothergill, *The Physiologist in the Household* (London: Balliere, Tindall and Cox, 1880).

37 Hall, *Adolescence* II, pp. 72, 333.

38 *Ibid.*, pp. 342, 349–54; cf. Arthur Daniels, 'The new life: a study in regeneration', *Am. J. Psychology* 6 (1893), 61–103. On the ethnological equation of the religious impulse and the social instinct, see: Henry Marshall, 'The religious instinct', *Mind* n.s. 6 (1897), 40–58; Marshall, 'The function of religious expression', *Mind* n.s. 6 (1897), 182–203.

39 For Starbuck, see his autobiographical essay: 'Religion's use of me', in Vergilius Ferm (ed.), *Religion in Transition* (London: Macmillan, 1937), pp. 201–60; H. J. Booth, *Edwin Diller Starbuck: Pioneer in the Psychology of Religion* (Washington DC: University Press of America, 1981). For Leuba, see his essay in Ferm, *Religion in Transition*, pp. 173–200; K. E. McBride, 'James H. Leuba', *Am. J. Psychology* 60 (1947), 645–6.

40 On the use of statistics in psychical research, see: Ian Hacking, 'Telepathy: origins of randomization in experimental design', *Isis* 79 (1988), 427–51.

41 Hall, *Adolescence* II, p. 342. On the questionnaire, see: Danziger, *Constructing the Subject*, pp. 75f.; Sheldon H. White, 'Child study at Clark University, 1894–1904', *J.Hist.Behav.Sci.* 26 (1990), 131–50.

42 E. D. Starbuck, 'A study of conversion', *Am. J. Psychology* 8 (1898), 269–70. Leuba's questionnaires were published in *The Presbyterian*, *The Christian*, *The Outlook* and non-denominational magazines such as *The Monist* and *The Open Court*. They covered almost identical material to those of Starbuck. See, J. H. Leuba, 'The psychology of religious phenomena', *Am. J. Psychology* 7 (1896), 371–85; Leuba, 'The psychology of religion', *Open Court* 14 (1900), 251–3; Leuba, 'The contents of the religious consciousness', *Monist* 11 (1901), pp. 536f.. Coe quizzed local YMCA members: *Spiritual Life*, pp. 261–76.

43 Starbuck, 'Religion's use of me', p. 225.

44 E. D. Starbuck, *The Psychology of Religion: An Empirical Study of the Growth of Religious Consciousness* (London: Walter Scott, 1899), p. 30. Cf. Leuba, 'Religious phenomena', 371.

45 Starbuck, *Psychology of Religion*, pp. 65, 66, ch. 6.

46 *Ibid.*, pp. 221f.

47 *Ibid.* chs. 6, 16–17. T. S. Clouston, *Clinical Lectures in Mental Diseases*, 2nd edn (London: Churchill, 1887); H. Havelock Ellis, *Man and Woman* (London: Walter Scott and Co., 1894), esp. ch 13. On this form of argument: Lorraine Daston, 'The naturalized female intellect', *Science in Context* 5 (1992), 209–35.

48 Starbuck, 'Religion's use of me'; Jeyhun Kim, 'The development of functional psychology of religion in America, 1900–1925', *Journal of Korean History of Society* 12 (1990), 110–12.

49 Starbuck, *Psychology of Religion*, p. 401. For psychiatry, see: W. Hammond, *Spiritualism and Allied Causes of Nervous Derangement* (London: H. K. Lewis, 1876), pp. 251f.; H. Maudsley, *The Pathology of Mind*, 3rd edn (London: Macmillan and Co., 1879), pp. 143–4. For literature, see: John Maynard, *Victorian Discourses on Sex and Religion* (Cambridge: Cambridge University Press, 1993). This tradition was censured by James (*Varieties*, p. 33fn.) and Trumbull Ladd, see his, *The Philosophy of Religion* (London: Longmans Green, 1905), pp. 292–301.

50 Josiah Moses [aka Morse], *Pathological Aspects of Religions* (Worcester MA: Clark University Press, 1906), ch. 3; Moses, 'The pathology of religions', *American Journal of Religious Psychology* 1 (1905), 228–33. Leuba later took up a mitigated version of this position, see his, 'Tendances fondamentales des mystiques chrétiens', *Revue Philosophique* 54 (1902), 1–36, 441–87; Leuba, 'A propos de l'érotomanie des mystiques chrétiens', *ibid.*, 57 (1904), 70–1; Leuba, 'On the psychology of a group of Christian mystics', *Mind* n.s. 14 (1905), 15–27; Bernard de Montmorand, 'L'érotomanie des mystiques chrétiens', *Revue Philosophique* 56 (1903), 382–93; de Montmorand, 'Des mystiques en dehors de l'extase', *ibid.* 58 (1904), 602–35; de Montmorand, 'Les états mystiques', *ibid.*, abstracted *J.Phil.* 2 (1903), 523–5. For an overview, see Hopkins, 'Critical survey', 29–33.

51 T. Schroeder, 'Religion and sensualism as connected by a clergymen', *American Journal of Religious Psychology* 3 (1908), 28; Schroeder, 'The sex-determinant in Mormon theology', *Alienist and Neurologist* 29 (1908), 208–22; Schroeder, 'Outline for a study of the erotogenesis of religion', *American. Journal of Religious Psychology* 5 (1910), 394–401. For Schroeder, see: J. Van Teslaar, 'Religion and sex', *Psychoanalytic Review* 2 (1915), 81–92; Nancy Sankey-Jones, *Bibliography of Théodore Schroeder etc.* (Cos Cob CT: n.p., 1934).

52 The formulation could also be seen as an advance on contemporary psychiatry and psychophysiology. Bain had depicted conversion as the sudden domination of a external idea which formed a new habit. This model left open the possibility of divine intervention: William Cyples, *An Enquiry into the Process of Human Experience* (London: Strahan and Co., 1881); [Anon.], 'On brain science in relation to religion', *Church Quarterly Review* 13 (1881), 107–28.

53 Starbuck, *Psychology of Religion*, p. 134.

54 Cf. L. P. Jacks's article of 1911, which described the misery produced in a young teacher by Starbuck and Leuba's work. Following the psychologists this earnest Christian had kept a personal chart of his soul's development secreted in a collar drawer. This academic preparation apparently thwarted his conversion: 'A psychologist among the saints', *Hibbert Journal* 10 (1911–12), 130–56.

55 James, *Varieties*, p. 214.

56 *Ibid.*, p. 368.

57 *Ibid.*, pp. 366–407. James's argument drew on Crichton Browne's interpretation of epilepsy given in his *Cavendish Lectures on Dreamy Mental States* (London: Balliere, Tindall and Cox, 1895).

58 T. Ribot, *The Diseases of Personality* [1887], trans. J. Fitzgerald, *Significant Contributions to the History of Psychology*, ed. Daniel N. Robinson (Washington DC: University Press of America, 1977).

59 Modern psycho-historians have argued that James's understanding of the sick soul derived from his personal experience of mental breakdown: Cushing Strout, 'William James and the twice-born sick soul', *Daedalus* 97 (1968), 1062–82; R. J. Richards, *Darwin and the Emergence of Evolutionary Theories of Mind and Behavior* (Chicago: University of Chicago Press, 1992), pp. 412–22.

60 Quoted in James, *Varieties*, p. 164.

61 *Ibid.*, p. 163. Similar conclusions had been reached by James's colleague Josiah Royce, 'The case of John Bunyan', *Psychological Review* 1 (1894), 22–34, 134–51, 230–40.

62 James, *Varieties*, p. 102; cf. James's attack on the evangelical consciousness of sin in *Principles* 1, pp. 311f..

63 James, *Varieties*, pp. 97–100; James, 'Talks to students', in *Talks to Teachers*, pp. 248–54.

64 R. Bucke, *Cosmic Consciousness: A Study in the Evolution of the Human Mind* [1901] (New York: E. P. Dutton, 1960), p. 232. On Bucke, see: S. E. D. Shortt, *Victorian Lunacy* (Cambridge: Cambridge University Press, 1986).

65 James, *Varieties*, p. 98.

66 Quoted in *ibid.*, p. 113.

67 *Ibid.*, pp. 121f..

68 *Ibid.*, pp. 212–13.

69 W. James, 'The hidden self', *Scribner's Magazine* 7 (1890), 361.

70 James, *Varieties*, p. 232; cf. his assessment of genius in Lecture VIII of *William James on Exceptional Mental States: The 1896 Lowell Lectures*, ed. Eugene Taylor (Amherst: University of Massachusetts Press, 1984), pp. 149–65; James, 'Degeneration and genius', *Psychological Review* 2 (1895), 287–94.

71 James, *Varieties*, lectures 11–13 on saintliness.

72 *Ibid.*, p. 242

73 *Ibid.*, pp. 267, 498.

74 *Ibid.*, p. 411; see also T. Flournoy, 'The varieties of religious experience', *Revue Philosophique* (1902), repr. *The Philosophy of William James* (London: Heinemann, 1911), p. 236; J. Arthur Hill, *Religion and Modern Psychology* (London: William Rider and Son, 1911), ch. 11.

75 J. Caird, *Introduction to the Philosophy of Religion* (Glasgow: James MacLehose 1880), p. 174, quoted in James, *Varieties*, p. 416. For John Caird, see: E. Caird, 'Memoir', in J. Caird, *The Fundamental Ideas of Christianity* 1 (Glasgow: James MacLehose, 1899), pp. xi–cxli.

76 Hall, *Adolescence* II, p. 293.

77 J. G. Hibden, 'The Varieties of Religious Experience', *Psychological Review* 10 (1903), 180–6; J. H. Leuba, 'Professor William James' interpretation of religious experience', *International Journal of Ethics* 14 (1904), 325f.; E. D. Starbuck, 'The Varieties of Religious Experience', *Biblical World* 24 (1904), 103–4.

78 James, *Varieties*, pp. 462–3.

79 Daniel Hack Tuke, 'Epidemic insanity', in Tuke (ed.), *Dictionary of Psychological Medicine* 1 [1892], repr. (New York: Arno Press, 1976), pp. 434–40; David W. Yandell, 'Epidemic convulsions', *Brain* 4 (1882), 339–50; Ronald L. and Janet S. Numbers, 'Millerism and madness', *Bulletin of the Menninger Clinic* 49 (1985), 289–320.

80 There was a long tradition of evangelical literature on psychic management in revivals: e.g. Jonathan Edwards, *Treatise on Religious Affections* [1735]; Charles G. Finney, *Lectures on Revivals of Religion* [1835] (London: Marshall, 1910); R. A. Torrey, *How to Conduct and Promote a Successful Revival* (Chicago: F. Revell, 1906).

81 John Jentz, 'Liberal evangelism and psychology during the Progressive Era', *Journal of Religious Thought* 33 (1976), 67–9.

82 Starbuck, *Psychology of Religion*, p. 176 and ch. 13 *passim*. Hall, *Adolescence* II, p. 301.

83 G. Coe, 'What does modern psychology permit us to believe in respect to regeneration?', *American Journal of Theology* 12 (1908), 361–2.

84 James, *Varieties*, pp. 229–36, 250.

85 G. Le Bon, *The Crowd* [1895] (London: Fisher Unwin, 1896); Berguer, 'Revue et bibliographie', 32–3. For the background of crowd psychology, see: Jaap van Ginneken, *Crowds, Psychology and Politics, 1871–1899* (Cambridge: Cambridge University Press, 1992).

86 F. M. Davenport, *Primitive Traits in Religious Revivals* [1905], repr. (New York: AMS Press, 1972), p. 280; Davenport, 'The religious revival and the new evangelism', *Outlook* 79 (1905), 895–9; A. C. Haddon, [Review of Davenport], *Mind* n.s. 15 (1906), 111. On Davenport (b. 1866), Professor of Law and Political Science at Howton College, see: *ABA* no. 402.

87 W. I. Thomas, *Sex and Society* (London: T. Fisher Unwin, 1907), pp. 115f..

On Thomas (1863–1947), Professor of Sociology at Chicago University, see: Roland Turner (ed.), *Thinkers of the Twentieth Century*, 2nd edn (London: St James, 1987), pp. 561–2.

88 B. Sidis, *The Psychology of 'Suggestion'* (New York: D. Appleton, 1903), p. 15. Cf. Freud's definition in 'Preface to the translation of Bernheim's *Suggestion*' [1888–9], in *SE* 1, p. 82; Janet's definition in his *The Mental State of Hystericals*, trans. C. R. Corson, repr. *Significant Contributions to the History of Psychology* Series C, II, ed. D. N. Robinson (Washington DC: University Press of America, 1977), p. 251. For Sidis (1867–1923), see: *AmericanDB* IX, pp. 152–3.

89 Sidis, *Suggestion*, p. 360, also chs. 17, 18, 23; B. Sidis, 'A study of mental epidemics', *Century Magazine* 52 (1896), 849–53. For a criticism, see: William Trotter, 'Herd instinct and its bearing on the psychology of civilised man', *Sociological Review* 1 (1908), 238f..

90 Coe, *Spiritual Life*, pp. 146f.; F. Granger, *The Soul of a Christian: A Study in the Religious Experience* (London: Methuen, 1900), pp. 74–80, 101–7; Morton Prince, 'The psychology of sudden conversion', *Journal of Abnormal Psychology* 1 (1906), 43–54; H. Woolston, 'Religious emotion', *Am. J. Psychology* 13 (1902), 73; Georges Dumas, 'Contagion mentale: épidémies mentales – folies collectives', *Revue Philosophique* 71 (1911), 225f..

91 Mikkel Borch-Jacobsen, *The Freudian Subject* (Stanford: Stanford University Press, 1988), pp. 135–231; on mimesis, pp. 13–51; Leon Chertok and Isabelle Stengers, *A Critique of Psychoanalytic Reason* (Stanford: Stanford University Press, 1992).

4

The self triumphant

Open wide our self-made prisons (*'R Hwn Sy'n Gyrru Mellt Hedeg*)

'Wales' read the headlines of the *Liverpool Echo* in January 1905, '[is] in the grip of supernatural forces'.[1] The country was in a state of millennial fervour. Across the principality the familiar pattern of religious life was rent asunder as women and workers were being driven into public ecstasies and seized by religious raptures. Chapels and communities were transformed. The familiar procedures of the Sunday meeting were abandoned for the marathon sessions of praise and prayer. Other papers reported how natural law seemed to have lost its jurisdiction across the Principality. The nation was riven by portents and omens, from the mysterious lights and fiery figures which illuminated the skies above Cardigan Bay to the many hauntings and prophecies. Predictions of a global religious awakening were uttered by a host of prophets that included the dying Dean of St David's and the talking baby of Bethesda.[2] Young children gave inspired Welsh sermons although it was claimed that they hardly knew a single word of the language.[3] It seemed as if the country was realising the biblical promises given in the Acts of the Apostles and the Book of Joel: 'I will pour out my spirit upon all flesh; and your sons and your daughters shall prophesy, your old men shall dream dreams, your young men shall see visions.'[4]

This twentieth-century Pentecost – the Welsh Revival of 1904–5 – was perhaps the last flourish of mass resistance to the triumph of the historicist perspective.[5] For a brief moment, the new rules of historical and psychological discourse were rent asunder. Their core assumptions – the narrative exclusion of the supernatural and the containment of the sacred within the field of memory – were challenged as miraculous events tore apart the fabric of everyday life. The movement began on the edge of industrial Wales, in Cardiganshire and Carmarthenshire, early in 1904. By the end of 1906 it was claimed that it had spread through Northern Europe, Russia and India, Madagascar, the West Indies and the United States.[6] It was characterised by charismatic worship and its converts were credited with the establishment of the Pentecostal Churches.[7] Yet today the revival's story has been largely forgotten. It gains only brief mentions in books on Welsh history and politics, with its close study largely relegated to the work of wistful evangelicals or latter-day chroniclers of the supernatural.[8] In these accounts, the revival tends to achieve merely an anecdotal presence. Most of the evangelical histories of the awakening are content simply to catalogue the thousands of conversions and transformed services that accompanied the acknowledged leaders of the movement. They structure their accounts around the inspired itinerary of Evan Roberts (1878–1951), the trainee minister and sometime farrier who was widely seen as the revival's figurehead, detailing the trials and triumphs of his missions across Wales and Merseyside.[9] While some writers attempt to trace the social context of the awakening, noting the widespread disruption wrought by the industrialisation of the South Wales valleys and the concomitant migration from the rural west, there is little agreement as to the revival's extent or its immediate causes.[10] The movement's emergence has been attributed variously to the power of secret prayers, a conservative reaction to the decline of Welsh culture, the psychological frustration of the disenfranchised, the work of the Presbyterian Forward Movement, the appearance of new media and transport technologies, the example of the Keswick Holiness Movement, the oppressive effects of English colonialism and the unsettling effects of Roberts's sexual magnetism.[11]

These attempts to trace an evangelical or sociological explanation for the revival sit uneasily with the beliefs and aspirations of the movement's participants. Although its causes were widely debated at the time and many claimed a constitutive role in the awakening, the general consensus was that its origins lay outside the compass of human understanding. As one enthusiastic supporter proclaimed during an impromptu debate on the revival held at Tylorstown railway station in December 1904: 'Originate be hanged! . . . Every Johnny is trying to hang his hat on the peg of the revival and wants to put up his little self as having set the ball rolling. It is too mean and paltry a question to be answered. Who cares where it originated so long as it has come.'[12]

This suspicion of historical explanations is a recurring feature of early commentaries on the awakening. The Cwmavon minister Howell Elvet

Lewis argued that no narrative or chronology could be attached to the revival since 'dates, places and persons were only the outward and visible symbols of a wave ... that has no everyday name, no secular explanation'.[13] Rhys Bevan Jones, a prominent Welsh evangelist, believed that: 'The very most that has been (or can be said) can only be glimpses after all, and glimpses too of that which has come *within the ken of a finite human being*. God alone can unfold what He has done.'[14] Evan Roberts himself denied his own role in the awakening, saying simply: 'We do not know how the revival originated; ... nobody knows how: nothing but the day of judgement will reveal it.'[15]

The suspicion of history that characterises so many of the revival reports is bound up with a particular version of selfhood. This is a model of subjectivity that stood in direct opposition to the dominant ideals of nineteenth-century Britain, as described in previous chapters. As a contributor to the *Contemporary Review* noted:

> Our working conceptions of psychology and sociology are permeated with ideas of causation, of the self-identity of human beings, of the essentially gradual character of growth that is to be thought of as permanent or real. But if we attempt to understand what revivalism means to those actively engaged in it, we find that they set forth the possibility and the necessity of a sudden and fundamental change in human personality, and further, that they wholly repudiate the notion that personal influence can itself bring about such change.[16]

This oppositional aspect of revivalism may in part be traced back to the eighteenth-century theology of Welsh Calvinist Methodism. The doctrine of sovereign grace, developed in the evangelical writings of Daniel Rowlands and William Williams Pantycelyn, had long insisted on the futility of human action and the individual pursuit of salvation.[17] Yet the intense hostility to notions of historical causation and selfhood that characterised the 1904–5 revival marked a new departure. This innovation, which would lend the awakening most of its radical and antinomian aspects, was bound up with the career and ideas of Evan Roberts.[18]

The ecstatic theology of Evan Roberts

Roberts's role in the awakening has been widely disputed. Certainly, successful revival meetings were being held long before his mission began. Few doubted however that his participation changed the nature of the revival and many claimed that his spiritual baptism on 29 September 1904 marked the true point at which the movement took hold. It happened in the Cardiganshire village of Blaenanerch during a mission meeting led by the New Quay Christian Endeavour Group, under the guidance of their minister, Joseph Jenkins, and the lay preacher, Seth Joshua.[19] Although Roberts was only 26 years old and still training for the ministry, his experience and the media attention later devoted to it, were to transform him into a leader of the revival. He provided a vivid description of the service to a reporter from the *Western Mail*:

> The meeting having been opened was handed over to the Spirit. I was conscious that I would have to pray . . . I felt a living force come into my bosom. It held my breath and my legs shivered . . . The living force grew, and grew and I was almost bursting . . . I would have burst if I had not prayed. What boiled me was that verse 'God commanding his love'. I fell on my knees with my arms over the seat in front of me, and the tears and perspiration flowed freely. I thought blood was gushing forth. Mrs Davies, New Quay came to wipe my face . . . For about two minutes it was fearful. I cried 'Bend me! Bend me! Bend us!' Then 'Oh! Oh! Oh! Oh!' What bent me was God commending his love and I not seeing anything in it to commend. After I was bent a wave of peace came over me.[20]

Roberts's conversion was significant, not so much because it marked the spiritual birth of the future 'leader' of the revival, but because it demonstrated how such experiences allowed marginal individuals to assume control of religious services. As Eliseus Howells, a minister present at the Blaenanerch meeting, wrote afterwards:

> As the Revival proceeded, Jenkins and the other brethren who had been concerned with these conventions, were worried because they thought the word was being dethroned, and that men were readier to speak to God rather than to listen to what God had to say to them through the preaching of the word . . . The leadership passed to a young man's hands, to the hands of one considered less suitable than themselves . . . The Revival took a very different path from the one they wished it to take.[21]

This transfer of power and the pastorate's loss of control over the revival movement was bound up with the critique of history and self-hood developed in Roberts's theology.

Roberts's theology was born out of the conventional Christian distinction between the individual self and the divine soul, yet his teachings reveal none of the sympathy or celebration of human personality that animates the work of his Protestant contemporaries.[22] In his very first sermon, written while studying for the ministry in June 1904, Roberts denounced the self as a chimerical creation. It was a mixture of worldly opinion and carnal desire that divided man from his real relationship with God. Thus he concluded his lesson by warning his audience that 'the rejection of Christ may be looked at as resting upon two things (i) a sense of sufficiency and (ii) a sense of independence'.[23]

The autonomy and plenitude of this selfish ego stands in marked contrast to the emptiness and dependence of the divine soul. As Roberts makes clear, the soul lacks any real content or definition: it is simply that aspect of the individual which stands in direct relation with God. 'God, through Adam's transgression left his home in the soul, and that therefore left a depth of emptiness to be felt in us ... The feeling of emptiness is in our soul and it needs to be filled ... it is impossible for anything visible to the senses, finite, carnal and temporal, to satiate the deep inward longing of an immortal soul.'[24]

Roberts's teachings place the fundamental aspect of the individual outside the ambit of conventional knowledge and possibility of historical representation. Indeed he makes the transcendence and destruction of personal history a necessary step in the achievement of individual salvation. He urged his followers to escape the snares of personal identity by engaging in a process of continuous conversion: a process in which the accreted memories and desires of the incipient self are repeatedly cast over. This process is exemplified in the crucifixion of Christ, which Roberts understood as an allegory of the process of conversion: 'The Cross is the power of God, the power of God even to deliver us from self. It works death to the life of the self ... Face the Cross, and you will trample on sin, self, and all the powers of darkness. But before we realise this conquest we must do what God did. He gave his all to the Cross. We too, must yield all, that is give up your will to God.'[25]

Yet Roberts did not believe that the promise of conversion could ever be entirely fulfilled. There was always a risk that self would return if the individual relaxed or took pride in his or her achievements. This danger was driven home by Roberts during a discussion with students at the Theological College, Bala: 'Do not think you will be entirely rid of sin in this life even after the baptism of the Spirit. Self will persist; you can never shake hands with self and bid it good-bye.'[26]

Because of this risk, the revivalist urged a form of perpetual vigilance, in which one's actions and desires are endlessly scrutinised for signs of self. In a letter to his college friend Sidney Evans, Roberts explained how the Holy Spirit aided the ongoing process of surveillance during a revival service:

> Like Moses, may you be allowed . . . to speak the *Words of God*. The Evil One often tempts me to speak *my own words*: but, Praise Him! the Holy Spirit through His wisdom overcomes me, overcomes the world, and the Devil, in all his wiles: and so He gives me words and ideas to answer to the need of the crowd . . .

> . . . Another way he has, is to try to get me to push myself to the front. But! Oh! that would be a curse to me, would spoil the work and rob God of glory. Really is it not important to keep ourselves in the background? I remember how in a meeting a voice said to me, 'Cry out the word, Judgement. Judgement!!' But, Praise be to the Spirit, I was prevented from doing so, else 'Mr Self' would have manifested himself at once.[27]

In his attempts to escape from 'Mr Self', Roberts claimed to have been led by the Holy Spirit to a series of techniques which would turn conversion from a singular event into a continual practice. These techniques were revealed to the public during his first revival service in his home town of Loughor. Roberts entitled these methods the 'amodau diwygiad', literally the 'conditions of revival', but widely rendered into English as the 'Four Articles of Faith'.

First   The past must be cleared: every sin must be confessed to God
Second   Everything doubtful must be removed once and for all from out of our lives
Third   Obedience prompt and implicit to the Holy Spirit
Fourth   Public confession must be made of Christ.[28]

Modern commentators following Michel Foucault will probably see the 'Four Articles' as 'technologies of the self', for they provide a series of practical and intellectual techniques through which individuals can engage with and transform their own identities.[29] The first two articles are intended to create a distance between the personal self (our felt memory and identity) and lived experience. In contrast to the Victorian romantics, Roberts did not believe that autobiographical narration instils a sense of personal coherence or self-identification: rather, the practice reveals the ego as something quite removed and foreign.[30] Roberts's own life was to develop into a struggle to overcome his finite self. As he wrote in a letter to his future biographer, Rev. D. M. Phillips:

What a commotion there is in the tents! My soul is a kind of tabernacle, and self dwelling in innumerable tents around it, and what takes place is the slaughtering of the troublesome, howling, thankless rebellious inhabitants, and so on ... I see today that 'self' has its houses, palaces and dens. But how cunning this can be in his den! But away, after him! Behold he fleeth into his cave! Here cometh the divine searchlight on its strong wings. Satanic, Ha! Ha! Ha! Lo, self is made a corpse by the pointed arrow.[31]

This inner struggle achieved a very public presence. In revival services across South Wales, Roberts relived the dramatic experience of self-crucifixion he had first suffered at Blaenanerch. Audiences described him writhing in agony during meetings and often collapsing to the ground.[32] The only relief from these sufferings lay in the achievement of Roberts's third article of faith, the practice of obedience.

Obedience to the Holy Spirit was the central tenet of Roberts's ministry. During his spiritual baptism at Blaenanerch, Roberts had repeatedly beseeched the Holy Spirit to 'bend' him ('plygu fi') before Its will. In his sermons, he frequently stressed the need for 'total and implicit obedience to the Holy Spirit ... You must do anything and everything; anywhere and everywhere.'[33] In his private advice to friends he argued that, 'Obedience must be given in the smallest thing. It looks small to us: but when obeying the blessing comes.'[34] And in his widely reprinted message to the churches, the young evangelist urged that they could only be redeemed if 'they will but learn the great lesson of obedience to the voice of the Holy Spirit. Obedience! Obedience! Obedience!'[35]

Such acts of obedience, Foucault argues, provide an effective strategy for self-transformation in so far as they remove the individual's autonomy and surrender his or her body to an external agency. As with the spiritualist trance or historical writing, obedience creates a situation in which the narrative of another runs through the body and guides future action.[36] It is a moment at which, in Foucault's words, 'You will have become the *logos* or the *logos* will have become you.'[37] Roberts believed he had achieved this state. As he noted in his diary: 'I carry not the gospel, the Gospel carries me.'[38]

However, the analogy between Roberts's position and the transformative practices that Foucault identified in the ethical systems of the Stoics and the Church Fathers can only be pushed so far. Whereas the early Christians achieved obedience through reference to an acknowledged set of rules, Roberts's pursuit of passivity was complicated by the fact that he depended on the ineffable instruction of the Spirit. Lacking any point of institutional or doctrinal reference, he was forced to rely on psychological and quasi-magical techniques.[39] At the beginning of his mission he experimented with bibliomancy, writing out questions for the Paraclete on small scraps of paper in the hope that the Spirit would deign to reply.[40] Although this ritual failed, the evangelist was rescued by the appearance of new forms of internal inspiration. His life and mission were to be guided by a series of religious visions and the felt presence of the Holy Spirit.

The majority of Roberts's visions occurred in the early stages of his mission: of the twenty-one recorded, fourteen occurred while he was still in his student lodgings.[41] Most of these visions were simple portents of the revival's success. In the gardens of his tutor's house in Newcastle Emlyn, Roberts witnessed the triumph of Christ over Satan; in his home chapel, Moriah in Loughor, he saw the final defeat of the four horsemen of the Apocalypse; and, on three separate occasions, he was encouraged by the appearance of a misty figure, like the Angel of Revelation, promising the imminent redemption of 100,000 souls.[42]

As well as encouraging Roberts in his mission, these visions provided an ostensible demonstration of his submission to a higher power. As the Jesuit historiographer Michel de Certeau has argued, the religious vision reverses the priority of sight. Whereas normal vision demonstrates our dominance over another, since it is an act in which we impose our apprehensions and interpretations onto an object, the religious vision always escapes objectification and instead impresses its own meaning upon us. The vision provides an oblique demonstration of the ways in which the mystic has changed from one who acts upon others to one who is acted upon.[43] Moreover, the unlikeliness of the visionary juxtapositions experienced by Roberts, in which apocalyptic scenes were played out in familiar domestic environments, provided a striking demonstration of the fragility of our common-sense apprehension of the world.[44]

Roberts's apparent achievement of this selfless state of mediumship turned him into a powerful yet unaccountable figure. He was pursued by devotees and journalists as a religious leader yet he denied his own role in the awakening. He urged his followers to ignore his life and character, explaining: 'When you go to the window, you do not go to look at the glass but through it to the scenery beyond. Then look through me and see the Holy Spirit.'[45] Similarly, he told reporters who questioned him about his life: 'I have nothing whatever to give you, not even a photograph. I have nothing whatever to tell you. I know nothing except what I am told by the Holy Spirit.'[46] In his interviews he refused to divulge any biographical details, telling the *Western*

Mail correspondent, 'Awstin' (Tom Davies), that 'I would rather keep myself in the background.'[47] W. B. Hodgson of the *London Daily News* recorded that '[Evan Roberts] was a little afraid of me', adding that 'he regards journalists as some kind of cold, passionless vivisectors'.[48] This judgement was endorsed by a writer for the Liverpool magazine *Porcupine,* who remarked on the fact that Roberts 'hates being photographed, and declines to speak into a gramophone'.[49]

This refusal of history, identity and agency had a series of political effects. Roberts's delegation of his speech and will to the command of the divine placed his actions outside the jurisdiction of the traditional leaders in the community. A good example of this process was provided in an exchange between Roberts and John Morgan Jones, the minister of Pembroke Terrace Chapel, Cardiff:

> Mr Jones asked the revivalist if he was coming to Cardiff on the morrow.
> 'No' replied Evan Roberts with considerable emphasis.
> 'Are you still too unwell to come?' questioned Mr Jones.
> 'No it isn't that,' returned Mr Roberts, 'I am feeling quite well and strong.'
> Obvious surprise was depicted on Mr Jones' face, and he again asked the revivalist why he was not coming to Cardiff.
> 'The Cardiff meetings have been on my mind for five days,' replied Mr Roberts. 'I have prayed constantly for guidance, and the answer of the Spirit is thou art not to go.'
> Mr Jones observed that there was a close connection between the body and the mind. Was Mr Roberts sure that he did not mistake bodily weakness or reluctance for the answer of the Spirit?
> 'I am as certain that the Spirit has spoken to me,' returned the revivalist still speaking in Welsh, 'as I am of my own existence.'
> Mr Jones wanted to know if Mr Roberts would come in the future.
> 'Yes as soon as I get permission,' was the reply, 'and not before.'
> 'What about the girls? Shall they come?' asked Mr Jones.
> 'No!' with emphasis, 'they shall not, I have asked the Spirit about that too.' . . .
> . . . In the course of a conversation with a local ministerial friend, Mr Roberts declared that the voice said 'If you go I shall not go with you' and on its being pointed out to him that his non-appearance would be a serious disappointment to many in Cardiff he said: 'I can't help it I'm not going with this voice ringing in my ears.' He was then asked 'What about the crowds that will be expecting you' and he replied 'That is it I want to be kept in the background', 'Is it that you do not want to go to Cardiff?' 'Oh no, I will go anywhere he leads, but I will not go anywhere without him.'[50]

Through reference to the desires of the Holy Spirit, Roberts's personal responsibility is dissolved. His motivation is ascribed to a force which lies beyond the criticism and authority of others. The Holy Spirit bestowed power without responsibility. As de Certeau has argued, 'it is all the more authorising precisely because It is authorised by no reason or system of thought'. Unlike the conventional claims of scientific authority there is no point of reference against which such divine claims can be judged. Rather, as de Certeau has it – 'it is not the experience that guarantees the existence of God: God, on the contrary, guarantees the experience'.[51]

As the revival progressed, Roberts's political and psychological transformation became more marked. At the end of February 1905, the Paraclete ordered him to retire from his mission for one week. The seven days of silence which followed were presented by the press as an episode akin to Christ's forty days in the wilderness, although Roberts's inspired exile was limited to one week in a bedroom in Neath.[52] From the beginning, he felt assured of the presence of the Spirit after an inner voice directed him to read Isaiah 54.10.[53] In his solitude he became conscious of a closer communion and a need for greater vigilance as he surrendered to the Lord, in 'every matter, however insignificant'.[54] Through this practice, he was led to a deeper sense of inspired authority. Just after 5.20pm on 2 March, he was led to write:

> 5.21 – Voice: Take thy pen and write: – Lo, I am the Lord, Who hath lifted thee up from the depth . . . Open thine hand, and I will fill it with power. Open thy mouth, and I will fill it with wisdom. Open thy heart and I will fill it with love . . . To kings turn thyself and say, 'Bend.' To knights, 'Submit ye.' To the priests, 'Deal out judgement, pity, forgiveness.' Ye islands, seas and kingdoms, give ear unto Me, I am Almighty.[55]

The message, which reflects the Old Testament prophecies in its form and delivery, encouraged Roberts to take up a more combative relationship both with the Churches and with his followers. He gave up his personal savings and withdrew from his family.[56] The most minor decisions and requests were met with reflective silence as Roberts sought guidance from the Holy Spirit. He began to demonstrate a new series of supernatural gifts, the most marked being a kind of pastoral telepathy through which he was able to scrutinise the inner consciences of his congregation.[57] This newly bestowed ability did little to endear him to his audience. His meetings degenerated into a series of personal confrontations as he denounced laymen and ministers for their private doubts and secret lack of faith.

These contests reached their height at the beginning of April 1905 during his mission to Merseyside.[58] After a bitter encounter with a vaudeville hypnotist's assistant and a Liverpool minister whose imminent paralysis he predicted, Roberts's prophetic critique began to strain public tolerance and credulity.[59] The strain reached breaking point when the evangelist denounced the Free Church of Wales, claiming that the organisation had 'fallen from the Rock' and no longer stood with Christ.[60] A few weeks later Roberts, encouraged by friends and ministers, retired from his mission. The newspapers attributed his withdrawal to the onset of nervous strain. The various supernatural manifestations which accompanied his mission were now seen as evidence of a physiological degeneration. As the *Cambrian News* editorialised: 'When he [Evan Roberts] thinks that he hears voices and fancies he is hearing divine messages, and is enabled to look into the intentions of those who attend revival services, he is probably on the borderland of nervous breakdown and ought to be under medical care . . . The revival is a real and emotional outbreak, but it is in strict accord with well known spiritual and mental conditions.'[61] Under the strain of his evangelical leadership and spirit possession, Roberts's flesh was seen as betraying his mission and intentions. Howell Elvet Lewis complained in the *British Weekly* that '[w]hat is written down as eccentricity or worse is simply the constitutional equipment of the man. Surely a personality like his has some laws of its own, which every casual onlooker cannot decipher?'[62]

In the eyes of the pastorate and the press, Roberts underwent a kind of involuntary *kenosis*. His transgression of the rules of public expectation reflected Adam's transgression of the law of God: it led to the surrender of his divine power to the finite law of personality. Perhaps the most telling example of the changed perception of Roberts occurred three days after his Liverpool outburst. In a report widely publicised by the newspapers, Roberts was granted a certificate of health by four Merseyside doctors: James Barr, William Williams, Thomas H. Bickerton and William McAfee.[63] The young revivalist who had once been authorised through the presence of God was now legitimated through the power of medicine.

Had the Welsh Revival been limited to Roberts's mission it would be easy to dismiss it as simply the familiar story of the rise and disgrace of a charismatic preacher. However, as noted before, the revival was a mass movement and it was in the widespread imitation of Roberts's rhetoric and actions that the awakening achieved its political effect. Throughout the cities, towns and villages that the movement touched, those who had been disenfranchised within their communities – women, youths and children – were allowed to cast off their debilitating identities and assume a new authority as inspired prophets acting under the command of God.

The politics of ecstasy

The rapid movement and spread of the revival, as many observers noted, seemed to defy rational explanation. Although the advent of new communication and transport technologies (the trains, telegraphs and newspapers) may have helped propagate the awakening, the pattern of conversions and outbreak of inspiration seemed to bear little relationship to media reports or the movement of missionaries.[64] Its progress was compared to actions of mysterious force, a 'Holy Fire' or 'spiritual hurricane' which could not be contained.[65] Towns far from the centre of the revival, like Bethesda and Llanfairfechan in the slate-working districts of North Wales, succumbed to impromptu awakenings. Other towns such as Llanelli in the revival's epicentre in south-west Wales remained largely unmoved by the efforts of missionaries.[66] This capricious dispersal of the revival's power extended from the geographical to the individual. Many devout and ardent worshippers remained untouched while the sceptical and the reprobate were redeemed. The unpredictability of the movement created a sense of uncanniness in the towns and villages it touched. This sense of the unearthly was remarked on by the spiritualist and social reformer W. T. Stead:

> Well, you have read ghost stories, and can imagine what you would feel if you were alone at midnight in the haunted chamber of some old castle, and you heard slow and stealthy steps stealing along the corridor where the visitant from the other world was said to walk. If you go to South Wales and watch the Revival you will feel pretty much like that. There is something there from the Other World.[67]

Stead believed that the distinct realms of the sacred and the profane had collapsed together. The Holy Ghost was no longer a distant entity: It now moved through the streets and chapels of Welsh towns and villages, and through the minds and hearts of the population. As Stead explained: 'You cannot say whence it came and whither it was going, but it moves and lives and reaches for you all the time. You see men and women go down in sobbing agony before your eyes as the invisible Hand clutches at their heart. And you shudder. It's pretty grim, I tell you.'[68] This sense

of the proximity of the divine was brought out very vividly in the collo-
quialisms people used to testify to their revival experiences. The most
common statement was that Jesus or the Holy Spirit was now living in
the convert's town or village; one believer asked for a linen shirt so that
he could cut bread and butter for Christ at the chapel tea, others stated
that Christ or the Holy Spirit now dwelt beside them, or inside them
('God now sits in the armchair of my heart').[69] This popular demotic
could be seen as deeply sacrilegious; certainly the aged Meirionethshire
man who advised God to rid his ears of wax so that he might better
hear the people's prayers raised nothing but consternation.[70] On another
level, however, such metaphors helped to spiritualise the landscape of
early twentieth-century Wales, binding together the religious and the
mundane in the popular imagination.[71]

The entry of the sacred into the individual was also expressed inversely
by people emphasising the unreality of the everyday. Some Carmarthenshire workers declared that they 'were now living in a different world'.[72]
One minister in Maesteg reported that during the revival his young
parishioners 'became very pale, and their eyes wore a far-away listless
look. One young man told me that for some days after a certain service
in which he prayed, he saw people move like ghosts in the street, and
thought there was a thick mist.'[73] It was this conflation of the sacred and
the mundane that undid the familiar hierarchies of town and village life.
The shared histories which tied individuals to a known identity and a
place in the social order were rendered meaningless by the capricious
presence of the supernatural.

The most obvious demonstration of the political effects of this confusion of the divine and the familiar occurred within the churches and
chapels touched by the awakening. Traditionally these institutions had
reflected the distribution of status and power within a community, with
local hierarchies being reproduced in the symbolic organisation of the
place of worship.[74] Ministers and deacons, figures of authority and
power, sat in the front of the chapel in the *sêt fawr* ('big seat') while
influential families occupied the foremost pews.[75] In the excitement of
the revival meeting, however, these figures were pushed aside. David
Hughes describes the confusion wrought by Roberts's appearance at
Bethel Chapel, Pontycymer, with people 'wildly excited, some on their
feet, some on their seats, some on their knees beneath their seats, some
lying at the bottom of their seats looking helpless and failing to breathe'.[76]
It was a drama repeated many times. Confronted by such excitement the
ministers often gave up control of the services, and instead encouraged

contributions from the congregation.[77] This renunciation of ministerial authority was almost seen as a necessary condition for encouraging the presence of the Holy Spirit.[78] Seth Joshua noted this in his tour of south Cardiganshire.[79] R. B. Jones similarly reported that his Rhosllaner-chrugog mission was unsuccessful until he 'invited the congregation to take the reins'.[80] As Stead observed:

> The most extraordinary thing about the meetings which I attended was the extent to which they were absolutely without any human direction or leadership. 'We must obey the Spirit' is the watchword of Evan Roberts . . . it is go-as-you-please for two hours or more . . . People pray and sing, give testimony; exhort as the spirit moves them. As a study in the psychology of crowds I have seen nothing like it.[81]

When a minister would not give up the service it often became necessary for the meeting to 'shunt them to the sidelines'.[82] In the Rhondda, one congregation prayed that their minister would stop preaching, while an American evangelist declared that God 'had told the ministers to stand on one side and let Him have a try'.[83] This rhetoric frequently led to confrontations and resignations. In Cardigan, the Leipzig-educated minister, Moelwyn Hughes, and his deacons refused to lend public support to the revival, while in Loughor, the minister of Roberts's old chapel resigned after £60-worth of damage was done to the chapel during a revival meeting.[84]

Perhaps the most obvious demonstration of the carnivalesque logic of the revival was the new role played by youth in the religious life of the community.[85] Young men and women organised their own prayer meetings and tried to enforce a new religious sensibility among their friends and neighbours. Occasionally this popular celebration of Protestant morality led enthusiasts into conflict with criminal law. In Rhosllanerchrugog, North Wales, police were called when revivalists bidden by the Holy Spirit picketed a ball organised by the local army volunteers.[86] In Liverpool, a revival march degenerated into a riot as inspired converts attacked passing Catholics.[87] Violence or the suggestion of violence could extend the ambit of the revival when consensus failed. The agricultural scientist T. J. Jenkins was threatened by local youths when he denied the reality of the awakening.[88] The parliamentarian James Williams complained that the fruits of the revival were achieved through collective blackmail.[89]

Children too were enfranchised by the supernatural logic of the awakening. During revival services they entered the *sêt fawr*, taking control of meetings and interrupting the chief evangelists.[90] The chapel provided a space where they could openly criticise their parents and work for their conversion. In Kenfig Hill, a boy of eight prayed for the salvation of his father's soul: 'the meeting was electrified. The father sobbing, thanked God that his little son had led him to the Cross.'[91] This seems to have been a general phenomenon. In Cwmbwrla a meeting was devoted to recounting tales of children converting parents in Clydach Vale and Pontypridd.[92]

Children organised their own prayer meetings independent of any ministerial supervision. At Pen-y-Wern, one teacher testified that in her school, 'children . . . were filled with the Spirit, and when in school turned from their lessons to sing and pray the moment the backs of the teachers were turned'.[93] At Cefn in Glamorgan, children held clandestine prayer meetings on a nearby mountain-top.[94] J. Vyrnwy Morgan recorded how Newcastle Emlyn children held a secret meeting in a pigsty to ask the advice of the Holy Spirit (rather than their parents) on visiting a circus. The Spirit refused permission but later allowed them to go on a merry-go-round. 'When asked the reason why they had chosen such a place for their meeting, the answer was that their parents were not likely to look for them in an empty pigsty, and they did not want the "old-folks" to intrude.'[95]

The idea of spirit guidance undid the responsibility of the child. Roberts's former tutor, Evan Phillips, related how his four-year-old nephew took up this teaching, refusing to have supper with him since the Spirit had instructed him to go and visit his grandmother for tea instead.[96] Another child complained to God: 'O Lord, you know that mother is always after me . . . and I am terribly bored. O Lord, make her understand that she can do nothing against me, since I belong to you.'[97] Those narrative chains of identity which bound the child to his or her family and responsibility were severed through the supernatural presence of the Holy Spirit.

The most marked political transformation wrought by the revival was in the position of women. Howell Elvet Lewis emphasised the fact, claiming that 'Nothing was more noteworthy in the general course of the movement than the women's part. Those who had been faithful but silent for forty to fifty years suddenly found a voice.'[98] The process was widely commented on by journalists, many of whom saw the revival as part of a general process of emancipation. John Gibson, the pro-suffrage editor of the *Cambrian News*, used a psychodynamic model to explain the revival and critique the establishment. 'Nothing', he argued, 'is more certain than the Revival is the outcome of a general and widespread sense of a religious repression exercised by organised religion which excludes women from all activity in the Churches.'[99] Stead believed that the revival was a sure indication of the imminent emancipation of women: 'In the present revival women are everywhere to the fore, singing, testifying, praying and preaching ... as the revival of 1859 to 61 led to the enfranchisement of the male householder, the present Revival may be crowned by the recognition by the State of the full citizenship of women.' The movement, Stead thought, was a corrective to the imbalance of power, 'marking the swing of the pendulum back to the days of the matriarchate'.[100]

There is a level at which the enfranchisement of women in the revival seems to have relied on the subversion of the concept of female nervous instability that Alex Owen identifies in her analysis of Victorian spiritualism.[101] In the context of the revival, women's perceived weakness and passivity were celebrated as demonstrating their openness to the Holy Spirit and, like Deborah in the Book of Judges, they were seen as one of the seven weak things that fulfilled the will of God.[102] Under the apparent influence of the Holy Spirit, many women were driven to take control of church and chapel services and a number rose to prominence as revival leaders in their own right.[103] Two women in particular led missions which were completely unconnected to the campaign of Evan Roberts: these women were Mrs Jones of Egryn and Sarah Jones of Carmel.[104]

Mrs Jones of Egryn attained nationwide notoriety.[105] A farmer's wife, she had decided to dedicate her life to Christ after reading Charles Sheldon's devotional work, *In His Steps* (1898).[106] In December 1904, she experienced a vision of an angel instructing her to urge a friend to lead a local revival. When her friend refused this divine commission, Jones started a series of prayer meetings that led to the conversion of fifty-one neighbours. Her mission was guided by a series of visions which were remarkable in so far as they were witnessed by the general public. Neighbours reported fiery crosses and burning columns hanging over the houses where she was due to make a conversion and, more unusually, these were also witnessed by reporters from the English press. The *Daily Mail* despatched a special team headed by Bernard Redwood to investigate the claims. Although Redwood concluded that Mrs Jones 'is a religious maniac, and that no reliance could be placed on her statements', other journalists were more sympathetic.[107] The Welsh publisher E. W. Evans reported how a local poet had been saved from a group a wild Merionethshire animals when a vision of Christ appeared beside him.[108]

A year later, in the spring of 1906, an illiterate working-class house-wife, Sarah Jones from Carmel, Carmarthenshire, was part of a much more emotional awakening. She had been brought into a closer sense of spiritual communion after being blessed through the laying on of hands by Evan Roberts and anointment by the Glossop Pentecostalist Pastor Howton.[109] Like Mrs Jones of Egryn, she apparently mediated between the spiritual and the material realms. She identified strongly with the Virgin Mary, wandering through chapel services cradling an invisible child in her arms.[110] A reporter from the *South Wales Daily News* described how she had abandoned her domestic duties to pursue a life of constant prayer. He noted how 'she spends her whole day in communion with the Creator, when she speaks there is a strange light in her eyes . . . she is in a kind of reverie and she centres all her thoughts on things above'.[111]

As with Evan Roberts, this life of constant prayer made possible Sarah Jones's direct contact with the Godhead. Her ministry, however, was distinguished by a series of clairvoyant gifts. During a meeting at Pen-y-Groes chapel, she fell into a trance and declared: 'I was washing the feet of Christ yesterday and drying his feet with the hair of my head . . . I have been in Heaven with Christ and the disciples. I have been speaking with Jesus Himself. He is coming to the world again soon.'[112] This declared proximity to the spiritual realm went beyond that personal intercourse reported by the Christian mystics of the Middle Ages. Both these women mystics were somehow able to pass on their mystical gifts. At Maes-y-Pica and Ty'r Gas farms, Cwmtwrch, men broke down and wrestled with demons as Sarah Jones delivered live reports from heaven and Calvary. Others saw visions and spoke in tongues. One elderly choir master was able to interpret the new marks that appeared on Jones's hands as a message of Christ's imminent return.[113] The presence of Sarah Jones inspired and empowered her neighbours. One man declared that: 'he could raise the dead, split the mountains as well as the oceans in two, and that he was going to clear the parliament and the laws of the country out of the way'.[114]

For many observers such claims were more likely to raise the possibility of delusion than they were to raise the dead. Sarah Jones, like Evan Roberts, was criticised throughout her evangelising attempts. The press gleefully reported how she had allegedly climbed her garden hedge to fly to heaven but had fallen in the onion patch.[115] The attitudes of the newspapers demonstrated how the achievement of religious authority or spiritual truth was contingent upon the establishment of an audience of sympathetic believers. Jones, like the handful of revival converts who entered the county asylums, crossed the boundaries of conventional morality and, through this transgression, found her motivations ascribed to fleshly weakness rather than divine strength.[116]

This new narration of Jones's actions as a form of pathological delusion went to the heart of the revival. As with the criticisms of supernatural myths or spiritualist testimony, the concept of delusion opened up the possibility of new narrative paths behind the ineffable action of the ostensibly divine: new narratives that led back to that recalcitrant flesh and personal history which the revivalists had tried so hard to destroy. It placed them with 'the foolish prophets' of Israel as described in the Book of Ezekiel, who prophesied 'out of their own hearts' or 'follow their own spirit'.[117]

Invisible threads

By the time Sarah Jones began her ill-fated mission in the spring of 1906, this psychological critique had already found a firm place in public discussion of the awakening. Just over a year earlier, on 31 January 1905, the Reverend Peter Price, the Cambridge-educated minister of Bethania Congregational Church, Dowlais, had written to the *Western Mail* complaining that there were 'two so-called Revivals going on'.[118] 'The one', he argued, 'was undoubtedly from above, Divine, Real, intense in its nature, and Cymric in its form'; but there was 'another Revival – a sham Revival, a mockery, a blasphemy, a travesty of the real thing. The chief figure in this sham revival is Evan Roberts.'[119] Drawing on the writings of William James, Price suggested that a distinction could be made between the true revival, which was the product of a law-governed developmental process, and a sham revival which was a purely surface phenomenon: a cynical performance presenting itself as a divine but gratuitous break with the past:

> There is then, a Revival which is of God, of God alone, – yes an almighty Revival. I am not sure what ought to be said of the revival from a physiological point of view, but I am quite certain that psychologically speaking, there has been what Professor James would call 'subconscious incubation' due to the earnest prayers of godly men and women for many years ... But it is this other made revival – this exhibition – this froth – this vain trumpery which visitors see and newspapers report.[120]

Price's criterion for distinguishing the true and the false revival is the existence of a discernible history. By locating what is real about the revival within the framework of 'subconscious incubation' rather than an unknowable divine realm, Price makes its truth conditional upon the possibility of knowledge and hence the possibility of authority. This position will by now appear quite familiar, for it resurrects the rules of historical discourse established in Strauss's *Leben Jesu* seventy years earlier.[121] These criteria stand in direct opposition to the plebeian rhetoric of the revival: a rhetoric which, as we have seen, emphasised the essential ineffability of the movement and the impossibility of any historical knowledge of either its origins or the motivations of its participants.

Price's argument confronted the plebeian rhetoric. Through reference to the 'subconscious', he attempted to repair self-proclaimed breaks both in the history of the revival itself and in the life narratives of its converts. He relocated the real psychic drama within an unbroken narrative that had been successfully opened up to the authority of others. Furthermore, his argument demonstrated the necessity of pastoral authority and intervention, since he claimed the rhetoric deployed by his revivalist opponents demonstrated an obvious ignorance of psychological processes, revealing their disenfranchisement from their own history.

Price's letter divided the Welsh population.[122] The correspondence triggered by its publication ran to over 100 submissions in the *Western Mail* alone.[123] The majority of these letters were simple defences of Evan Roberts, or vitriolic attacks on Price himself. He was, however, defended by many ministers, most notably the Rev. J. Vyrnwy Morgan.[124] Their sympathy is understandable. The deployment of this psychological argument allowed the ministry to redescribe the apparently gratuitous events of the awakening, locating these within a human history that reflected their own ideas and interests. As the critic W. F. Alexander noted, the notion of the subconscious 'acquires great value because it enables us to perceive a thread of continuity which before was invisible'.[125] The clergy used this invisible thread to embroider their own narratives on the origins of the revival. As had been the case in psychical research, the characteristics of the subliminal imagined in these histories tended to vary according to the nature of the anomaly under investigation and the political interests of the investigator. Those non-conformist ministers who wrote histories of the revival, such as D. M. Phillips and H. E. Lewis, partially replicated Price's argument. They claimed that the Sunday school lessons of the Welsh child had created 'a stock of buried knowledge and expression', or a 'spiritual and moral reservoir', which resurfaced during the soul's awakening.[126] This explained the inspired and eloquent speeches produced by a number of apparently uneducated people 'in the excitement of the moment and under the contagion of the crowd'.[127]

Whereas the Welsh pastorate traced the revival back to a subliminal self constituted in chapel pedagogy, overseas observers such as the French theologian Henri Bois and his compatriot, the psychiatrist Jean Rogues de Fursac, pursued a more nationalistic analysis.[128] They emphasised revival phenomena such as the Welsh *hwyl* (a word that lacks a direct translation but is usually taken as referring to enthusiasm or a particular cadence of speech) and Roberts's repeated refusal to speak English when under the direction of the Holy Spirit, arguing that these were indications of revival's deep racial origins.[129] Bois, Rogues de Fursac and the Swiss pastor Roger Bornand believed that *hwyl* was 'a throwback to one of the most primitive forms of human expression, arising from the suppression of language and musical ability' and the supposed incipient telepathy of the Celtic race.[130] Within their schemas, the revival appears as the final uprush of a repressed Celtic consciousness which for years had been repressed under the yoke of Saxon domination.[131]

A different version of this racial model was developed by Alfred Fryer and Edgar Vine Hall, two clergymen fascinated by psychical research. Hall made a close study of phenomena associated with Mrs Jones of Egryn, arguing that the reptilian creatures which haunted her nightmares were a 'recrudescence of the cave man fears of beasts savage and serpentine'.[132] Fryer also posited a racial subconscious. He believed Mrs Jones's visions could be explained if one recognised that all those who shared such experiences (including Evan Roberts) were of Cardiganshire stock.[133] The county's population had been traced back to an Iberian origin by anthropologists, so the experiences of its people could be seen as a recapitulation of their Spanish mystical heritage.[134] The Catholic writer 'S. F. S.' believed that the appearance of glowing crosses could be seen as the 'revivification of types of consciousness' associated with pre-Reformation Catholic worship.[135]

The racial models of the subliminal were joined by a Fabian analysis which saw the revival as a manifestation of the country's social evolution.[136] According to the socialist economist Alfred Hook, the revival was a vivid demonstration of man's 'craving for human fellowship and sympathy' that 'individualistic systems of modern thought [hold] in check'.[137] In his person, Evan Roberts exhibited 'the poverty, the self-abnegation [and] the absence of individualistic qualities' that the collective instinct sought. 'At such a time,' Hook thought, 'the current of this social spirit long restrained by the individualist character of modern society must break down all opposition and sweep in restless flood over the men and women so brought under its influence. Herein we find ample explanation of the fervour, the enthusiasm, the frenzy which modern religious revivals display.'[138]

These psychological accounts locate the motivation of the revivalists in a history they believed they had escaped. This irony was most obvious in the case of Evan Roberts, whose flight from selfhood was mediated through obedience to the voice of the Spirit. Within the terms of psychological analysis, this 'voice' became a simple manifestation of his subconscious: a subconscious formed through his own racial and individual history. Thus Rogues de Fursac, having met Roberts after his seven days' silence in Neath, diagnosed intense automatism and psychic asthenia, brought about through his concentration on the idea of Christianity.[139] Likewise, Bois believed that Roberts's conversion had instilled in him an *idée fixe* of the revival which so dominated his subconscious that automatic discharges eventually took place. Those voices and visions which led him throughout his mission were depicted as fragments of forgotten memory returning to haunt him.[140] Within these accounts the young revivalist, who had tried to sever his relation with the past, was seen as a neurotic figure dumbly playing out the stories of his childhood and his nation.

The strategies which the pastorate used to narrate and historicise the supernatural events of the awakening anticipate the arguments deployed by historians today. The processes of subconscious incubation that ministers and critics identified in the revivalists may now have been superseded by the modern psychological mechanisms of fantasy and repression yet the implication remains the same. The failure of narrative declared by the mystic marks the point of departure for new constructions fashioned from the imaginative vocabularies of psychoanalysis and social theory. And as with the early twentieth-century descriptions of the revival, the 'invisible threads' which we discover in our attempts to narrate supernatural events reflect a certain set of interests and a certain conception of history. The interests vary between the political and evangelical agendas maintained by different commentators but the faith remains the same: it is a faith that an unbroken sequence of events can be recovered from the body or society.

This faith in the unbroken sequence of events serves a political purpose. It reminds us, as Fredric Jameson has maintained, that each aspect of our existence is constructed in history, and, following on from this, that each aspect of our existence remains open to contestation and negotiation. As Jameson argues in *The Political Unconscious*:

> To imagine that, sheltered from the omnipresence of history and the implacable influence of the social, there already exists a realm of freedom – whether it be that of the microscopic experience of words in a text or the ecstasies and intensities of the various private religions – is only to strengthen the grip of Necessity over all such blind zones in which the individual subject seeks refuge, in pursuit of a purely individual, a merely psychological, project of salvation. The only effective liberation from such constraint begins with the recognition that there is nothing that is not social and historical – indeed that everything is 'in the last analysis' political.[141]

Certainly, with the hindsight that this commitment to history brings, we can apprehend some of the limitations of the project pursued by Roberts and the other converts. Within the space of a few years, the effects of the revival seemed to have subsided and the structures denounced in the ecstatic furore of the awakening remained untouched. The few adherents who remained loyal to the movement's Pentecostal vision appeared as an isolated band, parading through the novels of Gwyn Thomas or Caradog Evans to the sounds of general derision. The rejection of self and the world which Roberts and the other revivalists so ardently promoted, appears to be little more than 'a false sortie': an attempt to transgress the boundaries of law and narrative which only succeeded in extending their ambit.[142] In the wake of the revival, those missioners and preachers who had once encouraged an ecstatic escape from the demands of the world and the flesh now found themselves committed to the invention of new forms of self-government. Troubled by the apparent anarchy that had accompanied the Liverpool Mission and the Carmel awakening led by Sarah Jones, evangelists such as Rhys Bevan Jones and Jessie Penn-Lewis began to search for methods and techniques which would allow for a policing of the sacred realm. Their investigations led them towards the literature of the new psychology and the old doctrines of demon possession, which they combined to construct 'a saving theology' that would surrender the turmoil of the inner life to new forms of political subordination.[143] Like the British idealist theologians and the American psychologists of religion, they began to imagine the transcendent as a kind of polity: a space populated by conflicting forces demanding suppression and control.

Jones established the Porth Bible Training College, instructing his students in the arts of demonic detection. Pastor Howton, who had once anointed Sarah Jones, retired to his home in Glossop, Derbyshire, where he established a kind of Black Country *Zauberberg*, providing a refuge for the sick and the possessed, publicly wrestling with manifest devils and disease.[144] Evan Roberts, said to be suffering from 'nervous exhaustion', was taken into Penn-Lewis's care.[145] The two of them devoted themselves to uncovering the secret law which had governed their experiences in the revival. As one visitor to Penn-Lewis's Leicester home reported, Roberts now believed that revivals operated according to 'fixed and definite laws that should be understood and obeyed . . . So he delves into theology, anthropology and demonology and constructs therefrom, with prayer and plentiful meditation, a system of "Saving Theology".'[146]

These researches reached their conclusion in 1912 with the publication of *War on the Saints*, a practical manual of demonology.[147] Within this text, spirit invasion no longer appeared as an extra-mundane force, insulated from treatment by a death drawn through the body. It was now caught up in the medical apparatus of Jacksonian neurology, asylum psychiatry and the new psychology. Indeed, in *War on the Saints* we can discern the gradual combination of the various strands of thought I have described throughout this book: the surrender of the spiritual life to psychological and historical explanation; its representation as a kind of subliminal self, and the opening up of this subliminal self to new forms of control. And although *War on the Saints* was not the final apotheosis of these various movements, it retains a certain significance. It marks the victory of human interiority over eschatology: in it, the final cosmic struggle between God and the Devil is relocated at last in the fleshbound personality of man.

If we view *War on the Saints* within the terms of Roberts's biography, it is a document heavy with sadness. Its repeated injunctions against the cultivation of passivity and self-negation appear deeply at odds with the vision that had originally inspired his mission. It is hard to reconcile the book's admonition of those who request the Paraclete's presence with its author, who once sang 'O Anfon Di yr Ysbryd Glan' (Oh send us the Holy Spirit).[148] Roberts's behaviour during the revival stands at odds with his later vision of good spiritual government. The contradiction also raises a more unsettling suggestion. It implies that Roberts, in the midst of his apparent breakdown, had engaged upon a kind of gloomy narrative reconstruction. The life which had once been led by the bidding of the Holy Spirit was revealed as the dupe of deceiving demons.

The ease with which Roberts moves between these two narratives, slipping from saint to sinner, returns us to Jameson's argument. It demonstrates the hollowness of a narrative disconnected from the social world. The subversions and ruses practised by both ecstatics and psychologists became possible because they lacked any anchor into the material life, and in the end it was this lack of any anchor which became their undoing. The true basis for self-transformation lay not in private adventures of the interior life but in the individual's engagement with society. Memory and narrative could only be sustained through cooperation with others. It is tempting to think that Roberts also came to believe in this. Towards the end of his life, he seemingly gave up the Pentecostal preoccupation with the self, pursuing a more everyday escapism. He took up pipe-smoking and followed the fortunes of Cardiff City FC. Cared for by friends he had known since his college days, he died in 1951.

The failure of Roberts's attempt to resist history should not be taken as a kind of moral parable, illustrating the infallibility of our modern faith in the unbroken sequence of events. His life and the lives of his fellow mystics left their own peculiar legacy. In part, of course, they established a series of transformative techniques that are still in use today.[149] More importantly, their actions, like those of the hysteric and the spiritualist before them, helped shape contemporary notions of the unconscious and so contributed to the developing rhetorics of psychoanalysis and dynamic psychiatry that are foundational to modern historical writing. Returning to their supernatural encounters helps to remind us of the fragility and contingency of the tools we bring to bear in our interrogation of past.[150]

These tools, as F. H. Bradley pointed out over a century ago, rest on their own set of critical assumptions and systematic exclusions.[151] Well-attested miracles, such as the mysterious lights seen by revivalists and sceptics in Egryn, fall outside the scope of historical narrative, while minor disruptions to the historical record are recuperated (as we have seen) through reference to unconscious or subconscious forces. Our ideas of the nature of historical reality, the shape of the historian's self and the notion of the unconscious have been co-constituted in a series of political struggles over interpretive authority. In the critical responses to the religious ecstatic's refusal of history or the hysteric's disavowal of the past, these concepts have been continually extended and redefined.

A whole battery of procedures, from the hermeneutic strategies of the biblical critics through to the hypnotic techniques of the psychical researchers and the statistical investigations of the psychologists of religion, have been deployed to repair any threatened break in the worldly past. Yet the sheer inventiveness of these techniques has led to a situation where just about any motivation can be ascribed to human actions.[152] Although we might disavow it, our actions can be narrated in myriad new ways: as instances of sublimation, displacement, transference, fantasy and projection.[153] The endless possibilities opened up by the mystic's act of transcendence persist in the endless possibilities of the unconscious when fielded as an explanation. The waywardness that once characterised miraculous episodes is now inherent in the psychological tools that were developed to contest them. History has triumphed over the supernatural, but it has not come away unscathed.

Notes

1 *Liverpool Echo* (18 January 1905), 2.
2 On the deathbed prophecies of Dean Howells of St David's, see: H. Elvet Lewis, *With Christ among the Miners* (London: Hodder and Stoughton, 1906), p. 38; Henri Bois, *Le réveil au Pays de Galles* (Toulouse: Société des Publications Morales et Religieuses, 1906), p. 18. On the talking baby of Bethesda, see: *Western Mail* (21 January 1905); [Anon.], 'The journalist at large in psychical research', *J.SPR* 12 (1905), 66–7. For ghost episodes connected to the revival, see: *Cardigan and Tivyside Advertiser* (10, 17 February 1905); 'Revival delusions', *Cambrian News* (24 February 1905). For the role of prophecy in the revival, Rhodri Hayward, 'From the millennial future to the unconscious past: the transformation of prophecy in early twentieth-century Britain', in Bertrand Taithe and Tim Thornton (eds), *Prophecy of the Power of Inspired Language in History* (Stroud: Sutton Publishing, 1997).
3 On these apparent cases of xenoglossia, see: J. M. Jones, 'The religious revival in Wales', *The Times* (31 January 1905), 7; C. G. Williams, *Tongues of the Spirit: A Study of Pentecostal Glossolalia and Related Phenomena* (Cardiff: University of Wales Press, 1891), pp. 53–4.
4 Joel 2. 28; Acts 2. 16–21. Cf. *South Wales Daily News* (14 November 1904).
5 The best account of the revival remains, R. Tudur Jones, *Ffydd ac Argyfwng Cenedl: Cristionogaeth a diwylliant yng Nghymru, 1890–1914, vol. II, Dryswch a Diwygiad* (Swansea: John Penry, 1982). For a slightly abridged translation, Robert Pope (ed.), *Faith and the Crisis of a Nation: Wales 1890–1914*, trans. S. P. Jones (Cardiff: University of Wales Press, 2004). Where possible I have provided cross-references to the English edition.
6 On the spread of the revival, see: Jones, *Ffydd* II, pp. 188–200; Pope (ed.), *Faith*, pp. 337–45; Noel Gibbard, *On the Wings of a Dove: The International Effects of the 1904–05 Revival* (Bridgend: Byntirion Press, 2002).
7 Joe Creech, 'Visions of glory: the place of the Azusa Street Revival in Pentecostal history', *Church History* 65 (1996), 405–24; William Kay, *Pentecostals*

in Britain (Carlisle: Paternoster Press, 2000), ch. 1; J. E. Worsfold, *The Origins of the Apostolic Church in Great Britain* (Wellington: Julian Trust, 1991). Cf. the creed of the Apostolic Church in *The Apostolic Church: Its Principles and Practices* (London: Apostolic Publications, 1961), p. 11.

8 Evangelical accounts of the revival include, R. Ellis, *Living Echoes of the Welsh Revival* (London: The Delyn Press, [1954]); Mabel Bickerstaff, *Something Wonderful Happened* (Liverpool: Committee for the 1904–5 Revival Fund, 1954); Gibbard, *On the Wings of a Dove*; B. P. Jones, *Voices from the Welsh Revival* (Bridgend: Evangelical Press of Wales, 1995). A more critical assessment is offered by Eifion Evans, *The Welsh Revival of 1904* (Bala: Evangelical Movement of Wales, 1969). For supernatural phenomena associated with the movement, Kevin McClure and Sue McClure, *Stars and Rumours of Stars* (Market Harborough: McClure, 2002); X. Phillips, 'Rolling in the aisles', *Fortean Times* 77 (October 1994), 24–8. The great chronicler of strange phenomena, Charles Fort, claimed that the revival marked the high tide of paranormal phenomena in Britain, *Lo!* [1931] (London: John Brown, 1996), ch. 14.

9 Kevin Adams, *A Diary of the Revival: The Outbreak of the 1904 Welsh Awakening* (Farnborough: Crusade for World Revival, 2004); Brynmor Jones, *An Instrument of Revival: Complete Life of Evan Roberts, 1878–1951* (South Plainfield NJ: Bridge Publishing, 1995).

10 See the essays in D. Smith (ed.), *A People and a Proletariat* (London: Pluto Press, 1988); T. Herbert and G. E. Jones (eds), *Wales, 1880–1914: Welsh History and its Sources* (Cardiff: University of Wales Press, 1988).

11 On the organising power of prayer, see: Jessie Penn Lewis, *The Awakening in Wales and Some of its Hidden Springs* (London: Marshall Bros., 1906). For portrayals of the revival as a conservative movement, see: C. R. Williams, 'The Welsh religious revival, 1904–5', *British Journal of Sociology* 13 (1962), 242–59; E. Howells, 'Toriad y Wawr yn Ne Aberteifi', in S. Evans and G. Roberts (eds), *Cyfrol Goffa Diwygiad, 1904–5* (Caernarfon: Llyfrfa'r Methodistaidd Calfinaidd, 1954); John G. Jones, '"Ebychiad mawr olaf anghydffurfiaeth yng Nghymru": Diwygiad 1904–05', *Transactions of the Honourable Society of the Cymmrodorion* n.s. 11 (2002), 105–43. On the revival as an attempt to renegotiate individual identity, see David Jenkins, *The Agricultural Community in South West Wales at the Turn of the Twentieth Century* (Cardiff: University of Wales Press, 1971), ch. 9; Rhodri Hayward, 'Popular mysticism and the origins of the new psychology, 1880–1910' (Ph.D. dissertation, Lancaster University, 1995), ch. 4. On the Forward Movement and F. B. Meyer's claim to have originated the revival, see: Rosina Davies, *The Story of my Life* (Llandyssul: Gomerian Press, 1942); Howell Williams, *The Romance of the Forward Movement* (Denbigh: Gee and Son, [1949]); and for criticisms, see: *South Wales Daily News* (13 December 1904), 6; Evans, *Welsh Revival*, pp. 169–70. On the role of new technologies, see:

Edward Gitre, 'The 1904–5 Welsh Revival: modernization, technologies and techniques of the self', *Church History* 73 (2004), 792–827. On the Keswick Movement, see: John Kent, *Holding the Fort* (London: Epworth, 1986); J. C. Pollock, *The Keswick Story: The Authorised History of the Keswick Convention* (London: Hodder and Stoughton, 1964). On the revival as an expression of repressed nationalism, see: J. Rogues de Fursac, *Un mouvement mystique contemporain: le réveil religieux du Pays de Galle* (Paris: Felix Alcan, 1907), ch. 8; Bois, *Le réveil*, pp. 202–10. On sexual magnetism, see: Chapman Cohen, *Religion and Sex* (Edinburgh: T. N. Foulis, 1928), pp. 240–1.

12 [Anon.], 'Secret of success', *South Wales Daily News* (13 December 1904), 5.

13 Lewis, *Miners*, p. 5.

14 R. B. Jones, *Rent Heavens: The Revival of 1904* (London: Stanley Moulton, 1931), p. 7. For Rhys Bevan Jones, see: B. P. Jones, *The King's Champions* (Newport: B. P. Jones, 1968).

15 Quoted in Lewis, *Miners*, p. 10.

16 W. F. Alexander, 'Revivalism and mysticism', *Contemporary Review* 89 (1906), 350.

17 Derec Llwyd Morgan, *The Great Awakening in Wales*, trans. Dyfnallt Morgan (London: Epworth, 1988), pt II, ch. 6.

18 Jones, *Ffydd* II, p. 133; Pope (ed.), *Faith*, p. 293.

19 Seth Joshua, 'Diary, 1904' [NLW, Calvinist Methodist Archives General Collection no. 17916] (29 September 1904). For Joseph Jenkins (1861–1929) minister of Siloh Chapel, New Quay, see: Ellis, *Living Echoes*, ch. 2. For Seth Joshua (1858–1925), see: T. Mardy-Rees, *Seth and Frank Joshua: The Renowned Revivalists* (Wrexham: Hughes and Sons, 1926).

20 'Awstin', *Religious Revival in Wales*, no. 3, p. 31; R. H. Brewer, 'The collier revivalist', *Good Words* (1905), 414–15; D. M. Phillips, *Evan Roberts: The Great Welsh Revivalist and His Work* (London: Marshall Bros., 1906), pp. 123–5; Joshua, 'Diary, 1904' (29 September 1904); 'Idriswyn', *Y Diwygiad a'r Diwygiwr* (Cardiff: Evan ac Williams, 1905), ch. 3; T. Francis, *Yr Diwygiad a'r Diwygiwr* (Dolgellau: E. W. Evans, 1906), p. 41. An eyewitness account is given in 'Mr Roberts baptism', *Evening Express* (19 November 1904).

21 Howells, 'Toriad y Wawr', p. 38.

22 See chapter 1.

23 Written on 1 June 1904, reproduced in Phillips, *Evan Roberts*, p. 473.

24 Phillips, *Evan Roberts*, p. 469.

25 Address given in Bangor 24 April 1906, in *ibid.*, p. 478. This language of self-annihilation was also vividly deployed in a letter sent to David Lloyd, a month earlier: 'Remember the blood. Count yourself dead. Count and then what will the enemy do with the dead ones? The dead are good for nothing but the grave. Hence to the cross with us, and then to the grave, and let Christ our resurrection come to quicken us', in *ibid.*, p. 454.

26 Lewis, *Miners*, p. 158; Phillips, *Evan Roberts*, p. 438.

27 Letter dated 27 January 1905, repr. in Phillips, *Evan Roberts*, p. 353. Roberts's emphasis.

28 This is from a verbal account given by Roberts to W. T. Stead, see Stead, *The Revival in the West* (London: Review of Reviews Office, 1905), p. 53. Other accounts appear in Lewis, *Miners*, p. 70; Phillips, *Evan Roberts*, p. 195; Jones, *Rent Heavens*, p. 57; Jones, *Ffydd* II, p. 134; Luise Oehler, *Die Bewegung in Wales* (Stuttgart: Gundert, 1905), p. 37.

29 For a clear definition, see: M. Foucault, 'Technologies of the self', in Luther H. Martin et al. (eds), *Technologies of the Self* (Amherst: University of Massachusetts Press, 1988), p. 18. For a similar statement, see: Foucault, 'About the beginning of the hermeneutics of the self', *Political Theory* 21 (1993), 203. A useful introduction to this aspect of Foucault's work is provided by James W. Bernauer in 'Michel Foucault's ecstatic thinking', in J. Bernauer and D. Ramussen (eds), *The Final Foucault* (Cambridge MA: MIT Press, 1988), pp. 156–93.

30 Compare to the practice of *exomologesis* described by Foucault, 'Technologies of the self', pp. 41–3; Foucault, 'On the government of living', repr. Foucault, *The Essential Works*, vol. 1, *Ethics*, ed. Paul Rabinow (London: Allen Lane, 1997), pp. 81–3. See also Pierre Hadot, 'Reflections on the notion of the cultivation of the self', in Tim Armstrong (ed.), *Michel Foucault: Philosopher* (London: Harvester Wheatsheaf, 1992), pp. 228–9; Tom Webster, 'Writing to redundancy: approaches to spiritual journals and early modern spirituality', *Historical Journal* 39 (1996), 33–56, esp. 40–4.

31 From a letter (9 October 1905) to D. M. Phillips, reproduced in *Evan Roberts*, p. 448. Compare the language of one of the most popular revival hymns, 'R Hwn Sy'n Gyrru Mellt Hedeg': 'Send the arrow of conviction // To these hearts we Pray to Thee // Open wide our self-made prisons // Send the firebrand from the flame', in S. B. Shaw, *The Great Revival in Wales* (Chicago: S. B. Shaw Publishing, 1905), p. 2.

32 This happened at Hirwaun (18 January 1905), 'Awstin', *Religious Revival in Wales*, no. 3, p. 21; Shaw, *Great Revival*, p. 173; on his return to Blaenanerch, *Cambrian News* [Supp.] (17 March 1905); at Pontycymer, *South Wales Daily News* (18 November 1904), 6. For the idea that these spectacular agonies were the product of a subconscious imitation of Christ, see: Bois, *Le réveil*, pp. 410–12.

33 Sermon at Siloh Chapel, Pentre (4 December 1905), [Awstin], 'Enthusiasm at Pentre', *Western Mail* (5 December); 'Awstin', *Religious Revival in Wales*, no. 1, p. 25; for similar sermons cf. *ibid.*, p. 1; no. 3, pp. 6, 19; no. 4, pp. 5, 6, 24; no. 5, p. 20; no. 6, p. 3. See also Roberts's talk to Bala students, repr. in part in Phillips, *Evan Roberts*, pp. 434–5.

34 Advice to Rachel Phillips given in Phillips, *Evan Roberts*, p. 160.

35 E. Roberts, 'A message to the church', *Homiletic Review* (March 1905), 174–

5, also in Arthur Goodrich et al., *The Story of the Welsh Revival: As Told by Eyewitnesses Together with a Sketch of Evan Roberts and His Message to the World* (New York: Fleming H. Revell, 1905), p. 6.

36 Compare E. P. Thompson's statement: 'the historian has got to be listening all the time . . . If he listens then the material itself will begin to speak through him', quoted in R. J. Evans, *In Defence of History* (London: Granta Books, 1997), p. 116. See also the previous discussion in chapter 2, pp. 37, 68n.38, 39.

37 'The ethic of care for the self as a practice of freedom', in Bernauer and Ramussen (eds), *The Final Foucault*, p. 6.

38 Phillips, *Evan Roberts*, p. 485; cf. Margam Jones, *The Study of Nature* (Merthyr Tydfil: Joseph and Williams, 1905): 'Roberts did not start the Revival, the Revival started Evan Roberts' (pp. 143–4).

39 Bill Ellis has argued that Roberts's techniques were evolved from aspects of popular occultism such as the 'dumb supper'. This seems unlikely since this largely African-American tradition seems to have had little uptake in early twentieth-century Wales, see his, *Lucifer Ascending: The Occult in Folklore and Popular Culture* (Lexington: University Press of Kentucky, 2004), p. 201.

40 Phillips, *Evan Roberts*, p. 133. This mirrored the Jewish practice of casting lots as used by Justus and Matthias to decide the replacement of the twelfth apostle, John Jones, *The Natural or the Supernatural, or Man, Physical, Apparitional and Spiritual* (London: H. Balliere, 1861), p. 262.

41 Jones, *Ffydd* II, p. 131; Francis, *Diwygiad*, pp. 45–7.

42 Stead, *Revival in the West*, p. 49; Walter Percy Hicks, *The Life of Evan Roberts* (London: Christian Herald, [1906]), pp. 17–18; Bois, *Le réveil*, p. 404. For a discussion of the historical basis of these visions: John Harvey, 'Spiritual emblems: the visions of the Welsh Revival', *Llafur* 6 (1993), 75–93; Harvey, *Image of the Invisible: The Visualisation of Religion in Welsh Nonconformist Tradition* (Cardiff: University of Wales Press, 1999), pp. 59–74.

43 M. de Certeau, 'Surin's melancholy', in *Heterologies: Discourse on the Other* (Minneapolis: University of Minnesota Press, 1986), p. 107.

44 M. Foucault, *The Order of Things* (London: Routledge, 1988), pp. 9–10. For a good discussion, see: Gilles Deleuze, *Foucault* (London: Athlone Press, 1988), pp. 65–9.

45 Quoted in Jones, *Rent Heavens*, p. 55. Cf. 'The scenes at Loughor', *Western Mail*; 'Awstin', *Religious Revival in Wales*, no. 1, p. 2 (reported 11 November 1904).

46 'Dyfed', *Evening Standard* (27 December 1904); also *Western Mail* (27 December 1904), repr. 'Awstin', *Religious Revival in Wales*, no. 2, p. 19.

47 Western Mail (18 November 1904), repr. 'Awstin,' *Religious Revival in Wales*, no. 1, p. 11. 'Awstin' was T. Awstin Davies (1857–1934), sub-editor on the *Western Mail* and later President of the National Eisteddfod Association.

48 *London Daily News* (15 November 1904), repr. *South Wales Daily News* (16 November 1904); Phillips, *Evan Roberts*, p. 403.

49 Phillips, *Evan Roberts*, p. 403. Cf. 'In background', *South Wales Daily News* (19 November 1904), 3.

50 'Cardiff visit postponed', *Western Mail* (8 February 1905), repr. 'Awstin', *Religious Revival in Wales*, no. 4, p. 5. See also Bois, *Le réveil*, pp. 432–3. The Holy Spirit frequently prevented Roberts from complying with requests, see 'Ecclesiastical intelligence', *The Times* (31 January 1905), p. 7. He was often prevented from speaking English: Brewer, 'Collier revivalist', 416; W. G. Hall, 'More about the revival in Wales', *Friend* 45 (1905), 27; Bois, *Le réveil*, pp. 433–5. On John Morgan Jones (1838–1921), Moderator of the South Wales Calvinist Methodist Association, see: *DWB*, p. 486.

51 de Certeau, *Heterologies*, p. 111, also pp. 80–101.

52 'Full story of the seven days silence', *Western Mail* (3 March 1905), repr. 'Awstin', *Religious Revival in Wales*, no. 5, pp. 3–11; 'The silence of Mr Evan Roberts', *British Weekly* (2 March 1905), 403.

53 'For the mountains shall depart, and the hills be removed; but my kindness shall not depart from thee, neither shall the covenant of my peace be removed.'

54 'Awstin', *Religious Revival in Wales*, no. 5, pp. 5–6; Oehler, *Bewegung*, p. 81.

55 'Awstin', *Religious Revival in Wales*, no. 5, pp. 6–7; Phillips, *Evan Roberts*, p. 373.

56 'Awstin', *Religious Revival in Wales*, no. 4, pp. 15, 26.

57 See the services at Newcastle Emlyn and Blaenanerch on 13 and 15 March 1905, *ibid.*, no. 5; Jones, *Instrument of Revival*, chs 9–11.

58 On the Liverpool mission, see: Gwilym Hughes, *Evan Roberts, Revivalist: The Story of the Liverpool Mission* (Dolgelley: E. W. Evans, 1905); Jones, *Ffydd* II, pp. 169–72; Pope (ed.), *Faith*, pp. 321–5; Lewis, *Miners*, pt 3, ch. 2; Oehler, *Bewegung*, ch. 10.

59 'Awstin', *Religious Revival in Wales*, no. 6, p. 18; [Anon.], *British Weekly* (13 April 1905), 4; Hughes, *Liverpool Mission*, pp. 54–60; Oehler, *Bewegung*, p. 99. The hypnotist was a pupil of the magician and music hall star Dr Walford Bodie. Bodie had condemned revivalism as a form of sham suggestion in his popular work, *The Bodie Book* (London: The Caxton Press, 1905), pp. 85–7, and claimed that Roberts was a secret hypnotist: Bois, *Le réveil*, pp. 483–4. On Walford Bodie (1870–1939): *Variety* 62 (15 November 1939), 2.

60 'Awstin', *Religious Revival in Wales*, no. 6, p. 23; Hughes, *Liverpool Mission*, pp. 72–3.

61 [Anon.], 'Revival delusions' (24 February 1905), see also: 'Revival manifestations' (3 March 1905); 'The revival' (17 March 1905). See also the interviews with W. O. Jones and Caradoc Rees, in Hughes, *Liverpool Mission*, pp. 74–5; and the letter of Daniel R. Hughes in *ibid.*, pp. 85–7.

61 [Anon.], 'The Welsh Revival: Mr Evan Roberts', *British Weekly* (23 March 1905), 616.

63 *Liverpool Daily Post* (17 April 1905); 'Awstin', *Religious Revival in Wales*, no. 6, pp. 27–8; Hughes, *Liverpool Mission*, pp. 88–9. On Sir James Barr (1849–1938), Physician to Liverpool Hospital and later President of the BMA: G. H. Brown (ed.), *Lives of the Fellows of the Royal College of Physicians of London, 1826–1925, Munk's Roll* IV (London: Royal College of Physicians, 1955), pp. 434–5; William G. Williams (b. 1864), General Practitioner, *Medical Who's Who* (1914), repr. *BBA* no. 1175; Thomas Bickerton (b. 1857), Vice-President, British Medical Temperance Association: *BBA* no. 105.

64 For a fine attempt to relate the rapid spread of the revival to new technologies, see: Gitre, 'The 1904–5 Welsh Revival', 803.

65 Margam Jones, 'The power of the Spirit', *Western Mail* (17 December 1904), 4.

66 Jones, *Ffydd* II, p. 150; Pope (ed.), *Faith*, p. 309.

67 Methodist Times (15 December 1905), repr. in Stead, *Revival in the West*, p. 25. Charles Fort interwove his narrative of the revival with the story of an escaped wolf in Northumberland in an attempt to recapture this sense of dread and terror: *Lo!*, ch. 14. On Stead (1849–1912), see: Raymond L. Schults, *Crusader in Babylon: W. T. Stead and the Pall Mall Gazette* (Lincoln: University of Nebraska Press, 1972).

68 Stead, *Revival in the West*, p. 25.

69 Lewis, *Miners*, pp. 117, 215, 219; Jones, *King's Champions*, pp. 56–9. For a collection of such idioms, see 'Anthropos' [Robert David Rowland], *Perlau'r Diwygiad* (Caernarfon: Cwmni Gwasg Genedlaethol, [1906]).

70 [Anon.], 'Revival delusions', *Cambrian News* (22 February 1905).

71 On this effect of metaphor, see: David Leary, 'Psyche's muse' in David Leary (ed.), *Metaphors in the History of Psychology* (Cambridge: Cambridge University Press, 1990), p. 5.

72 South Wales Daily News (13 April 1906), quoted in D. R. Davies, 'A social history of Carmarthenshire' (Ph.D. dissertation, University College of Wales, Aberystwyth, 1989), p. 275.

73 A. Fryer, 'Psychological aspects of the Welsh revival', *Proc.SPR* 19 (1905), 123–4.

74 E. Jones, 'Tregaron', in E. Davies and A. D. Rees (eds), *Welsh Rural Communities* (Cardiff: University of Wales Press, 1960); Jenkins, *Agricultural Community*, pp. 179–94.

75 Davies, 'Carmarthenshire', p. 280; C. Ben Turner, 'Revivals and popular religion in Victorian and Edwardian Wales' (Ph.D. dissertation, University College of Wales, Aberystwyth, 1979), pp. 372–6.

76 David Hughes, 'Dechreuad y diwygiad i Mhontycymer', *Y Dysgedydd* n.s. 48 (1906), 521; Francis, *Diwygiad*, p. 68.

77 Detailed descriptions of meetings appeared daily in the popular press cf.

'Awstin', *Religious Revival in Wales*, nos 1–5: *passim*; Ilseley W. Charlton, *The Revival in Wales: Some Facts and Lessons* (London: Jarrold and Sons, 1905), ch. 5 etc.; 'Welsh Correspondent': 'The Welsh Revival', *Times* (3 January 1905), 12.

78 Janet Holmes, *Religious Revivals in Britain and Ireland, 1859–1905* (Dublin: Irish Academic Press, 2000), pp. 183–4, sees this as a unique departure in the history of British revivalism.

79 Joshua, 'Diary, 1904'.

80 Jones, *Ffydd* II, p. 128.

81 *Daily Chronicle* (13 December 1904), repr. Stead, *Revival in the West*, pp. 38–9.

82 Phrase from an idiomatic prayer given in John Vyrnwy. Morgan, *The Welsh Revival, 1904–5* (London: Chapman and Hall, 1909), p. 42: 'We thank Thee O Lord, that thou hast shunted the ministers to the sideline, so that we the people may come to the front. But Lord don't keep them there too long for fear they might become rusty.'

83 *South Wales Daily News* (26 December 1904); 'Awstin', *Religious Revival in Wales*, no. 2, p. 6.

84 For Moelwyn Hughes's attack on the revival: *Cardigan and Tivyside Advertiser* (3 February 1905); Jenkins, *Agricultural Community*, p. 239. For the Loughor incident: *Welsh Gazette* (19 January 1905); *British Weekly* (19 January 1905), 403. For examples of confrontations between ministers and their congregations cf. 'Awstin', *Religious Revival in Wales*, no. 1, pp. 5, 28–9, 30; no. 2, pp. 12, 14; no. 3, p. 26; no. 4, p. 24; no. 6, pp. 14, 18, 24; Jones, *Rent Heavens*, p. 56; Morgan, *Revival*, pp. 42, 184, 186; NLW, Calvinist Methodist Archives General Collection 28, 678: Capel Rehoboth, Taliesin, 'Atgofion am y Diwygiad', 11; [Thesbiad], 'Diwygiad a'r Weinidogaeth', *Y Geninen* (1906), 130–1; Basil Hall, 'The Welsh Revival of 1904–5: a critique', in G. Baker and D. Cummings (eds), *Studies in Church History*, vol. VIII, *Popular Belief and Practice* (Cambridge: Cambridge University Press, 1972), pp. 293–5.

85 For a very good discussion of the role of youth, see: Jenkins, *Agricultural Community*, pp. 228–34. For a personal reminiscence: [Capel Rehoboth, Taliesin], 'Atgofion'. For a criticism, Morgan, *Revival*, pp. 36f..

86 Robert Jones, 'The revival in Rhos', *British Weekly* (5 January 1905), 352; 'The revival', *Cambrian News* (20 January 1905).

87 *Liverpool Echo* (6 February 1905); Fort, *Lo!*, p. 665.

88 NLW, Minor Lists (1989): T. J. Jenkins Papers no. 296.

89 J. Williams, *Give Me Yesterday* (Newton Abbot: Country Book Club, 1973), pp. 86–7.

90 'Awstin', *Religious Revival in Wales*, no. 2, pp. 1, 11, 15; no. 3, pp. 6, 24, 26, 29; Morgan, *Revival*, describes 'young girls, naturally timid and shy, who had not previously spoken or prayed in public, moved by the Holy Spirit's

action, voluntarily went forward, some to read a chapter, others to pray'
(p. 165). For examples of Roberts being interrupted, see: *Evening Express*
(29 December 1904), 2; 'Awstin', *Religious Revival in Wales*, no. 3, p. 22.

91 *Evening Standard* (9 January 1905); George T. B. Davies, 'Evan Roberts and
   the Welsh Revival', *Independent* 59 (1905), 441– ?.

92 'Awstin', *Religious Revival in Wales*, no. 3, p. 6.

93 *Ibid.*, p. 26.

94 *Ibid.*, p. 28.

95 Morgan, *Revival*, p. 170.

96 J. J. Morgan, *Cofiant Evan Phillips* (Liverpool: Teulu Sunny Side and Huw
   Evans, 1930), p. 334. Phillips posited a more mundane motivation noting
   the grandmother's excellent cakes.

97 Bois, *Le réveil*, p. 316.

98 Lewis, *Miners*, pp. 184–5; Florence Booth, 'Ministry of women', *South Wales
   Daily News* (15 December 1904); David Adams, 'Y diwygiad – Sut i ddio-
   gelu ei ffrwyth?', *Y Dysgedydd* n.s. 29 (1905), 181–2.

99 [Anon.], 'The revival and organised religion', *Cambrian News* (3 February
   1905); 'Elementary religion', *Cambrian News* (17 February 1905). On Gibson
   and his proto-feminist views, see: W. Gareth Evans, 'Introduction', in Sir
   John Gibson, *The Emancipation of Women* (Llandyssul: Gwasg Gomer,
   1992).

100 Stead, *Revival in the west*, p. 56.

101 Alex Owen, *The Darkened Room: Women, Power and Spiritualism in
    Nineteenth-Century England* (London: Virago, 1989); I. M. Lewis, *Ecstatic
    Religion* (Harmondsworth: Penguin, 1972).

102 Turner, 'Revivals', p. 355; Fryer, 'Psychological aspects', 91; Mrs Stephen
    Menzies, *The Christian Woman* (London: Samuel Bagster and Sons, 1905),
    ch. 1.

103 For examples of services being taken over by women, see: 'Awstin', *Religious
    Revival in Wales*, no. 1, pp. 4, 9, 11, 24; no. 2, pp. 5, 15, 21; no. 3, p. 22; no.
    6, p. 17.

104 Other independent missioners included Rosina Davies who played a promin-
    ent role in the revival in Rhosllanerchrugog, see R. Davies, *The Story of my
    Life* (Llandyssul: Gomerian Press, 1942).

105 Beriah G. Evans 'Merionethshire mysteries', *Occult Review* 1 (1905), 113–20,
    179–87, 287–96; Bois, *Le réveil*, ch. 8; Lewis, *Miners*, pp. 236–9; Lewis, 'A
    mystic of the revival', *British Weekly* (26 January 1905), 424; Fryer, 'Psycho-
    logical aspects', 97–100; E. V. Hall, 'Some aspects of the Welsh revival', *Annals
    of Psychical Science* 1 (1905), 323–30; W. Morris Jones, 'Ymweliad a Mrs
    Jones Egryn', *Cymro* (2 March 1905); Francis, *Diwygiad*, pp. 210–13; Tom
    Davis, 'Mary Jones a Diwygiad yn Egryn', NLW, *ex* 1467.

106 'A mystic of the revival', *Barmouth and County Advertiser* (2 February 1905),
    2; C. H. Sheldon, *In His Steps* (London: H. R. Allenson, 1898).

107 His report was rejected by the *Daily Mail*, but was published in Fryer, 'Psychological aspects', app. pt 17. See also Bernard Redwood, 'Mysterious lights', *Barmouth and County Advertiser* (28 February 1905), 6–7.

108 *Y Goleuad* (6 January 1905). On E. W. Evans (1860–1925), *DWB*, p. 234.

109 Howton led a mission to the Carmarthenshire area in April 1906. He claimed to be the 'authentic voice of God', using public displays of exorcism, and the miracle of his raising a Glossop schoolboy from the dead, as evidence, see: *South Wales Daily News* (13, 14 May 1906); *Carmarthen Weekly Reporter* (4 May 1906). On Sarah Jones, see: Jones, *Ffydd* II, pp. 182–3; Davies, 'Carmarthenshire', pp. 275–7. On Howton, see: Hector Waylen, *An Apostle of Healing* (London: A. H. Stockwell, 1928).

110 Brynmor Thomas, *Llwybrau Llafur* (1970), p. 96, quoted, Jones, *Ffydd* II, p. 183; Pope (ed.), *Faith*, p. 335.

111 *South Wales Daily News* (14 April 1906), 6; 'Revival revived', *ibid.*, (13 April 1906), 6. These two articles were reprinted in *Carmarthen Weekly Reporter* (20 April 1906). She made similar claims at Gorseinion and Pantygwaith: 'Carmel revivalist', *South Wales Daily News* (23 April 1906), 6; 'The new revival', *ibid.* (25 April 1906), 6; 'The new revival', *ibid.* (26 April 1906), 6.

112 'Revival pandemonium', *ibid.* (18 April 1906), 6.

113 'Wonderful or what?' *ibid.* (16 April 1906), 6; 'Carmel revivalism', *ibid.* (17 April 1906), 5.

114 'Letter from W. D. Griffith', *ibid.* (21 April 1906), 6.

115 *Ibid.* (13 February 1906), 6. Likewise Mrs Jones of Egryn was lampooned in *Punch*, by a reporter who claimed that she had witnessed a luminous apparition which turned out to be a set of traffic lights: 'Practical inquirer' [Jessie Owen] 'More Welsh lights', *Punch* 52 (1905), 148.

116 Psychiatric support was usually based on the fact that revivalism was seen as a lesser threat than alcoholism: 'Revivals and lunacy', *South Wales Daily News* (22 December 1904); 'Religious mania in Wales', *Barmouth and County Advertiser* (19 January 1905), 3; the widely publicised April meeting of the North Wales Counties Asylum, repr. *in toto*: *Liverpool Daily Post* (18 April 1905); *Wrexham Advertiser* (22 April 1905); Bois, *Le réveil*, pp. 575–7; 'Report from Denbigh Asylum', *British Weekly* (19 January 1905), 403. Rogues de Fursac, *Mouvement mystique*, pp. 121–32. For a notable exception, see: *The Lancet* (26 November 1904), 1514–15. For examples of transgression and psychiatric incarceration, see: 'A pathetic incident', *Evening Express* (26 November 1904): on a Llanelli man who prayed for the conversion of local deacons and factory managers, who was sent to the asylum after refusing to work; *South Wales Daily News* (20 and 22 December 1904): on a Carmarthen woman committed to the asylum after she refused to stop singing.

117 Ezekiel 13.2, 3. Cf. Jeremiah 23.16, 26. For a contemporary commentary on this passage, G. Cunningham Joyce, *The Inspiration of Prophecy: An Essay in*

the *Psychology of Revelation* (Oxford: Oxford University Press, 1910), pp. 124–32.

118 On Price (1864–1940), see: D. J. Roberts, *Cofiant Peter Price* (Swansea: John Penry, 1970).

119 P. Price, 'Double revival in Wales/vigorous attack on Evan Roberts', repr. *The Rev. Peter Price and Evan Roberts* (Cardiff: The Western Mail, 1905), pp. 1–2.

120 *Ibid.*, p. 2.

121 See above, chapter 1.

122 'Ecclesiastical intelligence', *The Times* (2 February 1905), 5.

123 The majority were reprinted in [Price], *Price and Roberts*.

124 Cf. *ibid.* letter no. 42; Roberts, *Price*, pp. 95–101; Morgan, *Le Revival*, pp. 143–6; Bois, *Le réveil*, pp. 423–6. Bois attributed Roberts's late reliance on his 'telepathic' gifts to this attack.

125 Alexander, 'Revivalism and mysticism', 359.

126 Lewis, *Miners*, p. 16; Phillips, *Evan Roberts*, p. vi; 'S. F. S[mith]', 'The Welsh Revival', *Month* 105 (May 1905), 453. 'Native-born Cymro', 'Religious revival in Wales', *The Times* (4 February 1905), 8. This common strategy of tracing xenoglossic and glossolaic productions back to childhood experience is discussed in Marina Yaguello, *Lunatic Lovers of Language* (London: Athlone, 1991), p. 28.

127 Fryer, 'Psychological aspects', 91; John Morris Jones, 'The Welsh Revival', *British Weekly* (2 February 1905), 448; Emile Lombard, 'Essai d'une classification des phénomènes de glossolalie', *Archives de Psychologie* 7 (1907), 6–8, 45; Bois, *Le réveil*, pp. 230–2. Bois drew an explicit comparison with the speeches produced by Flournoy's patient, Hélène Smith.

128 On Henri Bois, Professor of Theology at Montauban, see: *Who's Who* (1918), p. 235.

129 Rogues de Fursac, *Mouvement mystique*, p. 141. *Hwyl* has subsequently developed a life of its own in Pentecostal and parapsychological literature. It appears as a unique racial characteristic connected to the Welsh love of singing, in: W. Hollenweger, *The Pentecostals* (London: SCM Press, 1971), p. 180; Cynolwyn Pugh, 'The Welsh Revival of 1904–5', *Theology Today* 12 (1955), 226–35; Leslie Shephard (ed.), *Encyclopaedia of Occultism and Parapsychology* 1 (Detroit: Gale Research, 1984), p. 693.

130 Bois, *Le réveil*, pp. 268–91; H. Bois, *Quelques reflexions sur la psychologie des réveils* (Paris: Librairie Fischbacher, 1906), pp. 104f.; R. Bornand, 'Quelques faits bibliques sur le réveil gallois', *Revue de Théologie et Philosophie* 11 (1907), 222–8. Cf. Bois, *Le réveil*, p. 321; Lombard, 'Essai', 11; 'Faits récents de glossolalie', *Archives de Psychologie* 7 (1907), 300. On Roger Bornand (b. 1871), Swiss pastor in Brussels, see: Marcel Godet et al. (eds), *Dictionnaire historique et biographique de la Suisse, 8 vols* (Neuchatel: Administration de Dictionnaire historique et biographique de la Suisse, 1921–34), 1, p. 246. The

idea of the Celt's telepathic ability probably stems from the SPR's investigation into Highland second sight, Trevor Hall, *Strange Things: Fr. Allan Macdonald, Ada Goodrich Freer and the Society for Psychical Research's Enquiry into Highland Second Sight* (London: Routledge and Kegan Paul, 1968).

131 Rogues de Fursac, *Mouvement mystique*, ch. 8; Bois, *Le réveil*, pp. 202–10. References to Celtic emotionalism as a contributory factor were widespread. For examples of such attitudes, see: Jones, *Rent Heavens*, pp. 34, 74–5; A. T. Fryer, 'The revival in Wales', *East and the West* 3 (1905), esp. 174–5; Sir Edward Russell, 'Leader', *Liverpool Daily Post and Mercury* (8 April 1905); 'The inwardness of the revival', *ibid.* (12 April 1905); W. D. Shields, 'Evan Roberts, the Welsh revivalist', *Outlook* 79 (1905), 802; *Sunday School Chronicle*, repr. *South Wales Daily News* (26 December 1905); Jones, *Study of Nature*, p. 129; J. Tylor Fox, 'The revival in South Wales', *Friend* 45 (1905), 6.

132 Hall, 'Aspects', 325; Thomas Lindsay, 'Revivals', *Contemporary Review* 88 (1905), 344–67.

133 On the anthropology of the Welsh, see: Hayward, 'Popular mysticism', pp. 278–82.

134 Fryer, 'Psychological aspects', 102 (Mrs Jones); 86 (Evan Roberts). See also the contributions of A. Fryer and S. Oliver to an SPR debate on the subject: 'Private meeting for members and associates', *J.SPR* (July 1905), 107–8.

135 [S. F. S.], 'Welsh Revival', 465.

136 Alfred Hook, 'Religious revivals and social evolution', *Westminster Review* 165 (1906), 418–30; J. G. James, 'Religious revivals: their ethical significance', *International Journal of Ethics* 16 (1906), 332–40.

137 Hook, 'Religious revivals', 426.

138 *Ibid.*, 429–30.

139 Rogues de Fursac, *Mouvement mystique*, p. 102 – he notes the similarity between Roberts and Flournoy's patient Hélène Smith.

140 Bois, *Le réveil*, pp. 408–22; D. M. Phillips devotes the first twelve chapters of his biography of Evan Roberts (*Evan Roberts*) to detailing the mental and spiritual influences in the evangelist's childhood, which led to his spiritual awakening.

141 F. Jameson, *The Political Unconscious: Narrative as a Socially Symbolic Act* (London: Routledge, 1989), p. 22.

142 On the notion of the 'false sortie', see: J. Derrida, 'The ends of man', *Philosophy and Phenomenological Research* 30 (1969), 56.

143 On these developments, see: Rhodri Hayward 'Demonology, neurology and medicine in Edwardian Britain', *Bulletin of the History of Medicine* 78 (2004), 37–58.

144 See his autobiographical work, Richard Howton, *Divine Healing and Demon Possession* (London: Ward Lock and Co., 1905).

145 There was some contention over Roberts's convalescence with Penn-Lewis. Many Welsh authors believed that she had somehow abducted the young

evangelist for her own purposes: Morgan, *Revival*, app. A; *South Wales Daily News* (12 July 1909), 10; Evans, *Welsh Revival*, pp. 172f.; Jones, *Ffydd* II, pp. 181–2.

146 Prof. Cunningham Pike, 'Impressions of Evan Roberts', *Overcomer* 1 (1909), 64; I. V. Nepresh, 'The spirituality of the Welsh revivalist: personal glimpses of Evan Roberts' [1955], repr. in R. O. Roberts (ed.), *Glory Filled the Land: A Trilogy on the Welsh Revival of 1904–05* (Wheaton: International Awakening Press, 1989), pp. 181–200.

147 Jessie Penn-Lewis and Evan Roberts, *War on the Saints* (Leicester: Overcomer Bookroom, 1912). For discussion of this work, see: Hayward, 'Demonology, neurology', 52–7; Ellis, *Lucifer Ascending*, pp. 214–21.

148 Penn-Lewis and Roberts, *War on the Saints*, p. 64.

149 See, William Kay, *Pentecostals in Britain* (Carlisle: Paternoster Books, 2000).

150 Cf. Michel de Certeau, 'Psychoanalysis and its history' [1978], in *Heterologies*, p. 10.

151 F. H. Bradley, *The Presuppositions of Critical History* [1874], ed. Lionel Rubinoff (Chicago: Quadrangle Books, 1968), pp. 20–4.

152 Karl Popper, *Conjectures and Refutations: The Growth of Scientific Knowledge* [1963] (London: Routledge, 1996), pp. 34–5; A. C. MacIntyre, *The Unconscious: A Conceptual Study* (London: Routledge and Kegan Paul, 1958), pp. 214–15.

153 For interesting discussions, Katherine Kearns, *Psychoanalysis, Historiography and Feminist Theory: The Search for a Critical Method* (Cambridge: Cambridge University Press, 1997), pp. 110–14, 125–9; Karl Figlio, 'Getting to the beginning: identification and concrete thinking in historical consciousness', in S. Radstone and K. Hodgkin (eds), *Regimes of Memory* (London: Routledge, 2003), pp. 152–66; P. Gay, *Freud for Historians* (Oxford: Oxford University Press, 1985), pp. 163–71.

Index

abductive logic 35, 66n.24
Alexander, W. F. 125
Armstrong, David (1947–) 33
Arnold, Matthew (1828–88) 20–1
automatic writing 35–7, 41, 45, 46, 48, 51, 60
automatism 36, 41, 58–60

Balfour, Gerald (1853–1945) 54
Barrett, William (1844–1925) 44
Barrow, Logie (1945–) 38
Beard, George M. (1839–83) 42–3
Benjamin. Walter (1892–1940)
and historical methods 5
Biblical criticism 10, 14, 16, 26n.50, 26n.51, 31–2, 35, 42, 62
Bloch, Marc (1886–1944) 4
Bornand, Roger (1871–?)126
Bradley, Frances Herbert (1846–1924) 1, 130
Braid, James (1795–1860) 48
Britten, Emma Hardinge (1823–99) 37–8
Bucke, Richard (1837–1902) 92
Bunyan, John (1628–88) 91

Caird, John (1820–98) 94, 105n.75
Carpenter, William (1813–85) 41, 42, 43, 83
celts, 97, 126
Cerullo, John (1949–) 45
Charcot, Jean-Martin (1825–93) 57–9, 77n.136
Clodd, Edward (1840–1930) 44
Clouston, Thomas (1840–1915) 88
Coe, George (1862–1951) 82, 83, 85, 96
conversion 34, 86–90, 94, 103n.52
Cooper, Thomas (1803–92) 31–2
cryptomnesia 62–3

Davenport, Frederick M. (1856–1966) 96–7
Davies, T. Awstin (1857–1934) 114
death 32–6, 41, 46, 53, 63, 65n.15
de Certeau, Michel (1925–86) 114, 116
Deleuze, Gilles (1925–95) 2
demonology 129–30
dreams 52
Drummond, Henry (1851–97) 33

Eliot, George (1819–80) 10, 31
Ellis, Havelock (1859–1939) 88
eucharist 81, 89
Evans, Evan (1861–1931) 122
expectant attention 42–3

Fairbairn, Andrew (1838–1912) 17
Faraday, Michael (1791–1867) 42
Farrar, Frederic (1831–1903) 12, 16
Flournoy, Théodore (1854–1921) 60–3
Fort, Charles (1874–1932) 132n.8, 137n.67
Forward Movement 108, 132n.11
Foucault, Michel (1926–84) 2, 7
technologies of the self 112–14, 134n.29, 134n.30
Fox, Kate (1838–92) 35
Fox, Margaret (1836–93) 35
Freud, Sigmund (1856–1939)
psychoanalysis 6, 43, 63–4, 130–1

Gibson, John (1841–1915) 121
Gore, Charles (1853–1932) 19, 30n.109
Lux Mundi 19–21
Green, T. H. (1836–82) 18–19, 21, 30n.105
Gurney, Edmund (1847–88) 44, 45, 47, 51, 55, 59